PHYSICS REVISON GUIDE FOR CSEC® EXAMINATIONS

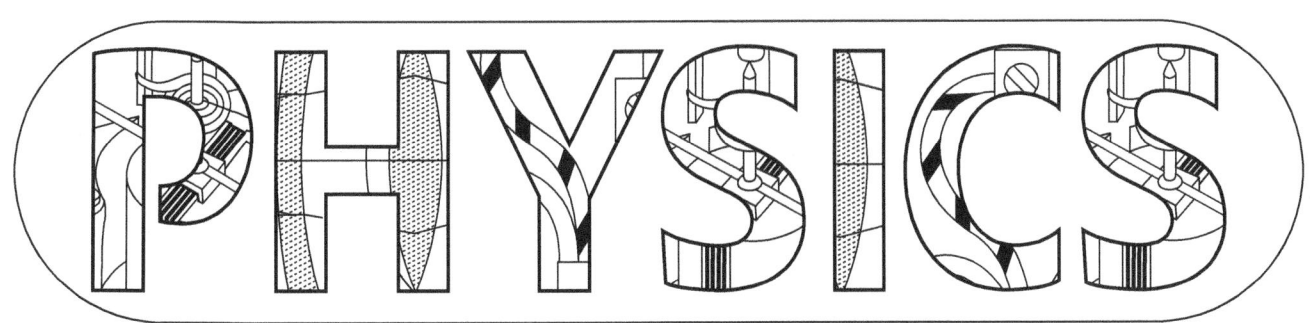

Revision Guide for CSEC® Examinations

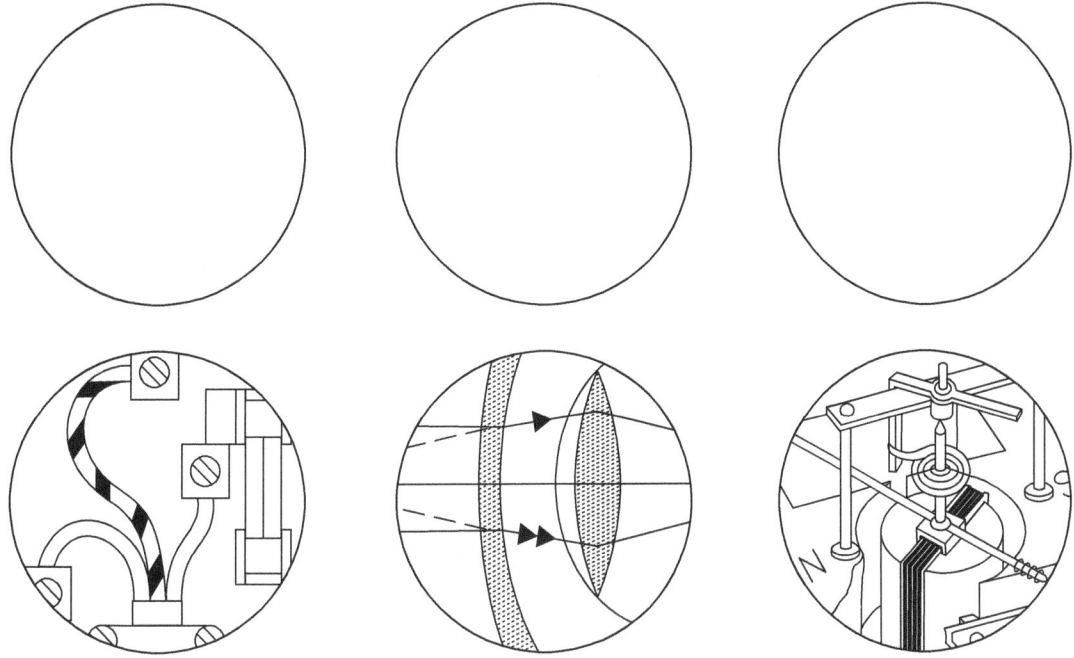

Peter Whiteley and Haydn Bassarath

CAMBRIDGE
UNIVERSITY PRESS

University Printing House, Cambridge CB2 8BS, United Kingdom

One Liberty Plaza, 20th Floor, New York, NY 10006, USA

477 Williamstown Road, Port Melbourne, VIC 3207, Australia

4843/24, 2nd Floor, Ansari Road, Daryaganj, Delhi – 110002, India

79 Anson Road, #06–04/06, Singapore 079906

Cambridge University Press is part of the University of Cambridge.

It furthers the University's mission by disseminating knowledge in the pursuit of education, learning and research at the highest international levels of excellence.

Information on this title: education.cambridge.org

© Cambridge University Press 2006

This publication is in copyright. Subject to statutory exception and to the provisions of relevant collective licensing agreements, no reproduction of any part may take place without the written permission of Cambridge University Press.

First published 1989
Second edition 2007
20 19 18 17 16 15 14 13 12 11 10 9 8 7

Printed in Great Britain by CPI Group (UK) Ltd, Croydon CR0 4YY

A catalogue record for this publication is available from the British Library

ISBN 978-0-521-69294-6 Paperback

Typesetter: DTP Impressions, Cape Town

Cambridge University Press has no responsibility for the persistence or accuracy of URLs for external or third-party internet websites referred to in this publication, and does not guarantee that any content on such websites is, or will remain, accurate or appropriate. Information regarding prices, travel timetables and other factual information given in this work is correct at the time of first printing but Cambridge University Press does not guarantee the accuracy of such information thereafter.

CSEC is a registered trademark of the Caribbean Examinations Council (CXC).

'Physics Revision Guide for CSEC® Examinations' is an independent publication and has not been authorised, sponsored, or otherwise approved by the Caribbean Examinations Council.

Contents

Introduction – preparation for examinations iv

1. Measurement and units 1
2. Measurement and mathematics 4
3. Motion 7
4. Force, mass and weight 12
5. Adding vectors and scalars 14
6. Motion and forces 15
7. Energy, work and power 19
8. Turning forces 21
9. Pressure 24
10. Upthrust and flotation 27
11. Temperature and expansion 28
12. Gas laws 31
13. Kinetic theory of matter 34
14. Transmission of thermal energy 38
15. Heat and temperature change 41
16. Heat and phase change 43
17. Light 46
18. Refraction 49
19. Lenses 52
20. Waves 56
21. Theories of the nature of light 60
22. Electromagnetic spectrum 61
23. Sound 62
24. Static electricity 65
25. Direct current 68
26. Electricity in the home 73
27. Magnetism 76
28. Magnetic effect of an electric current 79
29. Force on a conductor in a magnetic field 82
30. Electromagnetic induction 85
31. Electronics 89
32. Logic gates 91
33. Structure of atoms 93
34. Radioactivity 95
35. Some aspects of the historical development of physics 100

Sample examination questions 104
Numerical solutions 115
Index 116

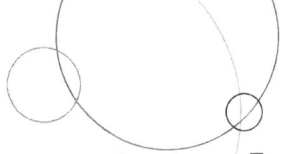

Introduction – preparation for examinations

Your school will enter you for your physics examination. If this is not the case, you should make your own arrangements.

1. Obtain the syllabus to help you with your revision. This document will probably provide examination dates and outline the form of the paper.
2. Obtain recent copies of the specimen papers for the examination.
3. Work out a program of revision and allow for a steady coverage during a period of 6–8 weeks before the dates of the examination.
4. Revise for a short period of 1–2 hours and then rest or go for a walk. When you feel refreshed, return for another session of work. Do not attempt to concentrate for long periods.
5. To achieve this programme of work you need to be fit. Achieve this by taking regular exercise, going to bed early and keeping regular hours. Do not smoke, take alcohol or use recreational drugs.

Revision hints

1. Try to work **on your own** without distractors such as radios, record players or the conversations of people.
2. **Sit at a table** with your books and work for the time suggested above. Do not sit in an easy chair. Remember that learning can be enjoyable but it is also hard work.
3. At this stage, it is important to **concentrate on the essential** points. The object is to learn facts, principles, theories, and practical techniques and, above all, to retain them throughout the examination period.

Methods of learning

You can learn with the help of your eyes, ears, and tongue.

1. **Read** the material aloud (aural memory).
2. **Write out** the material in note form (visual memory).
3. **Practise drawing** diagrams, flow charts, natural cycles and so on.
4. Use **memory aids**, such as key words, jingles and rhymes.
5. **Work through examination questions** by writing out the answers. Always check the answers if you are not sure (another form of revision).
6. Write minimum revision material on **index cards**. You can fit these into your pocket and look at them at any time. Do not take them with you into the examination hall.
7. **Revise topic by topic** through your notes and through this book. Do not use a textbook at this late stage.

The day(s) before the examination

1. Do not revise night after night without getting any sleep.
2. Do not cram up to the last minute the night before the examination. Get to bed early.
3. Check (and recheck) the subject, paper number, starting time and location of the examination room.
4. Make sure that you have all the writing and other instruments that you require. Put them in a clear plastic bag. This is often required to ensure that you have nothing hidden in a pencil case. Include pen, spare pen, pencil, ruler, eraser, compass, pencil sharpener, red and green-coloured pencils.
5. Write your centre name and number, as well as your own personal examination number and keep this on a piece of paper with your instruments. Remember that this information must be written at the top of each examination question book or writing paper.

The examination day

1. Allow **plenty of time** to reach the examination centre. Get up early and have a good breakfast.
2. **Check all the writing instruments** that you will take to the examination.
3. Allow extra time to get to the examination hall in case of traffic jams or other delays.
4. Go to the toilet.
5. Wait outside the examination hall until called in by the invigilator.
6. Make sure that you have **your identity card**, school pass or whatever means of identification is required.
7. **Go to your place** (usually numbered with your examination number).
8. Fill in the **book or paper heading** when it is given out and you are told to start.
9. **Read the paper instructions** very carefully and do exactly as it says. These instructions will establish:

a the time allowance;
b the number of questions to be answered;
c whether there is question choice.

Allow 5 minutes for reading time and then divide the remaining time by the number of questions to give an idea of the time to spend per question.

10 When **time is called** at the end of the examination you are to **put down your pen**. It is essential therefore that 5 minutes before the end of the examination, you ensure that:
   a all your papers are headed with your name and number;
   b your papers are in the correct order and numbered;
   c no papers have become mixed with your rough work and likewise no rough work is mixed in with your papers.

On no account write anything after you are told to stop.

Types of question

You will find each type of question to be asked illustrated in this book. To remind you, they are as follows:
Paper 1 Sixty (60) multiple-choice questions
Paper 2 Four (4) structured free-response questions and one compulsory data-anaylsis question
Paper 3 Five (5) extended-essay questions
Candidates are required to answer all three papers.

Multiple-choice questions

These are known as 'objective questions'. They are designed so that, of four responses given, only one is completely correct. The other three are known as distractors and you must eliminate these as incorrect, before marking the one correct answer. For example, Question 10 (Caribbean Examination Council Specimen Paper 1) is as follows:

10 Which of the following statements is TRUE for both diffusion and evaporation?
   (A) An increase in temperature occurs.
   (B) A decrease in temperature occurs.
   (C) A change of phase occurs.
   (D) Increased molecular activity occurs at higher temperatures.

Note that (B) and (C) are possible answers for *only* evaporation but the question specifies that the answer must also be true for diffusion. Thus only answer (D) is correct.

One hour and 15 minutes is allocated for all the multiple-choice questions.

Structured free-response questions

Paper 2 has **structured free-response questions** and all of these must be answered during the 1 hour available. There are five questions, which means that each one should be answered in 18 minutes. Each question has four or five sub-questions, so that a maximum time of about 3–4 minutes is allocated to each.

There is one compulsory data-analysis question. The **data** may consist of *diagrams, graphs, tables or statements*. The questions developed from these data will gradually increase in difficulty from easy, straightforward questions to short essays.

A useful guide to the type of answer required is given by the marks allocated to each sub-question (e.g. 1 mark); this shows that a very brief answer is required, which might consist of one or two words. A question that ends 'State your views on this matter' for 6 marks, requires an extended answer.

Paper 3 has five free-response questions. You only need to answer three of these. These questions are similar to those in Paper 2 but generally require more essay writing.

Terms used in questions on examination papers

(Presented in alphabetical order)

Annotated drawing or **diagram** – provide a large labelled drawing or diagram.
Calculate – clearly state formulae and show all workings in calculations.
Compare and contrast – state points of similarity and points of difference between items in the question. Each of these terms can be used separately, e.g. 'compare' means state the similarities and differences, while 'contrast' means just state the differences.
Define – only a strict definition is required here.
Describe – this is always a full, written description including all the main points of the topic.
Discuss – provide a balanced argument or critical account of all the points involved. This type of answer needs careful planning and no digression from the main argument is permitted.
Distinguish between – this concentrates on the differences between two or more concepts.
Explain – involves a detailed description of the topic so that it is clearly understood.
Give an account of – again involves a description of the topic.
Give an illustrated account of – must include a written account that refers to the included diagrams.

Graph – graph paper and tables of data are usually given. Remember the following:
1. Choose scales on the graph paper that will fill it, as nearly as possible.
2. The horizontal axis should represent the *variable* controlled by the *experimenter* (e.g. length of string, mass, etc.).
3. The vertical axis should represent the *variable under investigation* (e.g. time of oscillation, temperature reached, etc.).
4. Axes must be labelled at the extreme end (e.g. mass (g)), and the units entered along the axes (e.g. 0, 2, 4, 6, 8, etc.).
5. Enter the points in pencil as 'x' or ⊙.
6. Points should be joined approximately (i.e. using either a smooth curve or a straight line, to create a 'line of best fit' = see 2.5 Graphs, on page 5).
7. A 'sketch graph' may not require graph paper but the scales should be approximately correct and the shape of the graph should show clearly the way one variable influences the other.

List – produce a series of points or observations underneath each other. They should be numbered serially (e.g. (i), (ii), (iii), etc.).

Measure – refers to quantities that can be read directly from some measuring instrument (e.g. ruler, thermometer, balance, etc.).

Outline – requires only a description of the most important points.

State – requires a precise answer similar to a definition.

Suggest – an answer required that will draw on physical principles applied to a new or novel situation. The material may be outside the syllabus. Nevertheless the candidate should be able to answer from within his/her own knowledge.

Tabulate – using data supplied, or the candidate's own knowledge, construct a table showing the facts.

1 Measurement and units

[syllabus sections A.1.1–1.4, 2.8–2.12]

1.1 Fundamental quantities and units

In science there are five fundamental, or **base**, quantities – all other quantities are related to these. Mass (symbol m), length (l) and time (t) are three of these quantities. We will use two others later: electric current and temperature. All other quantities are **derived quantities**.

To measure a physical quantity we compare it with a standard known as the **unit** of the quantity. Each base quantity has a base unit (Table 1.1).

Table 1.1 *Names and symbols for base SI units*

Physical quantity	Name of SI Base unit	Symbol for unit
Length	metre	m
Mass	kilogram	kg
Time	second	s

A quantity is written as its value followed by its unit, e.g. the height of a girl might be 1.40 m. The system we use is called the Système International d'Unités or the SI system.

1.2 Derived quantities

We can multiply or divide base quantities with their units to produce derived quantities with their units. The area of a rectangle with sides 0.6 m and 0.5 m is given by the product of the sides, i.e. (0.6 m) x (0.5 m) = 0.3 m². Thus in the SI system the unit of area is the squared metre (m²).

The speed of an object is the distance, in metres, travelled each second. The unit of speed is metres per second. This is written m s^{-1}; s^{-1} means 'per second'.

1.3 Length

In your practical course you will use several instruments to measure lengths. A rule is one of the most common. With a rule we can usually measure length to the nearest millimetre.

A rule is not suitable for short distances such as the diameter of wires, thin sheets of material or round objects. In these cases we use a micrometer or calipers.

Micrometer

Figure 1.1 shows a micrometer screw gauge. The horizontal scale is marked in millimetres (mm). As the screw rotates once, the micrometer opens 0.5 mm. Each of the 50 divisions on the circular scale is 0.01 mm. To read the micrometer, we add the reading on the horizontal scale to the reading on the circular scale. We check and allow for any zero error when using a micrometer.

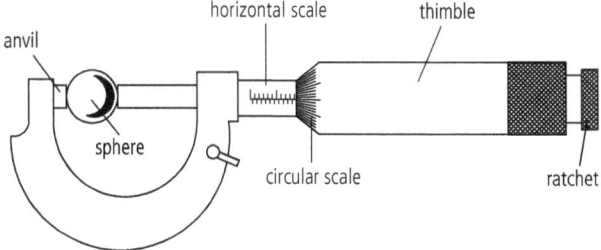

Fig.1.1 *Micrometer screw gauge*

Calipers

We use calipers to measure diameters of rods and balls. We then measure the distance between the caliper points using a rule (see Fig.1.2a).

(a)

Fig.1.2 *(a) Calipers*

(b)

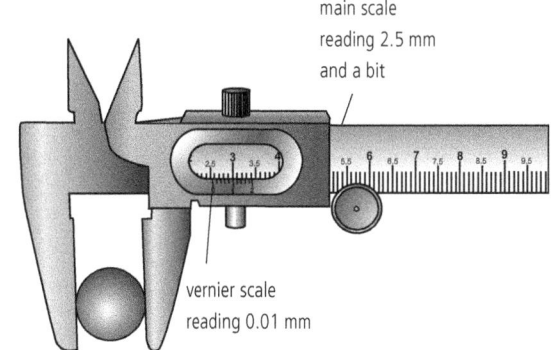

Fig.1.2 *(b) Vernier calipers*

We also use **vernier** calipers and the vernier scale permits greater precision, to 0.01 cm. A vernier scale is a small scale that slides along the main scale (see Fig.1.2b).

We see that one mark on the vernier scale coincides with a mark on the main scale. In Fig.1.2b the zero mark on the vernier indicates that the reading is 2.5 cm and a bit. The first mark on the vernier coincides with a mark on the main scale, showing the full reading to be 2.51 cm.

1.4 Area

The area of a square = (side)^2.

With irregular shapes we can divide the area into small squares, of known size, and estimate the total number of squares.

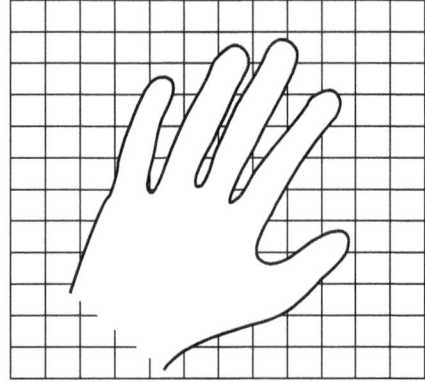

Fig. 1.3

1.5 Volume

To find the volumes of **rectangular solids** we measure the lengths of the sides. Then

volume = length × width × height

(For irregular solids see Section 1.7.)

We find the volume of **liquids** using a measuring cylinder and looking carefully at the meniscus. Remember: we read the base of the meniscus for water and the top of the meniscus for mercury.

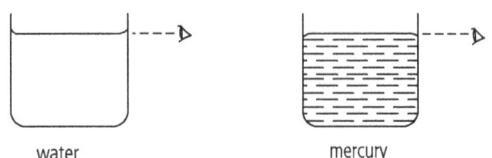

Fig. 1.4

We also use pipettes and burettes to measure volumes of liquids more accurately.

1.6 Mass

A chemical balance is used to measure mass very accurately but a **lever balance** is often accurate enough (Fig.1.5).

The scale on a lever balance is a **non-linear scale** – the marks are not evenly spaced. Most scales that we use are **linear scales** – the marks are evenly spaced.

In Unit 4 we look at the important distinction between mass and weight.

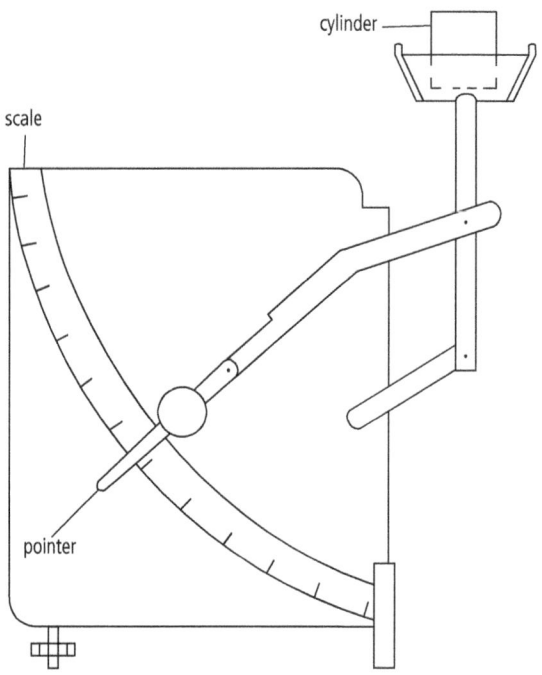

Fig.1.5 *Lever balance*

1.7 Density

Blocks of material can have the same volume but different masses. A wooden block may have a mass of 48 g while a block of iron of the same volume has a mass of about 420 g. The materials have different **densities**.

The density (ρ) of a material is defined as its mass per unit volume:

$$\text{density} = \frac{\text{mass (kg)}}{\text{volume (m}^3\text{)}}$$

The unit of density is kg m^{-3} (remember that the m^{-3} means 'per metre cubed'). The density of water is 1 000 kg m^{-3} or 1 g cm^{-3}. The latter unit is used in measurements involving small masses and volumes.

Determination of the density of solids

We measure the mass and volume of a sample and calculate the density. We use a lever balance to find the **mass** of the sample.

We find the **volume** of **rectangular solids** by measuring the lengths of the sides and finding the product of the length, width and height.

We immerse **irregular objects**, such as stones, in water. The volume of water that they displace equals the volume of the object. For a large object we use a 'eureka' or displacement can. We measure the volume of water that overflows (Fig.1.6.).

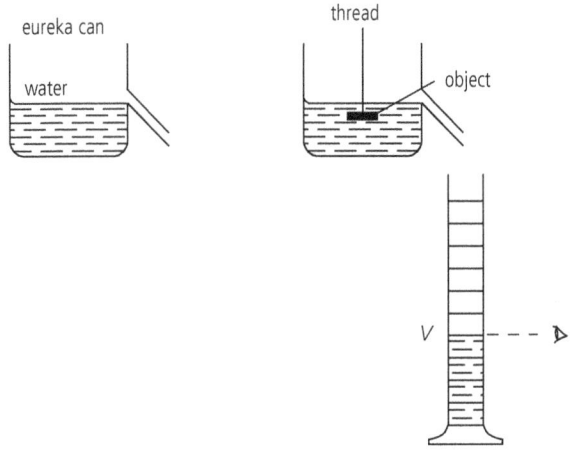

Fig. 1.6 *Using a eureka can*

We can add a *small* object directly to water in a measuring cylinder. The rise in the reading is equal to the volume of the object. Care must be taken to submerge the object carefully without splashing to prevent droplets from sticking to the sides of the container.

1.8 Time

You will use a stopwatch or stop clock to measure time intervals. Your reaction time causes inaccuracy in your timings. You should repeat timings and average your results. Many schools use stop clocks that have an error of ± 0.5 s.

Simple pendulum

A simple pendulum is a small mass hanging on a thin string. It oscillates from side to side.

The **time period** of a simple pendulum is the time taken for one oscillation. (A complete oscillation is from one side, across to the other side and back to the original point.)

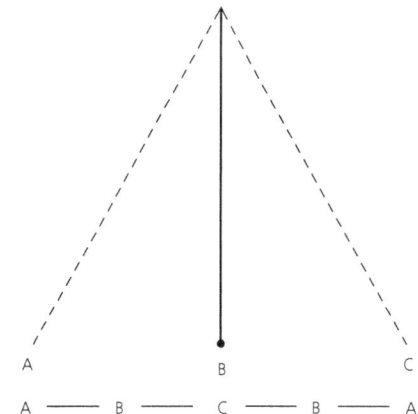

Fig. 1.7 *One complete oscillation*

The **amplitude** of the oscillator is the maximum distance of the bob from its rest position.

You will investigate the factors that determine the time period. You should time 20 or more vibrations, more than once, to improve the accuracy. You should consider changing the mass of the bob, the amplitude of the oscillation and the length of the string. You must change just one factor (or **variable**) at a time.

You will find that the time period depends only on the length of the string (as long as the amplitude is not too large i.e. <10° from vertical).

1.9 Relative density

It is useful to compare the density of a substance with the density of water.

Relative density (ρ_r) is defined as follows:

$$\text{relative density of a substance} = \frac{\text{density of the substance}}{\text{density of water}}$$

Relative density is a ratio and has no unit. We can also use the following expression:

$$\text{Relative density} = \frac{\text{mass of a volume of the substance}}{\text{mass of the same volume of water}}$$

1.10 Quality control

In order to protect the consumer, quality control standards are developed and enforced, e.g.
1. Regular checks are made of weighing machines.
2. Electrical appliances must meet strict safety standards. Safety standards are also applied to the construction and wiring of buildings.
3. The strength of milk or beer can be checked by measurements of their densities.
4. The amount of possibly harmful chemicals in processed food is monitored.

2 Measurement and mathematics

[syllabus sections A1.4–1.6, 3.1–3.3]

2.1 Measurement and significant figures

During your physics course you will record results of experiments. Look at Fig. 2.1. You can see that the length of side AB is somewhere between 2.0 cm and 2.1 cm and you might estimate the length to be 2.08 cm. However, the '8' is not very certain. The number of figures that you write gives an indication of your confidence in the result. It would not be sensible in this example to write 2.085 cm. It is best written 2.1 cm.

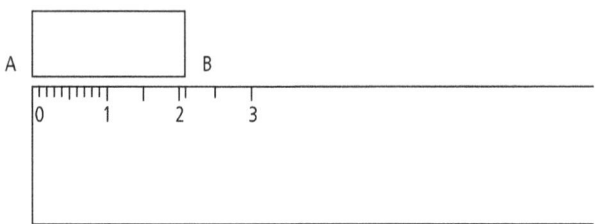

Fig. 2.1 *Approximate measurement*

Lengths measured with a metre rule can often only be written to the nearest millimetre. So we may write, for example, 24.2 cm (or 0.242 m). In each case here we have three **significant figures**. When we calculate a value from our results the answer should be written to the same numbers of significant figures as the original results.

If the two sides of a rectangle are measured as 24.2 cm and 18.3 cm, then

Area of rectangle = 24.2 cm × 18.3 cm
= 442.86 cm² (by calculator)
= 443 cm² (three significant figures)

In any calculation, the reading with the smallest number of significant figures determines the number of significant figures of the final answer.

2.2 Reading scales

Many readings you make in physics are taken from a scale on an instrument. Some were described in Unit 1; thermometers (temperature), ammeters (electric current) and spring balances (force) are other examples.

When reading a scale you make an estimate when the pointer is not actually on a mark on the scale. Fig. 2.2 is part of the scale of an ammeter used to measure current in amperes (A). This would be recorded as 1.35 A. Results can often be taken to three significant figures.

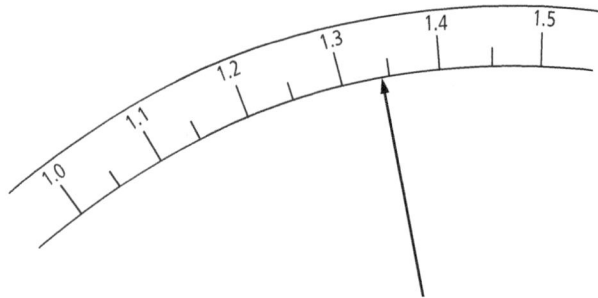

Fig. 2.2 *Ammeter scale*

2.3 Accuracy of results

For an experiment to be useful we must obtain accurate results. In any reading there is some uncertainty, which we can reduce as follows:

1. We can take the same reading more than once and calculate an average value.
2. We can measure a large number of a quantity and calculate the value for one. For example, if we have to find the thickness of a sheet of paper we can measure the thickness of 300 sheets. We then divide our result by 300 to find the thickness of one sheet.
3. We can select an instrument that is appropriate to the reading. If a current of about 0.4 A is being measured, we use an ammeter with a range of 0 to 1 A, not 0 to 5 A.
4. We take particular care to avoid 'parallax' (see Unit 17). We always read scales from directly over the mark (Fig. 2.3).

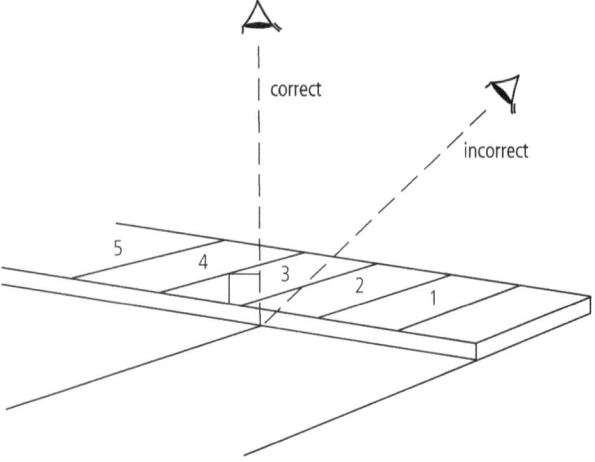

Fig. 2.3 *Reading a scale*

2.4 Large and small numbers

When we have very large and small numbers there are useful alternative ways to write them.

Standard form

In standard form we write numbers in two parts as follows:

$$100 = 10 \times 10 = 10^2 = 1.0 \times 10^2$$
$$240 = 2.4 \times 100 = 2.4 \times 10^2$$
$$3\,600\,000 = 3.6 \times 1\,000\,000 = 3.6 \times 10^6$$

$$0.3 = \frac{3}{10} = 3 \times \frac{1}{10^1} = 3.0 \times 10^{-1}$$
$$0.0024 = 2.4 \times \frac{1}{10^3} = 2.4 \times 10^{-3}$$

You should also be able to multiply and divide numbers in standard form:

$$(3 \times 10^2) \times (2 \times 10^3) = 6 \times 10^5$$
$$(4 \times 10^2) \times (6 \times 10) = 2.4 \times 10^4$$
$$(6 \times 10^4) / (3 \times 10^2) = 2 \times 10^2$$
$$(6 \times 10^3) / (3 \times 10^5) = 2 \times 10^{-2}$$

Prefixes

We also use prefixes for convenience. The following examples show their meaning.

1 MJ = 1 **mega**joule = 1 million joules = 10^6 J
1 km = 1 **kilo**metre = 1 thousand metres = 10^3 m
1 cm = 1 **centi**metre = 1 hundredth metre = 10^{-2} m
1 mm = 1 **milli**metre = 1 thousandth metre = 10^{-3} m
1 μA = 1 **micro**ampere = 1 millionth ampere = 10^{-6} A

Changing units from one to the other

$$1\,m^3 = 1\,m \times 1\,m \times 1\,m$$
$$= 100\,cm \times 100\,cm \times 100\,cm$$
$$= 10^6$$

i.e. $1\,m^3 = 10^6\,cm^3$

also $1\,m^2 = (100 \times 100)\,cm^2$
     $1\,m^2 = 10000\,cm^2$

Sometimes these conversions are necessary because we would not record the volume of a medicine bottle in m^3 but in the more convenient form of cm^3.

Density may be expressed in kg m^{-3}, but in a situation involving small quantities it may be more practical to express it in g cm^{-3}.

In converting 1 g cm^{-3} to kg m^{-3}, the following reasoning is used:

$$1\,kg = 1000\,g$$
$$1\,m^3 = 10^6\,cm^3$$

1 g is divided by 1 000 to covert to kg

and 1 cm^{-3} is multiplied by 10^6 to convert to m^{-3}

i.e. $1\,g\,cm^{-3} = \frac{1}{1\,000} \times \frac{1\,000\,000}{1}$

$1\,g\,cm^{-3} = 1000\,kg\,m^{-3}$

2.5 Graphs

A common way to present results is to draw a graph. The graph often provides us with extra information and helps our understanding.

When plotting a graph the axes are labelled with the quantities involved, their symbols and the units of the quantities. We choose a sensible and convenient scale so that the results occupy most of the graph. For instance, if a set of results of length has a range from 1.2 cm to 8.4 cm, the scale would be 0 to 10 cm, not 0 to 100 cm.

We use a small cross, or a dot with a small circle around it, to indicate the plotted points. We plot results as accurately as possible – we do not 'round off' to make them easier to plot.

Our results are often approximately in a straight line. We draw a **line of best fit**. This line goes as close as possible to as many points as possible. The points should also be 'balanced' about the line, with equal numbers above and below the line (if they are not exactly on the line). Sometimes the shape of a graph will be a smooth curve.

The line of best fit has the effect of averaging experimental inaccuracies.

Common graphs

If a graph is a straight line passing through the **origin**, this means that the two quantities are **proportional** to each other (Fig. 2.4).

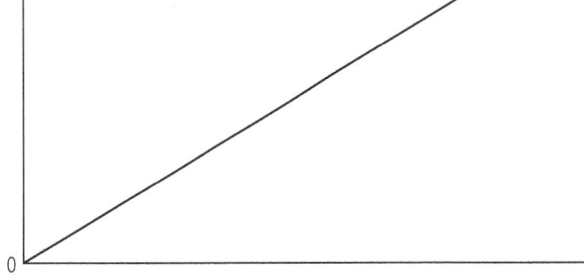

Fig. 2.4 *Straight-line graph passing through origin*

A graph can also be a straight line but **not** pass through the origin – the quantities are then **linearly related** to each other but are **not** proportional to each other (Fig. 2.5).

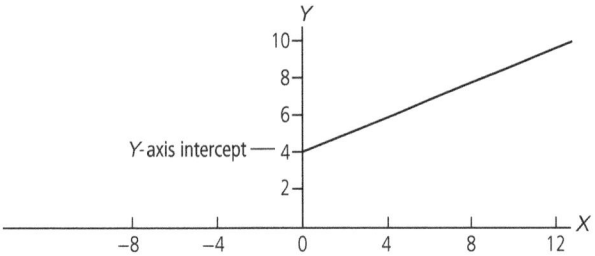

Fig. 2.5 *Straight-line graph not passing through origin*

Gradient and intercepts of a graph

Two important quantities of a straight-line graph are its gradient and its intercepts on the axes.

In Figs. 2.5 and 2.6 the intercept on the Y-axis is 4. If we draw the graph line until it hits the X-axis, the intercept is a **negative value** -8 (Fig. 2.6).

This triangle should be wider than half the width of the graph paper and the height should be greater than half the height of the page.

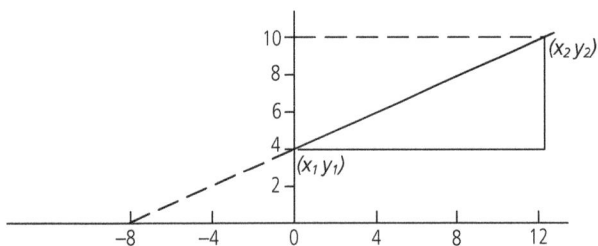

Fig. 2.6 *Intercepts on a graph*

$$\text{gradient} = \frac{\text{the change in the value of y}}{\text{the change in the value of x}} = \frac{y_2 - y_1}{x_2 - x_1}$$

In our example the gradient is:
$$\frac{10 - 4}{12 - 0} = \frac{6}{12} = \frac{1}{2}$$

Questions on Unit 2

1. Calculate the values of the following:
   a $(6 \times 10^3) \times (5 \times 10^4)$
   b $(4 \times 10^{-3}) \times (3 \times 10^2)$
   c $(6 \times 10^3) / (3 \times 10^5)$
   d $(4 \times 10^{-4}) / (2 \times 10^{-5})$

2. A student carries out an experiment to find the density of wood in a wooden block. The mass of the block is recorded as 163 g and its volume as 240 cm³. Which of the following values should the student write for the density of the material?
   a 0.7 g cm^{-3} b 0.68 g cm^{-3}
   c 0.679 g cm^{-3} d 0.6791 g cm^{-3}

3. Examine the graph drawn below.

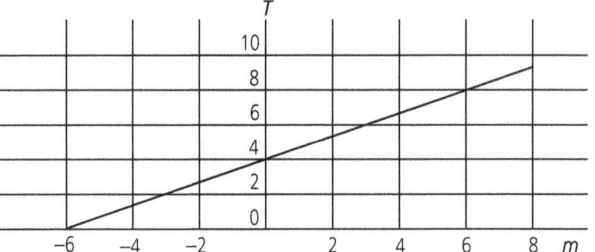

   a What is the gradient of this graph?
   b What is the value of T when m is 8.0?
   c What is the value of m when T is 0.0?
   d Does this graph indicate that m and T are proportional to each other? Explain your answer.

3 Motion

[syllabus sections B2.1–2.4, 3.2–3.4]

3.1 Vectors and scalars

Some quantities need to have both their size **and** direction stated to fully describe the quantity. These quantities are known as **vectors**. Examples of vectors are displacement, velocity, acceleration and force.

Other quantities, which only have size (but no direction), are known as **scalars**. Examples of scalars are distance, speed and mass.

In Unit 5 we discuss the addition of vectors and scalars.

3.2 Distance and displacement

When we calculate the total **distance** travelled by an object we take no account of the directions in which it travels. Distance is a scalar quantity.

The **displacement** is defined as the distance moved **in a particular direction**. Displacement is a vector quantity.

Figure 3.1 represents a man walking on a football field. He starts at P and walks 50 m due east – a displacement. He then walks 50 m due north. The total **distance** he has travelled is 100 m but his **displacement** is about 71 m north-east of his starting point.

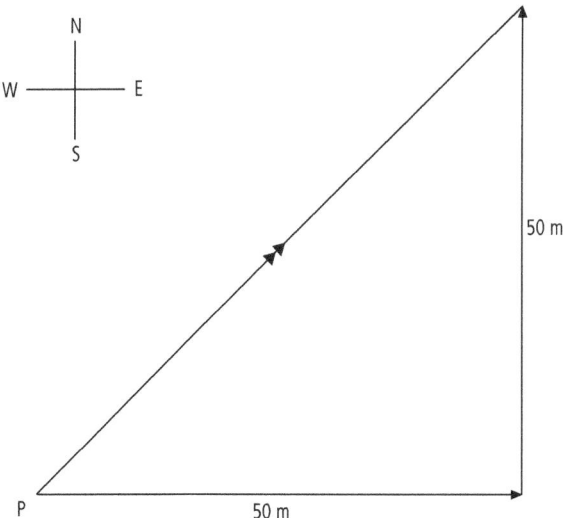

Fig. 3.1 *Distance and displacement*

We can draw a scale diagram to represent his movement. We could use a scale in which 1 cm represents 10 m. If we take north as being **up** the page we then obtain a diagram that is two sides of a triangle, similar to Fig. 3.1.

The length of the third side of this triangle, the hypotenuse, is measured and is about 7.1 cm. This represents the displacement in both size and direction.

3.3 Speed

Speed is defined as the distance moved per second. Speed is a scalar quantity.

If the speed does not vary (if it is **constant** or **uniform**) then

$$\text{speed} = \frac{\text{distance travelled}}{\text{time taken}}$$

Distance is measured in metres and time in seconds. The unit of speed is metres per second, m s^{-1}. Remember, in the unit m s^{-1} the -1 means 'divided by' or 'per'. The symbol for speed is v.

3.4 Velocity

Velocity is defined as the displacement per second. Thus the velocity is the distance moved per second in a particular direction. Velocity is a vector quantity. If the velocity is **constant**,

$$\text{velocity} = \frac{\text{displacement}}{\text{time taken}}$$

The unit of velocity is metres per second, m s^{-1}. The symbol for velocity is also v. For a velocity to be constant, both the speed and direction must be constant.

Changing m s^{-1} to km h^{-1}

$$20 \text{ m s}^{-1} = \left(\frac{20}{1\,000} \times \frac{3\,600}{1}\right) \text{ km h}^{-1}$$

we divide by 1 000 to change metres to seconds and we multiply by 3 600 to change 'per second' to 'per hour'. (There are 3600 s in 1 h.)

3.5 Acceleration

Acceleration is defined as the rate of change of velocity, i.e. the change of velocity per second.

If the acceleration is **constant**,

$$\text{acceleration} = \frac{\text{change of velocity}}{\text{time taken}}$$

The unit of acceleration is metres per second squared, m s^{-2}. This means a certain change of velocity, in m s^{-1}, each second.

Acceleration is a vector quantity and its symbol is a.

3.6 Representing motion using graphs

We use graphs to represent and analyse motion. The most useful to us are graphs of displacement against time, and velocity against time.

Constant velocity

If a car is moving at a constant velocity of 15 m s^{-1}, then each second it will travel 15 metres, in the same direction.

Two graphs can represent this motion:
1. **Displacement/time graph** – the graph (Fig. 3.2) represents the car's motion. The gradient of the line is $60/4 = 15$. The **gradient** of a displacement/time graph always represents the **velocity**.

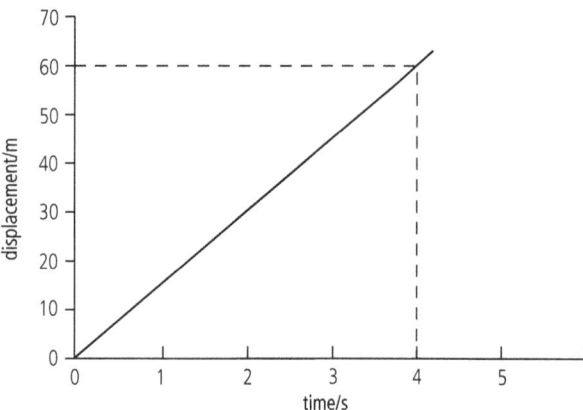

Fig. 3.2 *Displacement/time graph*

2. **Velocity/time graph** – the **gradient** of the graph represents the **acceleration**. In the example (Fig. 3.3) the velocity is constant, so the gradient and acceleration are zero.

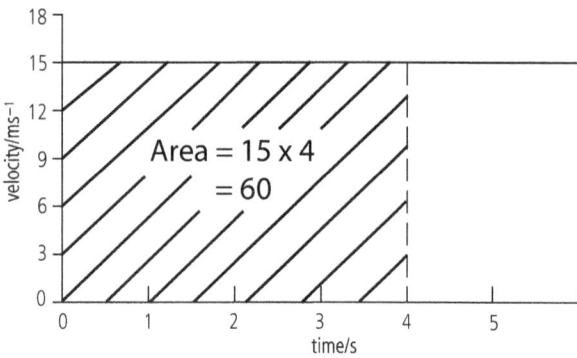

Fig. 3.3 *Velocity/time graph: constant velocity*

The **area** under a velocity/time graph represents the **distance travelled**. So in the 4 s, the distance travelled is 60 m.

Velocity/time graphs are more useful than distance/time graphs. All four quantities are represented on a velocity/time graph: velocity, time, distance and acceleration.

Uniform acceleration

If a car starts from rest and has an acceleration of 5 m s^{-1}, each second its velocity increases by 5 m s^{-1}. We represent this in a velocity/time graph (Fig. 3.4).

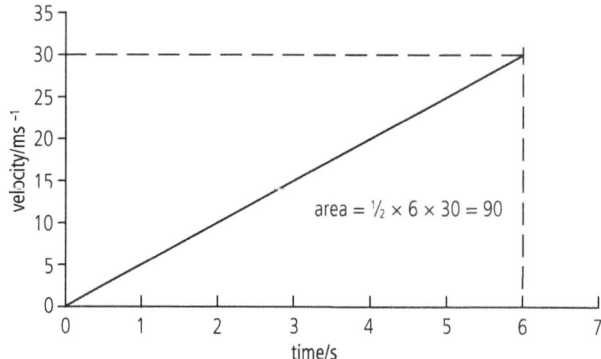

Fig. 3.4 *Velocity/time graph: uniform acceleration*

We can use the graph to calculate the distance travelled in 6 s. Remember that the distance travelled is represented by the area under the graph. The triangle has an area of

½ × base × height = ½ × 6 × 30 = 90

The distance travelled in 6 s is 90 m.

Example

A bus starts from rest and accelerates at 3 m s^{-1} for 5 s. It travels at a constant speed for 10 s and then quickly comes to a halt in a further 3 s.

Draw a velocity/time graph to represent this motion and calculate the distance between the two stops.

Answer

The distance travelled is equal to the area under the graph. We calculate this area by considering the three stages separately.
1. During the **acceleration** the area under the graph is the area of the triangle, ½ × 5 × 15 = 37.5 m².
2. During the **constant speed** the area of the rectangle is 10 × 15 = 150 m².
3. During the **deceleration** the area is again the area of a triangle:
½ × 3 × 15 = 22.5
The total area is 37.5 + 150 + 22.5 = 210
The distance travelled is 210 m.

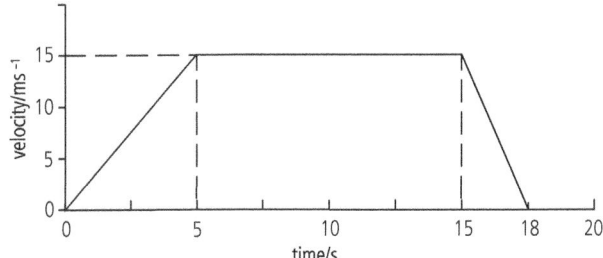

3.7 Equations of uniformly accelerated motion

When we have objects moving with a constant acceleration we can also use certain equations to solve problems. In these equations we use the following symbols:

initial velocity	u	final velocity	v
acceleration	a	displacement	x
time	t		

$$\text{acceleration} = \frac{\text{change in velocity}}{\text{time taken}}$$

$$a = \frac{v - u}{t}$$

Rearranging, $at = v - u$
and $v = u + at$ (1)

Also,

$$\text{velocity} = \frac{\text{displacement}}{\text{time taken}}$$

displacement = velocity × time taken

This is only true if the velocity is **constant**. If the velocity is **changing** then

displacement = *average* velocity × time taken

$$x = \frac{(u + v)}{2} \times t \quad (2)$$

We now substitute into equation (2).
As $v = u + at$

$$x = \frac{(u + [u + at]) \times t}{2}$$

Thus $x = ut + \tfrac{1}{2}at^2$ (3)

Also, substituting $t = \dfrac{v - u}{a}$ in equation (2)

$$x = \frac{(u + v)}{2} \times \frac{(v - u)}{a}$$

Rearranging, $2ax = v^2 - u^2$
and $v^2 = u^2 + 2ax$ (4)

Equations (1), (2), (3) and (4) are called the **equations of motion**. We can only apply them when the acceleration is constant throughout the motion.

In applying the equations of motion, the student should read the questions carefully, write down all data given and decide which variable has to be found. It is then easy to match up which of the four examples of motion he/she can use.

Examples of use of equations of motion

1. A racing car has a constant acceleration, from rest, of 4.0 m s^{-2}. How far does it travel in the first 10 s?
   The initial velocity is zero, $u = 0$, $a = 4.0$ m s^{-2}, $t = 10$ s, $x = ?$ m.
   We use the third equation of motion:
   $x = ut + \tfrac{1}{2}at^2$
   $x = 0 \times t + \tfrac{1}{2} \times 4 \times 10^2$
   $x = 2 \times 100 = 200$ m

2. What deceleration is needed to bring a car, with a velocity of 20 m s^{-1}, to rest in 80 m?
   The final velocity is zero, $v = 0$, $u = 20$ m s^{-1}, $s = 80$ m, $a = ?$ m s^{-2}
   $v^2 = u^2 + 2ax$
   $0 = 20^2 + 2 \times a \times 80$
   $= 400 + 160 a$
   $-400 = 160 a$
   $\dfrac{-400}{160} = a = -2.5$ m s^{-2}

A **deceleration** is a **negative acceleration**.

3.8 Measuring velocities and accelerations

In the laboratory we use a ticker-tape timer to measure velocities and accelerations (Fig. 3.5). It has a strip of metal that vibrates 60 times a second. A dot is printed at each 1/60th second on the paper that runs underneath.

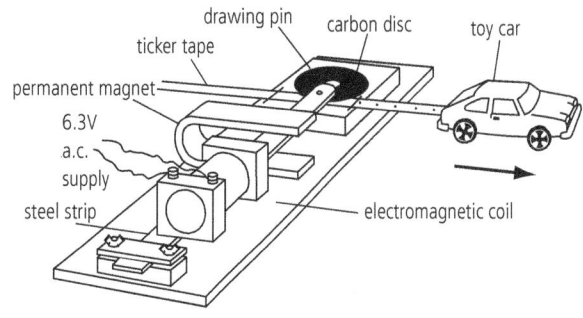

Fig. 3.5 *Ticker-tape timer*

The tape can be pulled at a constant speed through the timer. The tape is then cut up into sections of '10-dot' lengths, each 1/6th second. If the speed is constant then the sections of the tape obtained are the same length. The length of each of the strips is the distance travelled in 1/6th second.

The speed, distance per second, is calculated by multiplying by 6, the distance travelled in 1/6th second. A graph can also be made from the tapes (Fig. 3.6).

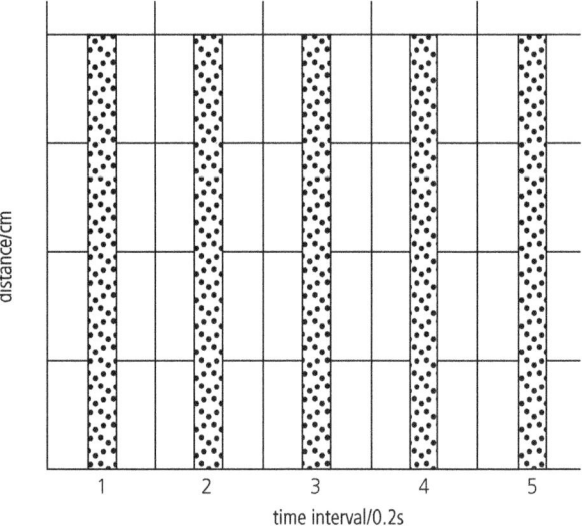

Fig. 3.6 *Graph from ticker-tape timer*

Calculating acceleration from the tapes

If the tape is pulled so that it accelerates through the timer, the spacing of the dots increases. We cut 10-dot lengths and make a new graph (Fig. 3.7). The lengths of the tapes increase as the speed increases. The rate of increase is constant if the acceleration is constant.

We calculate the acceleration by measuring the **change** of speed in a certain time. The initial velocity in Fig. 3.7 was 15 cm s^{-1} and after one second the velocity was 165 cm s^{-1}.

$$\text{acceleration} = \frac{\text{change in velocity}}{\text{time taken}}$$
$$= \frac{165 - 15}{1} = 150 \text{ cm s}^{-2}$$

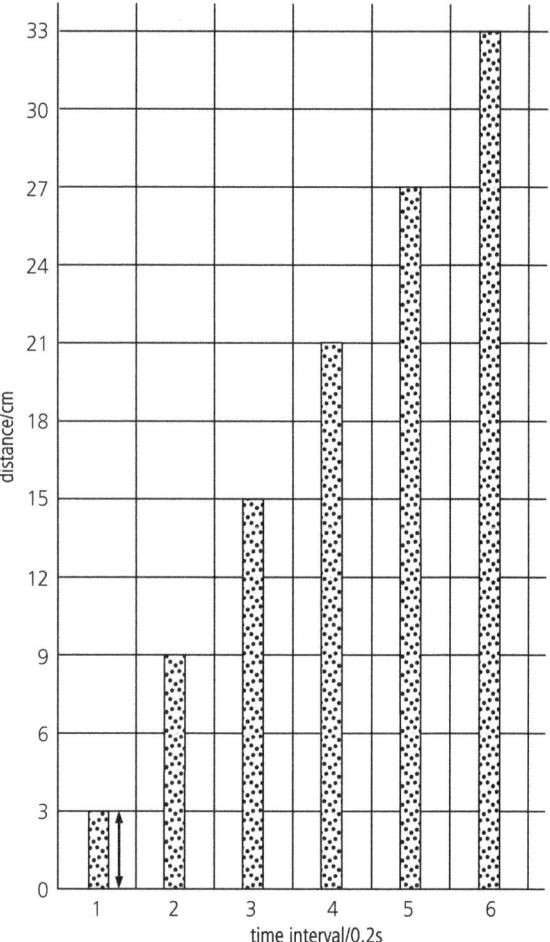

Fig. 3.7 *Calculating acceleration*

3.9 Falling objects

We can drop a large stone and a piece of chalk from a height of 3 or 4 m and they will land simultaneously. However, a stone will reach the ground faster than a piece of paper. If the stone and paper are allowed to fall **in a vacuum**, they fall together.

When objects fall in air, the resistance of the air has a greater effect on objects with larger surface areas, such as paper, than on heavy ones, such as the stone. Fluid friction (or viscous drag) always opposes the fall of objects through fluids, i.e. liquids and gases.

Acceleration due to gravity

If the effects of air resistance are eliminated or are negligible, then all objects fall with the same acceleration. This is called the **acceleration due to gravity**, g.

The acceleration due to gravity has slightly different values in different parts of the world but the average value is 9.81 m s^{-2}. We often take g as 10 m s^{-2}, as a convenient approximation.

An object falling vertically **gains** speed, 10 m s^{-1} in each second.

It will also **lose** 10 m s^{-1} each second as it rises vertically. If a stone leaves a person's hand moving vertically upwards with a velocity of 20 m s^{-1}, it will take two seconds to reach its highest point. It then stops and accelerates back towards the ground gaining 10 m s^{-1} each second.

The relation between mass, weight and acceleration due to gravity is discussed in Unit 6.

Measuring acceleration due to gravity

We use the apparatus shown in Fig. 3.8 to find the value of g. When the electromagnet is turned off the ball bearing falls. Simultaneously, the clock starts. When the ball bearing strikes the plate at the bottom, the clock stops. The time, t, and the height, h, of the fall are measured.

Thus $x = h$ and $a = g$ and, as it falls from rest, $u = 0$.
Using $\quad x = ut + \tfrac{1}{2}at^2$
$\qquad\qquad h = \tfrac{1}{2}gt^2$
leading to $g = \dfrac{2h}{t^2}$

The experiment is repeated and the results are averaged.

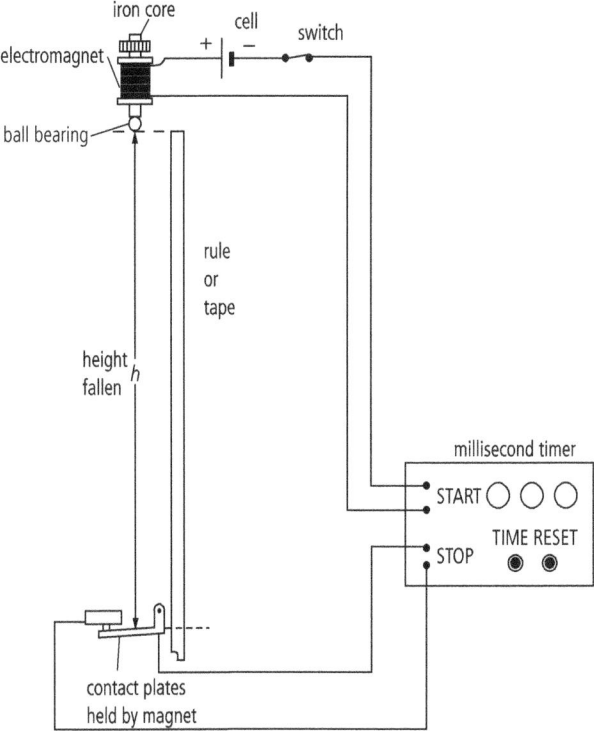

Fig. 3.8 *Measuring the acceleration of free fall by direct timing*

4 Force, mass and weight

[syllabus sections B1.1–1.4, 1.10–1.11]

4.1 Force

A force can be described as a push or a pull. It can change the size, shape or motion of a body. There are several different types of forces such as gravitational, electrical, magnetic and nuclear forces.

Measuring force

The instrument used to measure gravitational force is the spring balance (Fig. 4.1).

We use the fact that the extension is **proportional to the force** to calibrate the spring balance (see below). The unit of force is the **newton (N)** (see Unit 6).

Stretching a spring

We hang a wire spring from a retort stand. A pointer and a small pan are hung at the bottom of the spring. We set up a scale, marked in millimetres, vertically by the side.

We add a series of small, equal weights that stretch the spring. We measure the extension (i.e. the extra length) of the spring. Typical results are shown in Table 4.1.

Table 4.1 *Measuring extension of spring*

Force F/N	0	1.0	2.0	3.0	4.0	5.0
Extension e/cm	0	1.6	3.2	4.8	6.4	8.0

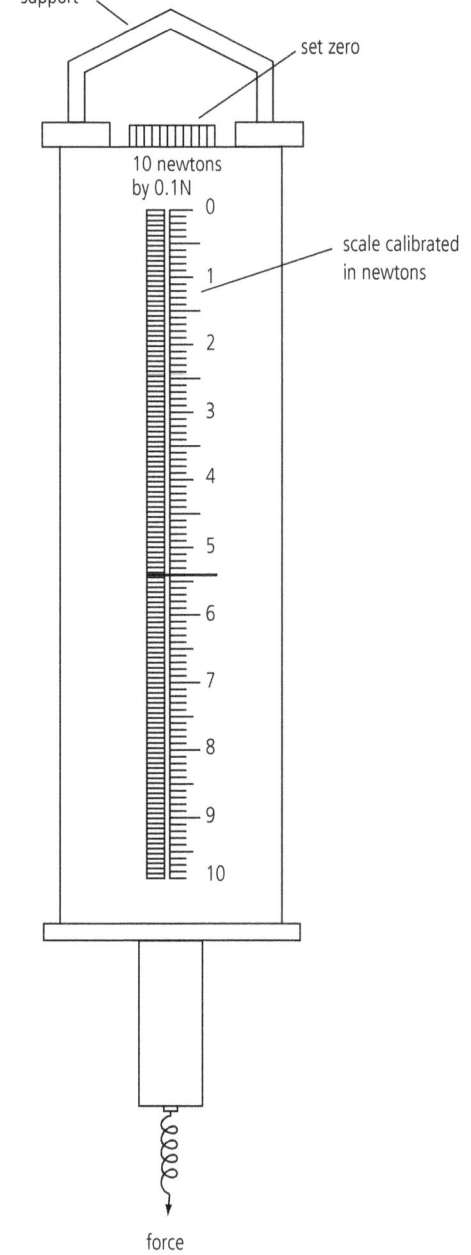

Fig. 4.1 *A spring balance*

We plot a graph of extension against load (Fig. 4.2). It is a straight line passing through the origin. This means that the extension is **proportional** to the load.

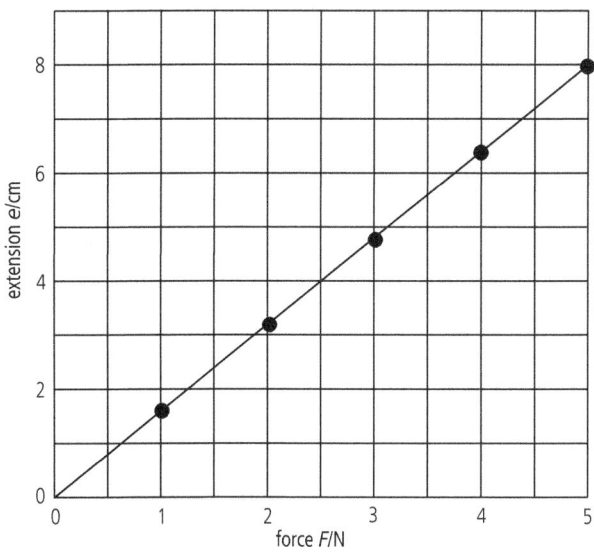

Fig. 4.2 *Extension/load graph*

4.2 Mass and weight

Mass

The mass of an object is a measure of the amount of matter it contains (i.e. the number and type of particles in the object).

The mass of an object is also a measure of its resistance to a change in its motion. This resistance is known as the **inertia** of the body.

We measure mass using a lever balance. The unit of mass is the **kilogram** (kg). The mass of an object is constant everywhere.

Weight

The weight of an object is the force of gravity on the object. It acts towards the centre of the Earth.

We measure weight using a spring balance. The unit of weight is the **newton** (N). A mass of 1 kg has a weight of approximately 10 N on Earth. The weight of an object changes if the force of gravity changes.

In outer space, where there is no gravity, a 1 kg mass has no weight. On the Moon, where the gravity is about ⅙ that on Earth, a 1 kg mass has a weight of about 1.6 N.

Elastic limit of springs

If we remove the weights the spring contracts to its original length. However, if we continue to add greater weights, the spring will stretch by different amounts. The extension is no longer proportional to the load. When we remove the larger weights the spring does not return to its original length. We have gone beyond the **elastic limit** of the spring. The new graph is shown in Fig. 4.3.

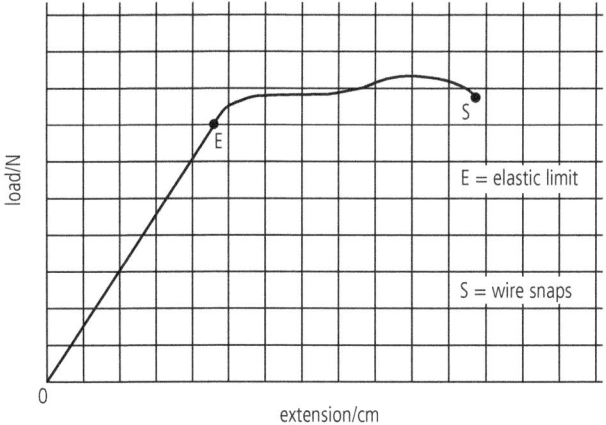

Fig. 4.3 *Extension for loads beyond the elastic limit for a wire*

Hooke's law

Hooke's law states that the extension of a spring is proportional to the load, provided that the elastic limit is not exceeded.

5 Adding vectors and scalars

[syllabus sections B2.1–2.3]

We already know that some quantities are vectors (force, velocity and acceleration) and some quantities are scalars (mass, speed and volume).

If we are adding scalar quantities, e.g. two masses, we just calculate the numerical sum, i.e. 3 kg + 5 kg = 8 kg. However, when we add vector quantities we have to take their direction into account.

5.1 Adding forces

We represent vectors by a line drawn to scale. Its direction is the direction of the vector quantity. If we have a force of 5 N east we might draw it as a 5 cm line (1 cm = 1 N) **across** the page (Fig. 5.1).

5 N east

Fig. 5.1

In Fig. 5.2 we have three examples. In each case we have to add forces of 3 N and 4 N.

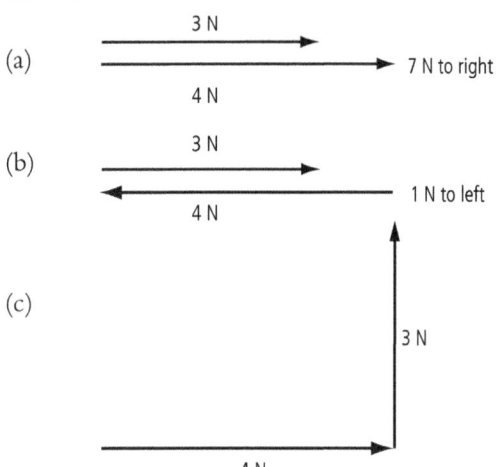

Fig. 5.2

In Fig. 5.2a the two forces are parallel, and in the same direction, and the net force is 3 N + 4 N = 7 N to the right.

In Fig. 5.2b the two forces are in exactly opposite directions (antiparallel) and so the resultant force is 4 N - 3 N = 1 N, to the left.

In Fig. 5.2c the two forces are acting in perpendicular directions. The resultant force has a magnitude between 7 N and 1 N and acts in a direction in between the two forces.

To find the resultant force of two forces that are not parallel or antiparallel we use the principle of the parallelogram of forces.

Parallelogram of forces

This principle states that if the two forces are represented in size and direction by the sides of a parallelogram drawn to scale, the resultant force is represented in size and direction by the diagonal drawn from the point where the two forces act.

In this case we would obtain the diagram shown in Fig. 5.3.

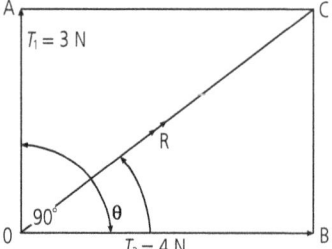

Fig. 5.3 *Finding the resultant force using trigonometry*

In the case of **perpendicular** forces the same result can be obtained using Pythagoras' theorem. Here,

$$OC^2 = OB^2 + BC^2$$
$$OC^2 = 4^2 + 3^2$$
$$OC^2 = 16 + 9 = 25$$
$$OC = 5N$$

The angle that the resultant makes with the two forces may be calculated using trigonometry, $\sin\theta = 3/5 = 0.6$, and $\theta = 36.9°$, or by direct measurement of the scale diagram.

You should note that a vector diagram is the **only** possible method at this level when the two faces are **not** perpendicular to each other.

5.2 Adding velocities

An aeroplane may have two components to its velocity, one due to the movement of the plane through the air and one due to the movement of the air itself.

Unless this is taken into account the plane will move far from the required course. Two velocities can be added in a way similar to that used for forces.

The two velocities are represented in a scale diagram and a parallelogram of velocities is drawn. The resultant velocity is represented by the diagonal as in the parallelogram of forces.

This resultant velocity is the velocity of the plane relative to the ground and gives the actual direction that the plane will travel.

6 Motion and forces

[syllabus sections B4.2–4.9]

6.1 Newton's first law of motion

The Ancient Greeks incorrectly thought that to maintain a constant velocity we need a **constant, net** (resultant or unbalanced) **force** (see Unit 35 for more on the history of physics). Newton realised that a resultant force causes an **acceleration** or **deceleration**.

Newton's ideas are stated in his three laws of motion.

Newton's first law of motion An object at rest remains at rest or, if in motion, continues to move in a straight line unless acted upon by an externally impressed force.

A good example of this law is a spacecraft in outer space. It travels at high speed in a straight line for many years without the need for an engine or any fuel. There is no friction (or any other force) to stop it so it just keeps moving.

On earth, friction opposes the relative motion of objects in contact with each other. We need a forward force to overcome this friction. If the velocity is constant this forward force is **equal** to friction, and the net force is zero.

6.2 Momentum and Newton's second law of motion

We define the **linear momentum** of an object as the product of its mass and velocity.

$$\text{linear momentum} = \text{mass} \times \text{velocity}$$

The unit of momentum (p) is kg m s^{-1}.

An unbalanced force causes a change in the momentum of an object.

Newton's second law of motion The rate of change of momentum of an object is proportional to the applied force and takes place in the direction of the force.

When the momentum changes, the object accelerates or decelerates and we can show that this leads to the equation

$$\text{force} = \text{mass} \times \text{acceleration}$$

This is an alternative form of Newton's second law: **A resultant force acting on a mass causes the mass to accelerate in the direction of the force.**

The unit of force is the newton (N).

A force of 1 N is that force that gives an acceleration of 1 m s^{-2} to a mass of 1 kg.

6.3 Force, mass and acceleration

We use the ticker-tape timer and trolleys on a runway to find experimentally the relation between force, mass and acceleration (Fig. 6.1).

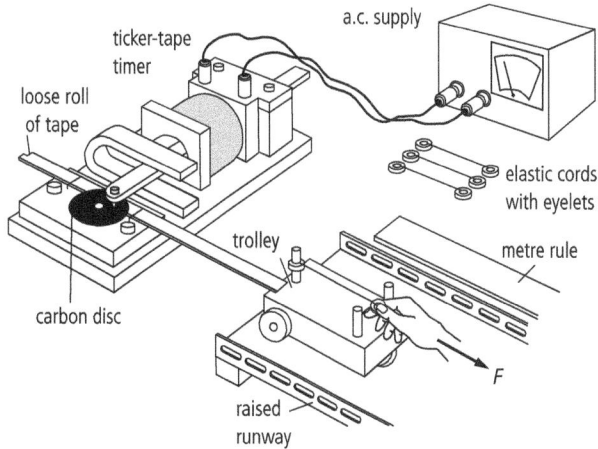

Fig. 6.1 *Ticker-tape apparatus*

We set the runway at an angle so that when a trolley is given a slight push it runs at a constant velocity – the dots are equally spaced. This means that no resultant force is acting on the trolley.

Constant mass

We first use one trolley and vary the force applied. We attach an elastic to the trolley and stretch it to a certain, constant length. This provides a **constant force**. We can calculate the acceleration of the trolley from the tape obtained (see Unit 3).

We now use two and three similar elastics, stretched to the same length, to provide double and triple the force. The new accelerations are measured. We can also make velocity/time graphs using '10-dot' strips of tape (Fig. 6.2).

The gradient of the graphs represents acceleration and the gradient increases as the force increases.

We find that the gradient is **proportional** to the force used, i.e. if the force doubles then the gradient also doubles.

As the acceleration is equivalent to this gradient, this means that the **acceleration** is **proportional** to the force.

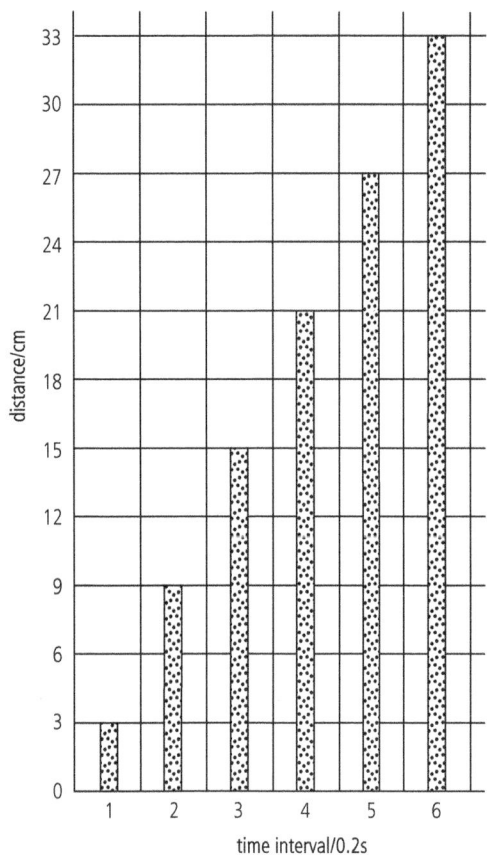

Fig. 6.2 *Velocity/time graph using 10-dot strips*

Constant force

When we use two or three trolleys on top of each other we find that with a greater mass the acceleration is **less** with the same force.

The acceleration is halved when two trolleys are used. With three trolleys, and the same force, the acceleration is one-third of the original value.

The acceleration is **inversely proportional** to the mass.

From these two experiments we have:

$$a \propto F$$

and $$a \propto \frac{1}{m}$$

Thus, $$a \propto \frac{F}{m}$$

and $$F = kma$$

where k is a constant of proportionality.

From the definition of one newton we see that $k = 1$ and thus

$$F = ma$$

6.4 Mass, weight and the acceleration due to gravity

We see that when a mass of 2 kg has only the force of gravity (20 N – its weight) acting upon it (i.e. it is falling freely), then the acceleration will be

$$a = \frac{F}{m} = \frac{20}{2} = 10 \text{ m s}^{-2}$$

A mass of 3 kg has a weight of 30 N and so also has an acceleration of 10 m s^{-2}.

In general, we see that

the weight of a body = mass of body $\times g$
weight = mg

Here we can think of g as 10 N kg^{-1}.

6.5 Newton's third law of motion

If object A provides a force on object B then object B provides an equal and opposite force on object A.

A jet engine is a good example of this law. Hot gases are forced out backwards by the jet engine. The gases push forward on the jet, with an equal force, so the jet accelerates forwards.

You may have seen garden water sprinklers that rotate. The water is forced out through a small nozzle and provides an equal force, but in the opposite direction, on the nozzle.

6.6 Conservation of linear momentum

The law of conservation of linear momentum states that when two or more bodies act on each other the total linear momentum of the bodies is constant, providing no external forces are acting.

Demonstration of conservation of momentum

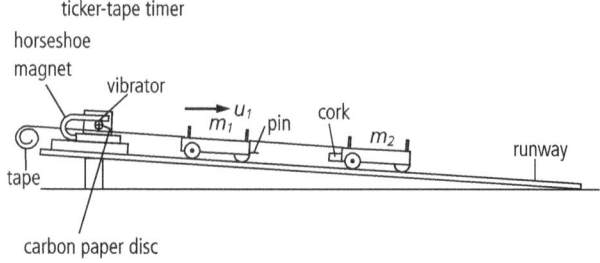

Fig. 6.3 *Apparatus to verify principle of conservation of momentum*

Two trolleys are used, each of mass m and attached to a ticker-tape timer, and collisions between them studied. The trolleys may separate or link up after the collision and the velocities before and after collision are measured (Fig. 6.3).

If before the collision the trolleys are moving with velocities u_1 and u_2, they have initial momenta mu_1 and mu_2.

After collision their new velocities are v_1 and v_2 and their new momenta are mv_1 and mv_2.

The **vector sum** of the momenta before and after the collision is found to be the same, thus proving the law of conservation of momentum, i.e. $m_1 u_1 + m_2 u_2 = m_1 v_1 + m_2 v_2$ (if u is the initial velocity and v is the final velocity).

(i) If the bodies separate after collision:
$m_1 u_1 + m_2 u_2 = m_1 v_1 + m_2 v_2$
(ii) If the bodies stop after collision:
$m_1 u_1 + m_2 u_2 = 0$
(iii) If the bodies coalesce after collision:
$m_1 u_1 + m_2 u_2 = (m_1 + m_2) V$
where V is the common velocity of two coalesced objects.

Further experiments may be carried out with trolleys of different mass and with one trolley initially stationary.

Example

A trolley of mass 3 kg is travelling at a speed of 2 m s^{-1} when it hits, and links up with, a trolley of mass 1 kg. They move off together. Calculate the speed at which they move off.

Initial momentum = mv_1, = 3×2 = 6 kg m s^{-1} where v_1 is the initial speed.

As the momentum is not altered by the collision, the final momentum is also 6 kg m s^{-1}.

The total mass is now 4 kg.

$u_1 = 2$ m s^{-1} $m_1 = 3$ kg
$u_2 = 0$ m s^{-1} $m_2 = 1$ kg
$V = ?$ m s^{-1}

Using $m_1 u_1 + m_2 u_2 = (m_1 + m_2) V$
$(3)(2) + (1)(0) = (3 + 1) V$
$6 = 4 V$

$V = \dfrac{6}{4} = \dfrac{3}{2}$ m s^{-1}

6.7 Circular motion

We can spin a stone at the end of a piece of string in a circle at a **constant speed**. However, as the direction of motion is changing, its velocity is changing: it is **accelerating**. A resultant force is needed to cause this acceleration. This force is directed towards the **centre** of the circle and is provided by the string.

Whenever we have an object moving in a circle, the force of the object is **towards the centre of the circle**. For example, the Moon moves around the Earth in a circle. The force of gravity between the Earth and the Moon provides the force needed towards the centre.

In general, we call the force towards the centre of the circular path the **centripetal force**. The actual force involved is different in different situations and can be gravity, the tension in a string, or friction, but they all act towards the centre. A car turning a corner is held on the circular path by friction.

Questions on Units 3 to 6

1. An electric train has a constant acceleration, from rest, of 2.5 m s^{-2}. Use a velocity/time graph to find
   a. the velocity after 5.0 s
   b. the distance travelled in the 5.0 s.
2. The velocity/time graph shown below represents the motion of an object.

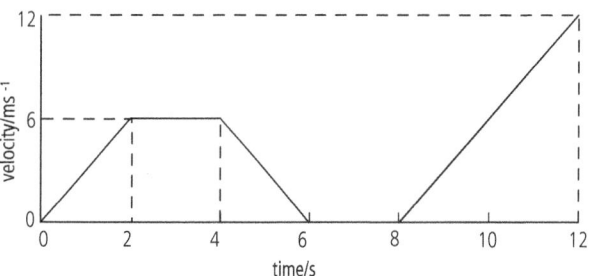

   a. Describe the motion of the object over the 12 s.
   b. Calculate the acceleration between the 8th and the 12th seconds.
   c. Calculate the distance travelled in the 12 s.
   d. Calculate the average speed over the 12 s.
3. A truck has a velocity of 8 m s^{-1} and then accelerates at a constant acceleration of 2 m s^{-2} until it has a velocity of 20 m s^{-1}. Using the **equations of motion**, find
   a. the time taken to reach 20 m s^{-1};
   b. the distance travelled during the acceleration;
   c. the distance travelled in the **next** two seconds if the truck continues to accelerate at 2 m s^{-2}.
4. A stone, dropped from a cliff, takes 2.0 s to reach the sea. Taking the acceleration due to gravity as 10 m s^{-2}, what is the height of the cliff?
5. The following table shows how the length of a spring changes when the spring is loaded.

Length of spring/cm	?	20	26	32	38	44
Load/N	0	20	40	60	80	100

Plot a graph of length of spring against load. Determine from the graph
   a the load that produces a spring length of 31 cm;
   b the spring length produced by a 35 N load;
   c the length of the unloaded spring;
   d the extension produced by the 80 N load.
6 Two forces, each of 50 N, act upon an object at an angle of 120° to each other. Find the size of the resultant force using a scale diagram.
7 A force of 60 N acts horizontally on a body. A second force of 80 N acts vertically on the same body. Find by either calculation or scale diagram the size and direction of the resultant force.
8 a   i What is meant by momentum?
       ii How is the resultant force acting on a body related to the **change of momentum** of the body?
       iii State which of the quantities mentioned are vector quantities.
    b A motorist, driving on a straight level road, suddenly notices a road block and nearly has a bad accident. Draw a speed/time graph for his motion given the following details:

    At 0 s the motorist, driving at 40 m s^{-1}, notices the road block. After 1.0 s, he applies the brakes. These produce a deceleration of 50 m s^{-2}. After a further 0.5 s his brakes fail. After another 2.0 s the car comes to rest.

    Given that the car stopped **just** at the road block, calculate how far away the road block was from the motorist when he first noticed it.
    c If the mass of the motorist and his car together is 1000 kg, calculate the value of the resultant force that retarded the car when the brakes were working. **In words**, define the unit of force used.

(CXC)

7 Energy, work and power

[syllabus sections B5.1–5.18]

Energy is the capacity to do work. The unit of energy is the **joule** (J).

Energy exists in different forms. **Heat**, **light** and **sound** are three forms of energy. When objects are moving they possess **kinetic energy**. **Electrical energy** is one of the most useful types of energy.

7.1 Potential energy

Energy can be stored for later use. We refer to stored energy as potential energy. Potential energy is defined as the energy stored by an object by virtue of its position or state. There are several different forms of potential energy.

A battery stores **chemical energy** and as we use the battery the chemical energy is transformed into electrical energy. Petrol is also a store of chemical energy, which is converted into kinetic energy as a vehicle moves.

When a catapult is stretched, **elastic energy** is stored. We can release it and change the energy into the kinetic energy of a stone.

Nuclear power stations use stored **nuclear energy** as their energy source (nuclear energy is discussed in Unit 33).

Finally, we can store energy by lifting an object to a higher position. This energy is **gravitational potential energy**. It may be converted into kinetic energy if we let the object fall.

7.2 Work

When we move a force through a distance we do work and transform energy from one form into another. **Work is defined as the force multiplied by the distance moved in the direction of the force.**

$$\text{work} = \text{force} \times \text{distance moved in the direction of the force}$$

The unit of work is the **joule**(J). One joule is the work done (or the energy transformed) when a force of 1 N moves through a distance of 1 m in the direction of the force.

When we lift an object vertically upwards, at a constant speed, the force used is the **weight** of the object.

7.3 Energy transformations

Common processes are often a series of energy changes.

A battery changes chemical energy into electrical energy. The electrical energy may then be used to drive a motor and obtain kinetic energy. Alternatively, the electrical energy may be converted to heat and light in a light bulb.

Thermal energy is produced when work is done against friction, e.g. when we push a block along a table, our stored chemical energy is converted to thermal energy as the work is done.

In all energy changes the principle of conservation of energy applies.

Principle of conservation of energy Energy can neither be created nor destroyed but it may be changed from one form to another.

If it appears that energy is lost then usually thermal energy will account for the 'loss', e.g. in machines (see Unit 8).

7.4 Gravitational potential energy

We can obtain a useful equation for **changes** in the gravitational potential energy of an object of mass, m. When we lift the object, through a height h, the force we use equals the weight of the object, mg.

$$\text{work done} = \text{force} \times \text{distance moved}$$
$$\text{work done} = mg \times h$$

The work done on the mass is equal to the increase in gravitational potential energy, ΔE_p, of the mass.

$$\Delta E_p = mgh$$

The Greek letter, Δ, delta, is used to represent a change in a quantity.

7.5 Kinetic energy

We can also show that the kinetic energy, E_k, of a mass, m, moving with a velocity, v, is given by

$$E_k = \frac{1}{2} mv^2$$

A falling object transforms potential energy into kinetic energy.

7.6 Power

The **rate** at which energy is transformed is often important. Power is defined as the work done, or energy converted, per unit of time.

$$\text{power} = \frac{\text{work done (J)}}{\text{time taken (s)}}$$

The unit of power is the **watt** (W). One watt is the rate of working of one joule per second.

Our own power may be measured approximately by timing a run up a flight of stairs. We measure the height gained, our weight and the time taken. We calculate the work done and from this the power output. A typical value for a fit young person is 500 W (0.5 kW).

7.7 Sources of energy

Energy is needed, in different forms, for all activities and processes in everyday life. It is only quite recently that we have begun to realise the importance of careful use of energy.

We obtain most of our energy in the Caribbean from oil and gas. These are both **non-renewable** sources of energy and the world's supply of energy will finish eventually.

Coal, which is used in many countries for producing electricity, will last for a longer time but will eventually also be finished.

We must look at alternative energy sources such as solar energy, geothermal energy and the energy in the wind and the waves.

Solar energy

The Sun's energy can be used directly. With the help of concave mirrors to bring the Sun's rays together (see Unit 17), high temperatures may be obtained. Solar water heaters, which absorb the heat radiation from the Sun, are becoming more common.

It is possible, but difficult, to convert the Sun's radiant energy into electrical energy, e.g. in solar-power calculators. This practice is not very common on a larger scale as the collecting plates are expensive and convert only a small fraction of the energy available.

Geothermal energy

Geothermal energy is the use of the large amount of thermal energy stored in rocks deep in the Earth. As we go deeper into the Earth the temperature rises substantially (at 6 km depth it is about 200 °C). It has been shown that it is possible to drill holes to these depths and pump down cold water which heats up and is used on its return to the surface.

Wind and wave energy

Winds have been used to drive large windmills which then drive an electrical generator. Similarly, wave energy can be used to provide the energy to turn a generator.

Nuclear energy

Nuclear energy is a possible long-term source of energy. However, there are problems of waste disposal and safety that have not yet been entirely solved (see Unit 34).

Questions on Unit 7

1. What is the work done by a force of 30 N if it moves through a distance of 80 cm in the direction of the force?
2. If a body of weight 40 N is moved vertically upwards a distance of 14 m, what is the increase in its potential energy?
3. What is the kinetic energy of a girl of mass 25 kg running at a speed of 8.0 m s^{-1}?
4. a A mass of 50 kg is 6 m from the floor. If the force of gravity is 10 N kg^{-1}, what is the gravitational potential energy stored?
   b The mass now falls to the floor. Use the principle of conservation of energy to find the speed of the object as it strikes the floor.
5. What is the energy used by a motor of power output 1.5 kW if it is used for 10 minutes?
6. A car needs a force of 550 N to push it at a steady speed along a horizontal road. If a man pushes this car a distance of 30 m in 22 s, what power is he supplying?
7. What device can be used to transform
   a sound into electrical energy
   b electrical energy into sound energy
   c chemical energy into electrical energy
   d electrical energy into kinetic energy
   e kinetic energy into electrical energy?

8 Turning forces

[syllabus sections B1.5–1.9, 5.15–5.17]

A force may cause an object to rotate if the object is pivoted at a point. This point is known as the **fulcrum**. Examples are water taps, doors, levers and screw tops on jars.

We can use a suspended metre rule to investigate turning forces. We find that the turning effect of a force depends on both the **size** of the force and the **distance** of the force from the fulcrum. This is why it is easier to close a door by pushing on the door far from the hinge. When we use a spanner to undo a tight nut we find it easier with a long spanner. This increases the turning effect of the force.

The size of the turning effect is called its **moment**.

8.1 Moment of force

The moment of force about a point is defined as the product of the force and the perpendicular distance of its line of action from the point.

moment of force = force × perpendicular distance from the point

The unit of moment of force is N m. The moment of force is also called the **torque** and is given the symbol T.

Equilibrium of moments

You will find that a simple rule for the equilibrium of moments can be derived from your experiments on balancing a metre rule. We see an example in Fig. 8.1.

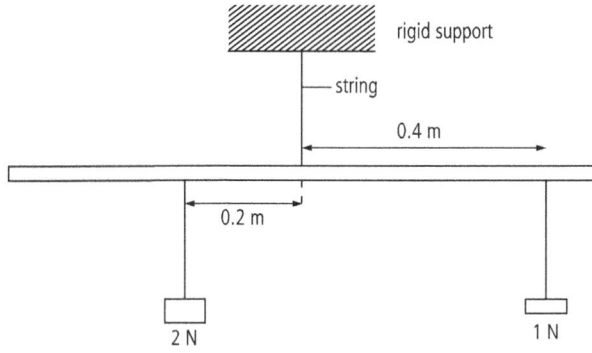

Fig. 8.1 *Balancing a metre rule*

The metre rule is balanced. There is a weight of 1 N on one side, a distance of 0.4 m away from the pivot. On the other side a weight of 2 N is 0.2 m away from the pivot. The moment of force of **each** weight is 0.4 N m. The 1 N weight provides a clockwise moment and the 2 N weight provides an anticlockwise moment. As the moments are in opposite directions and are equal, the rule balances horizontally.

The principle of moments

When a body is in equilibrium the sum of the clockwise moments is equal to the sum of the anticlockwise moments. We use this principle to solve problems.

If a light rod of 4 m length is suspended at its midpoint and a weight of 30 N is placed 0.5 m from one end, where would a weight of 75 N need to be placed to balance the rod (Fig. 8.2)?

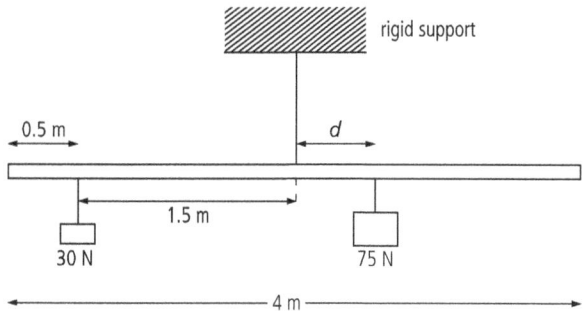

Fig. 8.2 *Principle of moments*

The moment in both directions has to be the same. The important distance is the distance from the fulcrum.

So, $\quad 75 \times d = 30 \times 1.5$
$$d = \frac{45}{75}$$
$$d = 0.6 \text{ m}$$

8.2 Centre of gravity

An unloaded metre rule only balances horizontally when suspended at one point. This point is called the centre of gravity.

The centre of gravity is the point on a body where its whole weight may be considered to act.

When the rule is not suspended at its centre of gravity we have to take account of the moment of force that the weight provides.

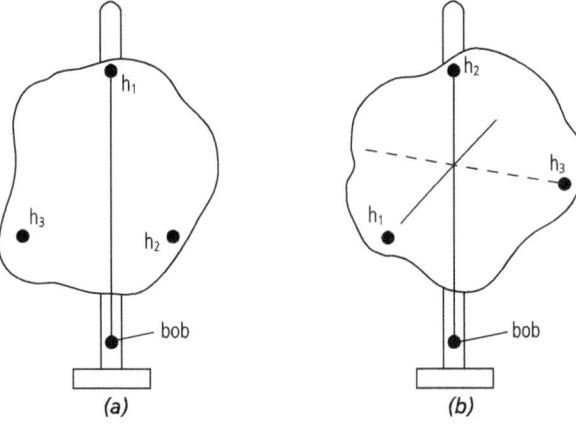

Fig. 8.3 *Finding the centre of gravity of a lamina*

Centre of gravity of a lamina

A lamina is a thin sheet of material such as cardboard or metal. We use a plumbline and bob to find the centre of gravity of the sheet. We make three or four small holes (h) at different points around the edge of the lamina. We suspend the lamina from a nail through one of the holes so that it swings freely and we hang the plumbline from the nail. We draw the rest position of the string on the sheet. We repeat this using the other holes. The lines intersect at one point, which is the centre of gravity (Fig. 8.3).

8.3 Stability

The stability of an object depends on the position of the centre of gravity. If the centre of gravity is high above the ground, the body is more likely to topple over, e.g. a bus loaded on top with heavy baggage. This can be investigated using blocks of varying mass and shape.

A body can be said to be in equilibrium when all forces acting balance off each other. The net force is zero and the body is at rest. There are three types of equilibrium:

Stable equilibrium When a body in stable equilibrium is displaced slightly, the centre of gravity returns to its original position (Fig. 8.4).

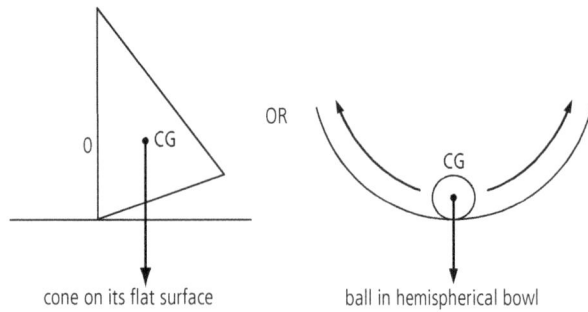

Fig. 8.4 *Stable equilibrium*

Unstable equilibrium When a body in unstable equilibrium is displaced slightly, the centre of gravity permanently moves from its original position (Fig. 8.5).

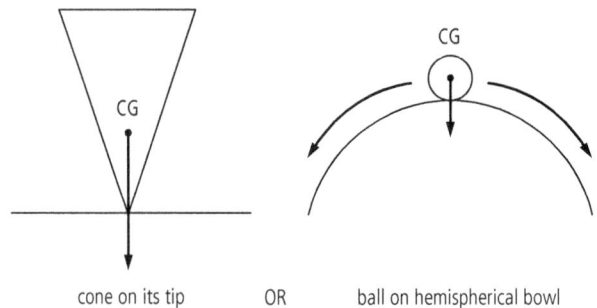

Fig. 8.5 *Unstable equilibrium*

Neutral equilibrium When a body in neutral equilibrium is displaced slightly, the centre of gravity changes spatial position but the height of the centre of gravity above the surface remains constant (Fig. 8.6).

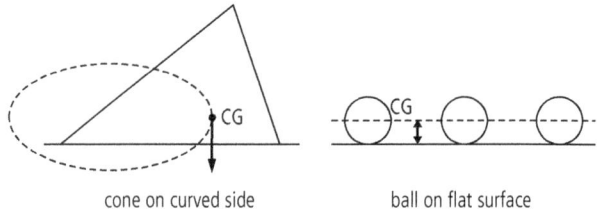

Fig. 8.6 *Neutral equilibrium*

8.4 Machines

A machine is a device in which a force – the **effort** – applied at one point is used to overcome another force – the **load** – at another point. Examples are levers, pulleys and gears.

The crowbar

We can use a crowbar to lift a large rock (Fig 8.7). The crowbar pivots on the ground. There is a large distance between the applied force and the fulcrum but only a small distance between the rock and the fulcrum. Our smaller force has a larger moment than the weight of the rock and is able to lift the rock. A crowbar is an example of a **lever**. This is a simple machine (see below).

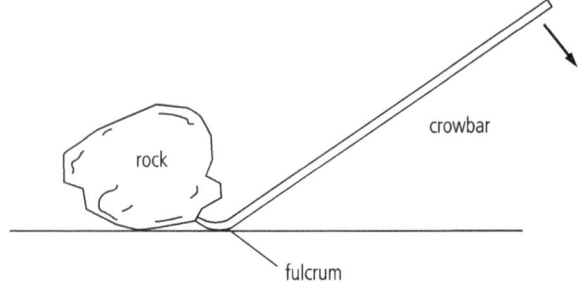

Fig. 8.7 *Using a crowbar*

Levers

The crowbar is one example of a lever. It is a **force multiplier** as the force applied to the load is much greater than the effort used. However, the effort moves further than the load.

The forearm is a **distance multiplier**. The biceps muscle provides the effort (Fig 8.8).

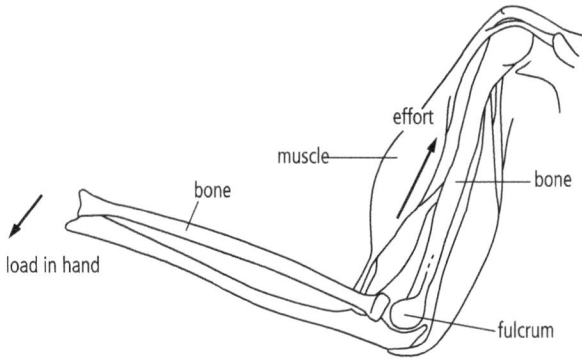

Fig. 8.8 *The forearm as a lever*

The force of the muscle is greater than the load (as it is nearer the fulcrum) but the load moves further than the effort.

Efficiency of a machine

A machine makes tasks easier but does not increase the amount of energy available. In fact, machines always waste some of the energy, mainly because of friction. The energy supplied **to** the machine is always more than the useful work done **by** the machine. The useful work can also be thought of as the energy output.

The efficiency is defined as follows:

$$\% \text{ efficiency} = \frac{\text{energy output}}{\text{energy input}} \times 100\%$$

or

$$\% \text{ efficiency} = \frac{\text{work output}}{\text{work input}} \times 100\%$$

The work input is the work done **by** the effort. The work output is the work done **on** the load.

Efficiency of a two-pulley system

A two-pulley system that you can set up is shown in Fig. 8.9. We place a small load in the pan hanging on the pulley and then add weights – the effort – until the loaded pan rises.

$$\text{mechanical advantage (MA)} = \frac{\text{load}}{\text{effort}}$$

This quantity is a ratio of two like terms and has no units.

We measure the distances travelled by the load, and the effort.

work input = effort × distance travelled by the effort
work output = load × distance travelled by the load

Also,

$$\text{Velocity ratio (VR)} = \frac{\text{distance moved by effort}}{\text{distance moved by load}}$$

$$\% \text{ efficiency} = \frac{\text{load} \times \text{distance travelled by the load}}{\text{effort} \times \text{distance travelled by effort}} \times \frac{100}{1} \%$$

$$= \frac{\text{MA}}{\text{VR}} \times \frac{100}{1} \%$$

Remember efficiency can never exceed 1, i.e. $0 \leq \% \leq 1$

We then calculate the efficiency of the pulley system. We can use larger weights as the load and find the efficiency for a series of values of the load. The efficiency is less than 100% as we waste energy in overcoming friction and in lifting the lower pulley itself.

You can extend this to larger pulley systems.

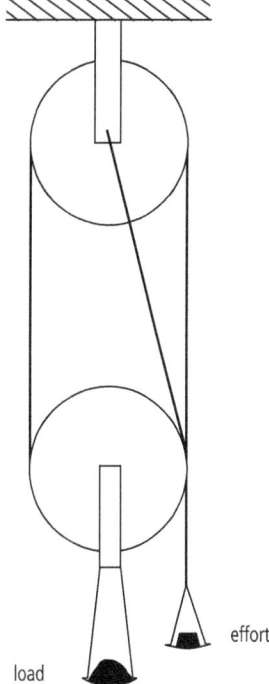

Fig. 8.9 *A two-pulley system*

Efficiency of an electric motor

The electrical energy supplied to an electric motor is converted to mechanical work. The amount of electrical energy used by the motor can be calculated (see Unit 25), and also the work done by the motor. The efficiency of the motor is then calculated as above.

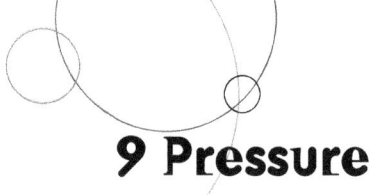

9 Pressure

[syllabus sections B6.1–6.4]

We often hear the words 'pressure' and 'force' used as if they have the same meaning. They are related but are distinctly different quantities.

We define pressure as the force acting perpendicularly per unit area.

$$\text{pressure} = \frac{\text{force (N)}}{\text{area (m}^2)}$$

The SI unit of pressure is the pascal, Pa. One pascal is one newton per metre squared, $1\text{ Pa} = 1\text{ N m}^{-2}$.

Non-SI units are also commonly used – we introduce them later.

When we concentrate a force on a small area the pressure is large. For instance, the area of the cutting edge of a sharp knife is small. The pressure is high under the blade with just a moderate force.

The small areas of the points of nails and drawing pins cause a large pressure under the point.

9.1 Pressure in liquids

In a liquid the pressure is greater the deeper we go. This is due to the greater **weight** of liquid above us. Scuba divers have to take great care that they do not remain in the high-pressure depths for too long.

We demonstrate this increase of pressure with a can with three holes in the side. We fill it with water and three jets of water are produced (Fig. 9.1).

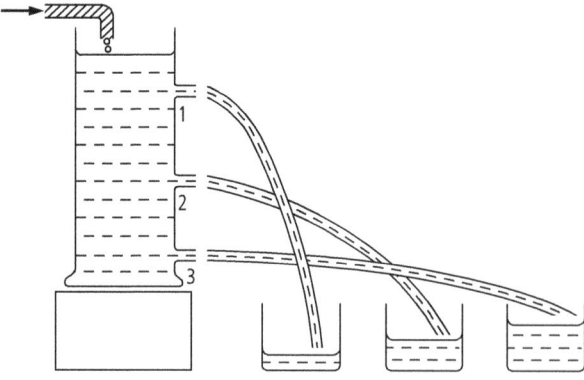

Fig. 9.1 *Pressure in a liquid increased with depth*

The water from the lowest hole comes out fastest owing to the greater pressure.

This also shows that the pressure does not only act downwards, it acts horizontally as well. The pressure at a point in a liquid actually acts in all directions.

9.2 Pressure, density and depth

Liquids with a greater density exert a greater pressure for the same depth of liquid.

A depth of liquid, h, with a density, ρ, is contained in a vessel of cross-sectional area, A (Fig. 9.2).

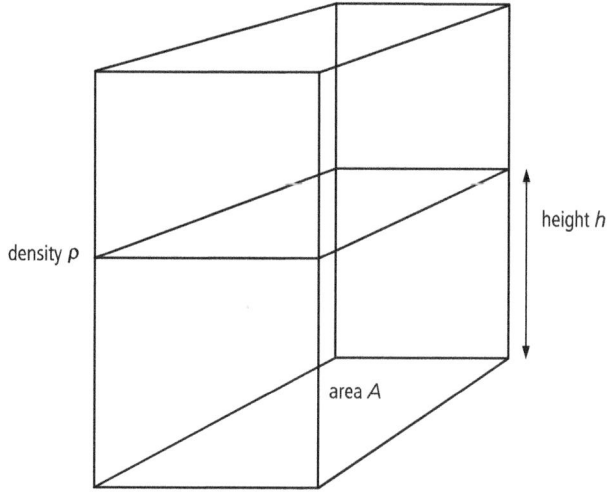

Fig. 9.2 *Pressure in a liquid depends on the height of the liquid above it*

$$\begin{aligned}
\text{volume of liquid }(V) &= \text{height} \times \text{cross-sectional area} \\
V &= hA \\
\text{mass of liquid }(m) &= \text{volume} \times \text{density} \\
m &= V\rho = hA\rho \\
\text{weight of liquid} &= \text{mass} \times \text{acceleration due to gravity} \\
\text{weight} &= hA\rho g \\
\text{pressure on base }(P) &= \frac{\text{weight}}{\text{area}} = \frac{hA\rho g}{A} \\
P &= h\rho g
\end{aligned}$$

We see that the pressure in a particular liquid depends only on the vertical height of the liquid above it. It does not depend on the cross-sectional area of the column.

When a liquid is at rest the pressure at all points at the same horizontal level is the same.

9.3 Transmission of liquid pressure

The pressure exerted on the surface of a liquid is transmitted throughout the liquid. This is used in the hydraulic braking system (Fig. 9.3). When we press the brake pedal the hydraulic fluid transmits the pressure to the brake shoes which are forced outwards and which rub against the wheel. When the brake pedal is released, springs return the brake shoes to the normal position.

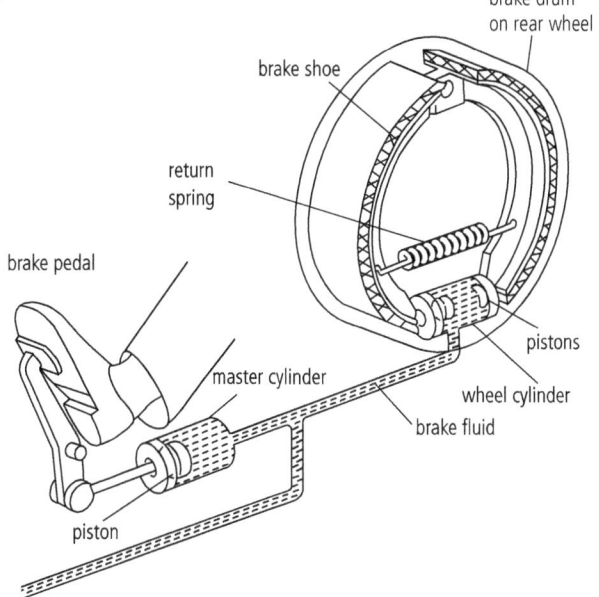

Fig. 9.3 *Hydraulic braking system*

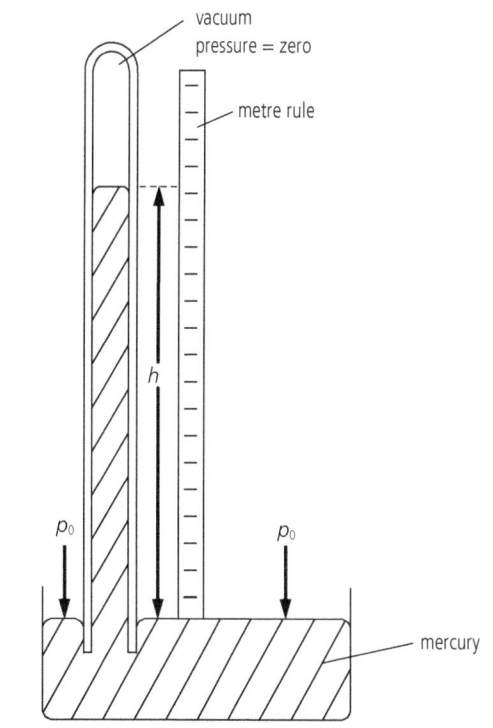

Fig. 9.4 *Simple barometer*

9.4 Pressure in gases

The atmosphere exerts a pressure upon us. The pressure in gases is due to the collisions of gas molecules with surfaces (see Unit 13). The gas molecules exert a net force over the internal surface area of the containing vessel.

Mercury barometer

We use a mercury barometer to measure atmospheric pressure (Fig. 9.4). To construct a mercury barometer we need a glass tube, length 0.9 m to 1.0 m, which is sealed at one end. We carefully fill the tube with mercury and place the open end, covered by a finger, under the surface of some mercury in a dish. When we remove the finger the mercury falls a distance in the tube. This leaves a vacuum above the mercury.

The atmosphere acts on the mercury surface and holds up the column of mercury, height h. Atmospheric pressure is equal to the pressure P of the column of mercury and is stated as, say, 75.3 cm of mercury. Standard atmospheric pressure is 76 cm of mercury. If atmospheric pressure changes, the height of the mercury also changes. Mercury vapour is dangerous; mercury must be handled with care.

We can also make a water barometer but its length is about 10 m as the density of water is much less than the density of mercury.

Effects of atmospheric pressure

Crushing can experiment

We can show the forces due to atmospheric pressure using a metal can. We connect a vacuum pump directly to the can. When the air is extracted the can collapses. Alternatively, some water is boiled in the can for a few minutes. The steam and the water vapour drive out most of the air. We now place a tight stopper in the can and allow it to cool. The steam and water vapour condense leaving a low pressure in the can. The air pressure on the outside crushes the can.

Atmospheric pressure acts in all directions

We take a flat-topped glass container filled with water and place a flat piece of card on top. When we carefully invert them the card stays on the container. This is due to the pressure of the air acting upwards.

Atmospheric pressure and the weather

Variations in atmospheric pressure help us to predict weather changes. If the atmospheric pressure falls quickly at a particular place then stormy weather is usually approaching the area. At the centre of a hurricane the pressure is very low.

Manometer

A manometer is a U-shaped, transparent tube containing a liquid, usually coloured water or mercury (Fig. 9.5a). A manometer measures a difference in pressure. We use a manometer to measure the pressure of a gas supply.

Originally the liquid levels are the same on both sides. When we attach the gas supply the levels change (Fig. 9.5b).

Points A and B are at the same level and thus at the same pressure. At A only gas pressure p_1, is acting but at B the pressure is the sum of the atmospheric pressure p_0, and the pressure due to the extra liquid. Therefore

gas pressure = atmospheric pressure + liquid pressure

$$p = p_0 + p_1$$

We measure the pressure of a gas supply in units of centimetres of water or mercury. The manometer tells us the **excess** pressure of the supply. A cylinder of gas, which we use in the Caribbean, has a pressure of 30–35 cm of water above atmospheric pressure.

$$p_1 = h\rho g$$

where ρ is the density of water.

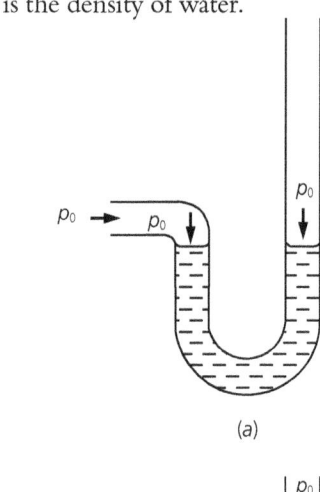

(a)

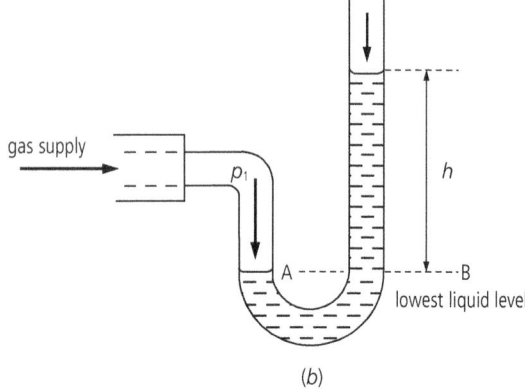

(b)

Fig. 9.5 *Manometer*

10 Upthrust and flotation

[syllabus sections B6.5–6.6]

When we place an object, hanging on a spring balance, into water, the reading on the spring balance goes down. This is because the water provides an upward force called the **upthrust**.

A Greek scientist, Archimedes, was the first to investigate the effects of upthrust in fluids (fluids are liquids and gases).

10.1 Archimedes' principle

Archimedes' principle states that when a body is partially or wholly immersed in a fluid it experiences an upthrust, which is equal to the weight of fluid displaced.

As we gradually immerse an object in a liquid it displaces more of the liquid. Therefore the upthrust increases with greater immersion.

10.2 Floating objects

With objects that float, such as rafts and boats, the upthrust is equal to the weight of the object. The net force is zero.

The **law of flotation** states that a floating object displaces its own weight of the fluid in which it floats.

10.3 Submarines

While floating on the sea's surface, a submarine displaces a weight of water equal to its own weight.

To dive it takes in water and increases its weight. Now, even when fully submerged, its weight is greater than the upthrust and it sinks.

While under the sea it may pump out some of the extra water and make the weight equal to the upthrust again. It now stays at a constant depth.

To rise it has to pump out more water and make the weight less than the upthrust.

You should note that once the submarine is fully submerged, the **upthrust is constant** and it is the weight of the submarine that is changed.

10.4 Balloons

Balloons experience an upthrust that is due to the weight of air they displace.

If we have a hydrogen-filled balloon it rises in air because the upthrust of the air is greater than the total weight of the balloon and the hydrogen.

Questions on Units 8 to 10

1. A uniform see-saw is pivoted at its mid-point. It is 4 m long and a girl of weight 240 N sits at one end.
   a. What is the moment of the girl's weight about the pivot?
   b. A boy sits on the see-saw and to make it balance he has to sit 1.6 m from the pivot. What is his weight?

2. A uniform plank 6.0 m long balances at a point 2.4 m from one end when a stone of weight 80 N is placed at that end. Find the weight of the plank.

3. A container, full of liquid of density 1500 kg m^{-3}, is 0.6 m in depth. The cross-sectional area of the container is 0.2 m^2. Find the volume, mass and weight of the liquid in the container. What is the pressure exerted by the liquid on the base of the container?

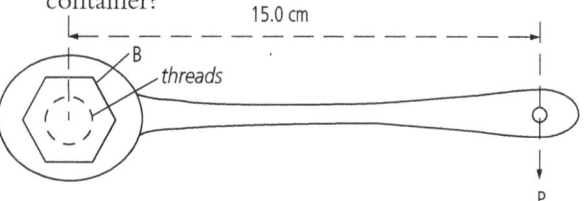

4. A mechanic uses the spanner shown in the diagram above to turn a bolt, B, into a threaded nut. The force, P, used to do this is applied in a **horizontal** plane and perpendicular to the length of the spanner.
   a. Sketch a simple, labelled diagram showing the forces acting in a horizontal plane on the spanner as it begins to turn the bolt.
   b. If an effort of 80 N is applied 15.0 cm from the axis of the bolt, calculate the moment of the forces opposing the effort as the spanner just begins to turn.
   c. Name the principle used in obtaining your result in (b) above. State this principle.
   d. Explain why, if the mechanic uses a longer spanner, the effort will be smaller but the energy he expends in turning the spanner through one revolution will be the same.
   e. Suppose the same spanner were used in a vertical rather than a horizontal plane. Describe, with a labelled diagram, how you would measure the effort that would now be needed just to turn the bolt.
   f. Would you expect the value for the effort in (e) to be greater or less than that used in (a)? Give a reason for your answer. (CXC)

11 Temperature and expansion

[syllabus sections C1.1–1.6]

The temperature of an object does **not** tell us how much energy it contains – this also depends on its size and the material of which it is made.

However, if the temperature of two objects, which are in contact, is **different**, energy flows from one to the other, from the higher temperature to the lower temperature. This flow of energy we call **heat** (see Unit 15).

A change in temperature often affects the size of an object. It expands or contracts.

11.1 Expansion of solids

We take a metal bar that just fits a gap in another piece of metal (Fig. 11.1). When we heat the bar it can no longer fit into the gap – it has expanded. You may also see this demonstrated with a metal ball that fits into a ring. These experiments show that solids expand, by small amounts, when heated.

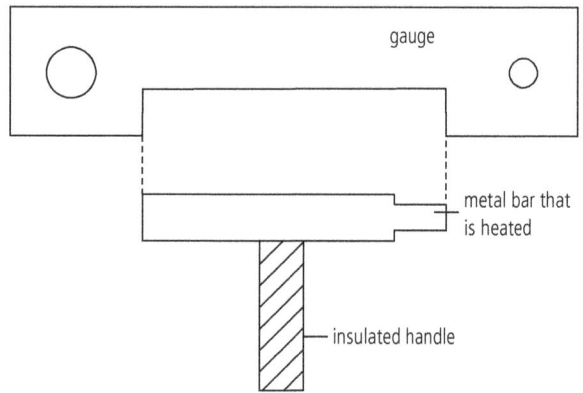

Fig. 11.1 *Bar and gauge*

When a glass bottle stopper is stuck, we heat the neck of the bottle. The neck expands and the stopper is now easily removed.

Bimetallic strip

A bimetallic strip is made from two metals that expand at different rates when heated. Brass and iron are often used (Fig. 11.2a). When heated, the strip bends so that the metal that expands more is on the outside of the curve (Fig. 11.2b). Brass expands more than iron and so is on the outside of the curved strip. Brass also contracts more than iron and so the strip bends in the other direction when cooled.

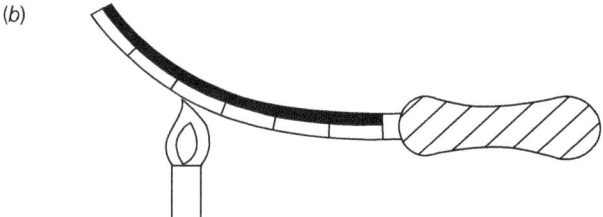

Fig. 11.2 *Bimetallic strip*

Applications of the bimetallic strip

The bimetallic strip is used to turn electric circuits on or off.

In a fire alarm the bimetallic strip heats up and bends to complete a circuit (Fig. 11.3).

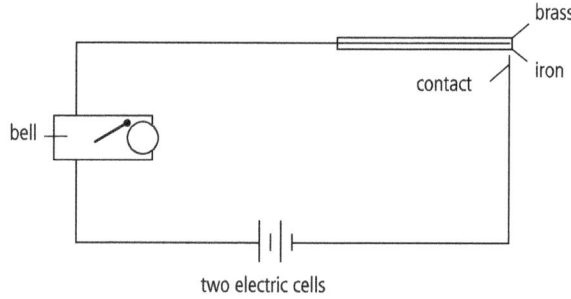

Fig. 11.3 *Bimetallic strip in a fire alarm*

In a cold-weather (frost) alarm, the bimetallic strip bends and turns on a circuit when it gets cold.

In a refrigerator the bimetallic strip bends and breaks contact, thus turning off the circuit, when the temperature is cold enough.

Similarly, in an electric iron the bimetallic strip breaks the circuit when the temperature is hot enough.

11.2 Forces in expansion and contraction of solids

Large forces are involved when solids expand. We use the apparatus in Fig. 11.4 to demonstrate this. The cast-iron rod A breaks as the steel bar B is heated. The steel bar is prevented from expanding until the internal forces become so great that they break the cast-iron rod.

If we place the cast-iron rod inside the steel frame, it

can be broken by heating the steel bar, securing the cast-iron rod and then allowing the steel bar to contract.

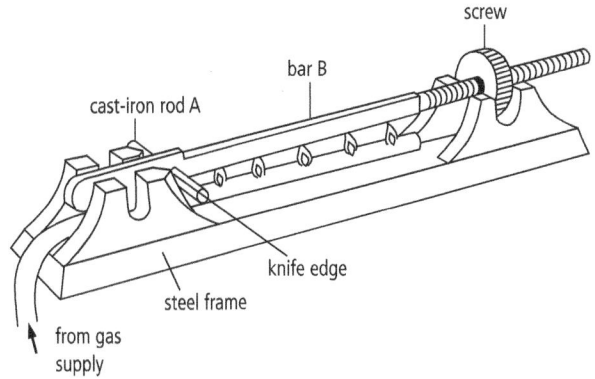

Fig. 11.4 *Bar-breaker*

Applications

The effects of the large forces when solids expand can be advantageous or disadvantageous.

Rivets are used to join two sheets of metal. The rivet is very hot when put in the hole in the two pieces of metal. It is then hammered to a head on each side. As it cools it contracts and pulls the pieces tightly together.

Thick glass containers may crack as hot water is poured inside. The glass on the inside expands but as glass is a poor conductor of heat (see Unit 14), the glass on the outside does not heat up or expand. The forces created crack the glass.

Concrete is often laid in sections with wood or pitch between the sections to allow for expansion. Bridges may be placed on rollers to allow for expansion and telephone wires are hung with spare cable to allow for contraction in cold weather.

11.3 Expansion of liquids

Liquids expand more than solids. This is seen using the apparatus in Fig. 11.5. We heat the water in the trough and see the liquid rise in the tube owing to its expansion. We also notice that different liquids expand by different amounts for the same temperature rise.

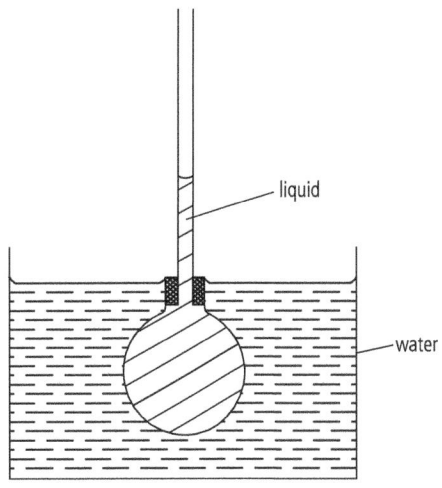

Fig. 11.5 *Expansion of a liquid*

11.4 Gases

We demonstrate the expansion of gases using the apparatus in Fig. 11.6. We warm the flask using our hands and we see that the thread of liquid moves rapidly up the stem. Gases expand much more rapidly and by much greater amounts than liquids or solids.

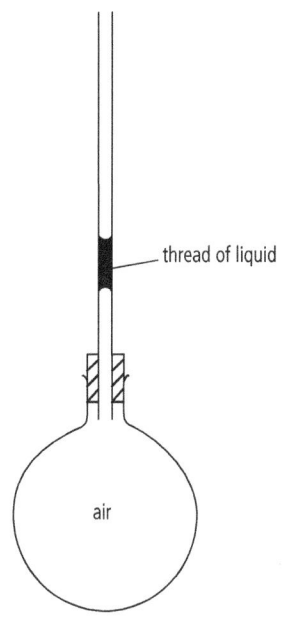

Fig. 11.6 *Expansion of air*

11.5 Measuring temperature

We measure temperature using some property of a substance that varies with temperature, such as the expansion of a liquid.

We establish a temperature scale by choosing two fixed points.

The **upper fixed point** is the temperature of steam from pure boiling water at standard atmospheric pressure (76 cm mercury). This is 100 degrees on the

Celsius scale (100 °C).

The **lower fixed point** is the temperature of pure melting ice at standard atmospheric pressure. This is 0 °C.

The two fixed points are marked on the scale of a thermometer and the interval between them is divided into 100 equal parts.

Laboratory thermometer

A laboratory thermometer is shown in Fig. 11.7. The mercury expands when heated and rises up the narrow capillary tube.

This is a convenient thermometer but it is not very accurate.

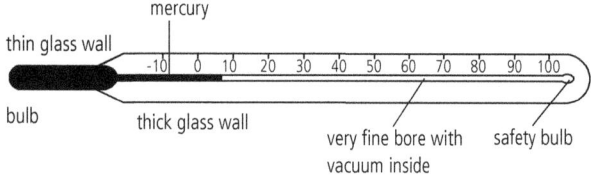

Fig. 11.7 *Laboratory thermometer*

After a thermometer has been removed from a hot substance the mercury in the stem may still continue to rise. The safety bulb holds some mercury and prevents the thermometer from shattering.

The range of the thermometer, −10 °C to 110 °C, is suitable for work in the laboratory.

No mercury thermometer can be used at temperatures above about 340 °C as the mercury then boils.

Clinical thermometer

We measure the temperature of the human body with a clinical thermometer. We need greater accuracy here and the thermometer is designed for a limited range of temperatures around normal body temperature (37 °C). Its range is usually from about 35 °C to 44 °C. (Fig. 11.8)

It has a very narrow capillary bore and is smaller than a laboratory thermometer. It also has a constriction in the bore that prevents the mercury running back into the bulb when the thermometer is taken from the patient.

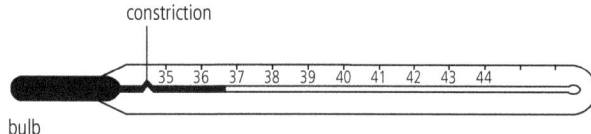

Fig. 11.8 *Clinical thermometer*

Thermocouple

A thermocouple is used to measure high temperatures and those that change quickly. When two dissimilar metals are wrapped together and heated, a small current flows if the circuit is completed (Fig. 11.9). The amount of current depends on the temperature and the scale is calibrated in degrees Celsius.

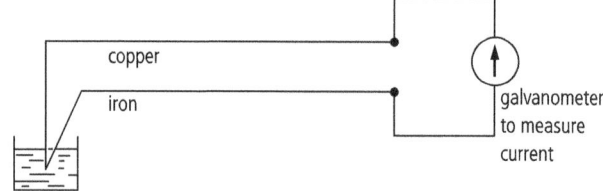

Fig. 11.9 *Thermocouple*

Other properties which can be used in thermometers are electrical resistance, the bending of a bimetallic strip or the change in volume of a gas.

Expansion of water upon freezing

Water expands as it freezes: 10 cm³ of water make about 11 cm³ of ice. Thus ice has a lower density than water and floats in water. In cold climates water pipes can burst if the water inside is allowed to freeze. Large forces are created as it freezes and expands.

12 Gas laws

[syllabus sections C1.7–1.10]

We consider three quantities when investigating the properties of gases: the **pressure**, **volume** and **temperature** of the gas. We perform three experiments, keeping one of the quantities constant each time.

12.1 Boyle's law

We use the apparatus shown in Fig. 12.1 to find the relationship between the pressure and volume of a gas at a constant temperature.

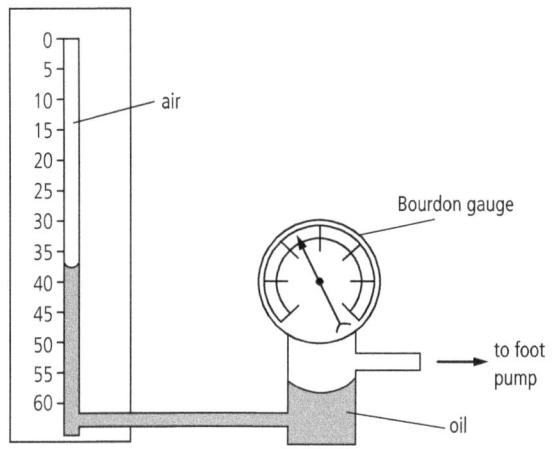

Fig. 12.1 *Apparatus for Boyle's law*

We have a fixed mass of air trapped and we measure its volume on the scale behind the tube. We measure the pressure of the air on the pressure gauge. We now reduce the volume of the air by pumping on the oil, which moves up the tube, and measure the new values of volume and pressure. We keep the temperature constant throughout the experiment.

We obtain a set of pairs of values of volume and pressure like those in Table 12.1. In the table we also have the product of the pressure and the volume. This product has a **constant value**.

Table 12.1 *Relationship between pressure and volume*

Volume/ cm³	Pressure/ Pa	Pressure × volume/ Pa cm³
30.1	1.0×10^5	30.1×10^5
23.2	1.3×10^5	30.2×10^5
16.9	1.8×10^5	30.4×10^5
13.4	2.2×10^5	29.5×10^5
12.0	2.5×10^5	30.0×10^5

Boyle's law may be stated as follows:

For a fixed mass of gas at a constant temperature the product of the pressure, P, and the volume, V, is a constant.

Mathematically,
$$P \times V = \text{a constant}$$

We can also state Boyle's law as follows:

For a fixed mass of gas at a constant temperature the pressure is **inversely proportional** to the volume.

If the original pressure and volume are P_1 and V_1 and the final pressure and volume are P_2 and V_2 then

$$P_1 V_1 = P_2 V_2$$

12.2 Charles' law

We use the apparatus shown in Fig. 12.2 to establish Charles' law. A fixed mass of gas is trapped in the syringe. We read the volume of the gas from the markings on the syringe. We take the temperature of the water, which is the same as the temperature of the gas.

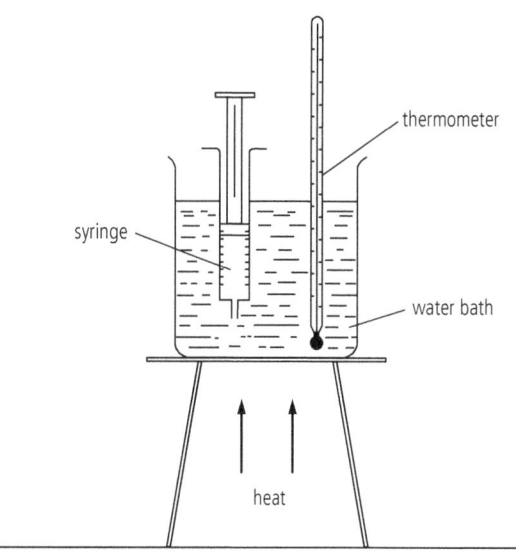

Fig. 12.2 *Apparatus for Charles' law*

We heat the water and obtain a temperature rise of about 20 °C. We wait a short while and note the new temperature and volume. The pressure is constant – it is equal to the pressure of the atmosphere outside the syringe.

We obtain a set of pairs of values of the temperature and the volume. Typical values are shown in Table 12.2.

Table 12.2 *Temperature/volume values*

Temp. T/°C	Volume V/cm³
25.0	10.8
45.2	11.6
72.1	12.3
90.4	13.2

We plot the results on a graph of volume against temperature (Fig. 12.3).

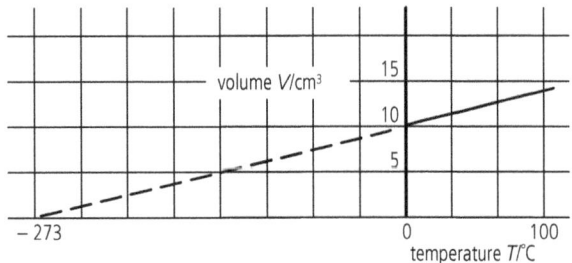

Fig. 12.3 *Volume/temperature graph (Celsius)*

The graph is a straight line. When we extend the line we obtain values of the volume that we would expect at lower temperatures. The volume would decrease and at a certain temperature the volume of the gas would theoretically become zero.

The temperature at which the volume of a gas would become zero is known as absolute zero. It is equal to −273 °C.

Kelvin scale of temperature

From the experiment to demonstrate Charles' law we can establish a new scale of temperature: the Kelvin or absolute temperature scale.

It begins at absolute zero (0 K). It rises at the same rate as the Celsius scale, i.e. 1 °C = 1 K, so

$$0 \text{ K} = -273 \text{ °C}$$
$$273 \text{ K} = 0 \text{ °C}$$
$$373 \text{ K} = 100 \text{ °C}$$

In general, $T/\text{K} = T/\text{°C} + 273$

If we redraw the graph of volume against temperature with the temperature in kelvin, then the graph is a straight line passing through the origin (Fig. 12.4).

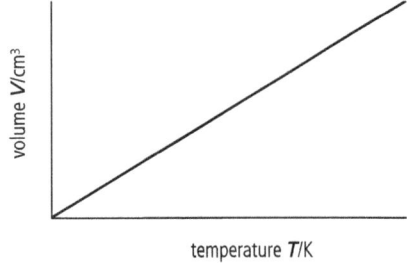

Fig. 12.4 *Volume/temperature graph (kelvin)*

Remember, a straight line through the origin means that the two quantities are proportional to each other.

Charles' law For a fixed mass of gas at a constant pressure the volume is directly proportional to its absolute temperature.

Alternatively we can show that:

$$\frac{V}{T} = \text{a constant (pressure constant, temperature in kelvin)}$$

If V_1 and T_1 are the original values of the volume and temperature and V_2 and T_2 are the final values, then

$$\frac{V_1}{T_1} = \frac{V_2}{T_2}$$

provided that the pressure is constant and the temperature is in kelvin.

12.3 Pressure law

The apparatus shown in Fig. 12.5 is used to investigate the variation of pressure with temperature at a constant volume. The flask only expands a very small amount, which we ignore.

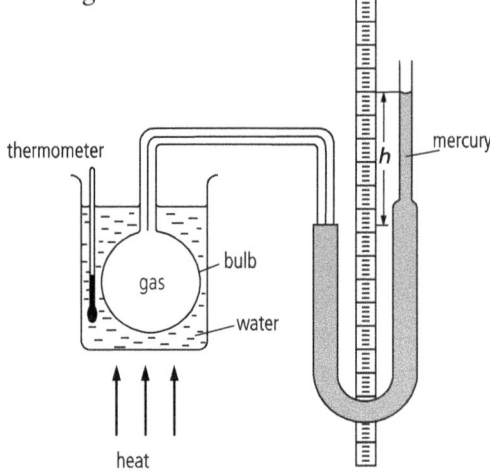

Fig. 12.5 *Apparatus for pressure law*

We obtain values of *h* for the pressure at various temperatures. When we plot a graph of pressure against kelvin temperature we obtain a straight-line graph similar to that in the previous section.

We find that at absolute zero the pressure of the gas would become zero.

This leads to the **pressure law**.

For a fixed mass of gas at a constant volume the pressure is directly proportional to the absolute temperature.

Alternatively, we can show that:

$$\frac{P}{T} = \text{a constant } (V \text{ constant, } T \text{ kelvin})$$

With P_1 and T_1 as the original pressure and temperature and P_2 and T_2 as the final values:

$$\frac{P_1}{T_1} = \frac{P_2}{T_2} \quad (V \text{ constant}) \quad (T \text{ kelvin})$$

12.4 Combined gas equation

We have three equations that describe the behaviour of gases. Each applies when one quantity remains constant. They are combined into one equation, which is true when all three quantities are varying (provided we have a fixed mass of gas).

Combined gas equation $\quad \dfrac{PV}{T} =$ a constant

Finally, as before, this leads to

$$\frac{P_1 V_1}{T_1} = \frac{P_2 V_2}{T_2}$$

13 Kinetic theory of matter

[syllabus sections C1.11–1.12, 2.1–2.2]

The gas laws discussed in Unit 12 do not explain **why** a gas behaves in that way. We now consider an important theory that can explain several properties of matter including the properties of gases. This is called the kinetic theory of matter.

13.1 Basic assumptions of kinetic theory of matter

1. Matter is composed of very many small particles called atoms or molecules.
2. The atoms or molecules in matter are vibrating or moving.

There are several experiments that support this theory.

Size of molecules

It is possible to obtain an idea of the size of an oil molecule from the following experiment.

We take a tray, with a few centimetres' depth of water, and put a fine dust of lycopodium powder or talcum powder on the surface (Fig. 13.1a).

We form an oil drop in a small loop and measure the diameter of the loop with the help of a magnifying glass. We then calculate the volume of the spherical oil drop from $\frac{4}{3}\pi r^3$, where r is the radius of the drop, which is half the diameter of the loop.

We now drop the oil on the water surface and it spreads out to form a circle just one molecule thick. This is a cylinder of radius R and a thickness t (Fig. 13.1b)

We measure the radius of this circular cylinder. The volume now is given by $\pi R^2 t$.

The two volumes are equal; only the shape is different. Therefore

$$\tfrac{4}{3}\pi r^3 = \pi R^2 t \quad \text{and}$$

$$t = \frac{4r^3}{3R^2}$$

The value t is the thickness of the patch of oil and gives an approximate value for the size of a molecule. In a typical experiment t is about 3×10^{-9} m.

This is not very accurate as the oil patch may be more than one molecule thick. It gives an **upper limit** for the size of the oil molecule.

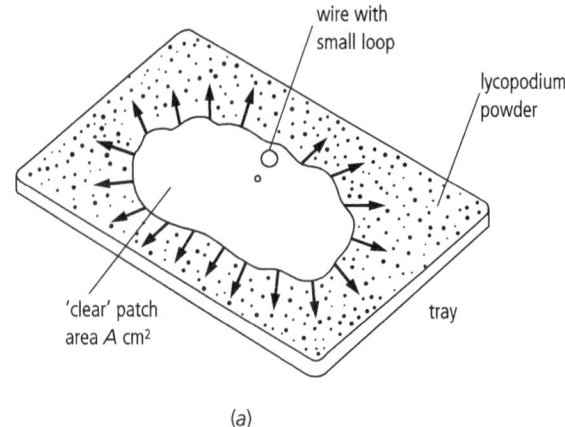

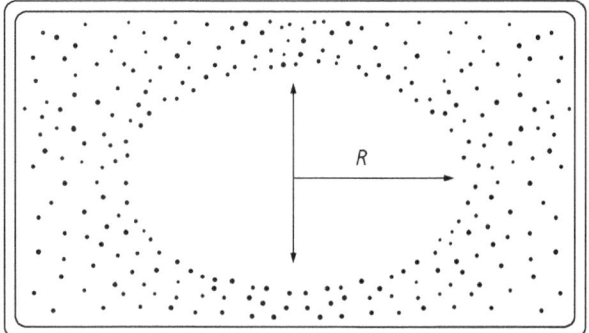

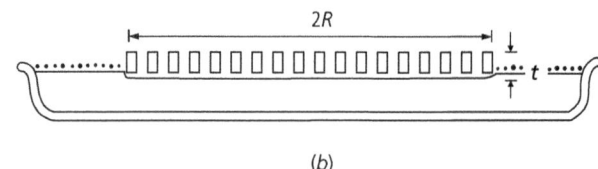

Fig. 13.1 *Estimating the size of a molecule*

Brownian motion

A botanist, Robert Brown, looking through a microscope, noticed that small pollen grains in water were continually moving.

We can observe the same effect by looking at a dilute solution of Indian ink, or brightly-lit smoke particles in a small cell. They are observed under a microscope and the particles perform a jerky, haphazard movement (Fig. 13.2).

We can understand these observations if we assume that the air or water surrounding the particles is made of very small, **invisible molecules**. These molecules are moving randomly and continually collide with the **visible particles**, causing the movements we see.

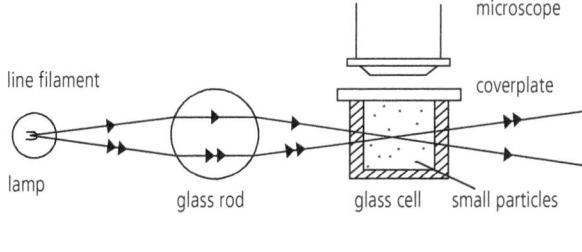

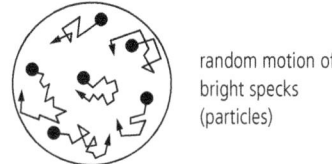

Fig. 13.2 *Brownian motion*

Diffusion in liquids and solids

Diffusion is further evidence that the molecules are moving.

Liquids

We pour water carefully onto a strong solution of blue copper sulphate in a beaker. The water floats on the solution (it is less dense). We leave them undisturbed for a few days and the colour of the copper sulphate slowly spreads upwards. This process, where two liquids mix without being stirred, is known as **diffusion**. The copper sulphate molecules are moving and gradually move in between the water molecules.

Gases

Diffusion also occurs in gases. We can use the apparatus in Fig. 13.3. One end of the cotton wool is soaked in ammonia solution and the other end in hydrochloric acid. The gases given off by these solutions give a white mist when they mix and react. After 15 to 20 minutes a white mist is seen along the tube. The gases have diffused down the tube and reacted.

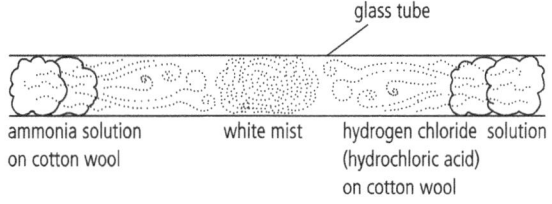

Fig. 13.3 *Diffusion in gases*

13.2 Forces between molecules

Solids are hard to stretch and compress. This suggests that there are strong forces between the molecules holding them in place. The forces are both attractive and repulsive. Normally they are in equilibrium.

In a liquid the forces between the molecules are not quite as strong. You can 'float' a needle on the surface of water by placing it on some tissue paper. If this is done carefully the needle rests on the surface. The forces between the liquid molecules create a surface tension, which holds up the needle.

Gases fill any container in which they are placed and are relatively easy to compress. This suggests that there are very weak forces, or no forces, between gas molecules.

13.3 Solids, liquids and gases

Solids, liquids and gases are called the **three phases of matter**. We understand the properties of solids, liquids and gases as due to differences in the arrangement and behaviour of the atoms or molecules.

The **temperature** of materials is proportional to the **average kinetic energy** of the atoms or molecules.

Solids

In a solid the molecules are fixed in position with strong forces (or bonds) between them. This gives a solid a fixed shape and size. The molecules are also often arranged in a regular pattern. This is best seen in crystals where the layers of atoms produce flat sides and sharp edges.

In solids the molecules are vibrating about a fixed point. When a solid is heated the molecules gain kinetic energy and vibrate faster and further from the fixed point. To allow this the molecules move apart – the solid expands.

Liquids

In a liquid the molecules are usually slightly further apart than in the solid of the same material. The forces between the molecules are slightly lower, which permits the liquid to flow – its size is fixed but not its shape.

The molecules are moving, with a range of velocities. When the liquid is heated the molecules gain kinetic energy and move faster.

Gases

When we change water to steam the volume of the steam produced is over one thousand times the volume of the water.

The molecules in gas are much further apart than in liquid. As a result there are almost no forces between the gas molecules and they move very fast and in all directions.

Figure 13.4 (overleaf) shows the arrangement and spacing of molecules in the three states.

The gas laws

The pressure of a gas is **not** due to its weight (as in a liquid). The pressure a gas exerts on a surface is due to the random collisions of the gas molecules with the surface.

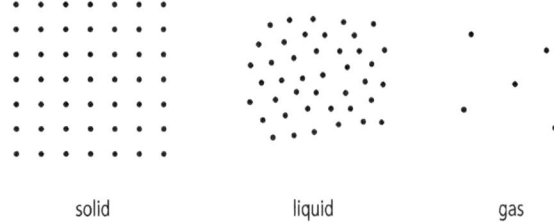

solid   liquid   gas

Fig. 13.4 *Molecules in solid, liquid and gas*

Boyle's law

When we reduce the volume of a gas, without changing the temperature, the average kinetic energy of the molecules is **not** altered. They do not move any faster. However, they have less far to travel and hit the walls more frequently. The pressure therefore rises.

Pressure law

If we keep the gas at the same volume but increase its temperature, the molecules gain kinetic energy and move faster. They now hit the walls of the container more frequently **and** harder. Both of these result in an increase of pressure.

Charles' law

When we heat a gas we can maintain a constant pressure by allowing it to expand. Now, although the molecules hit the wall harder, they hit much less frequently. Therefore the pressure stays the same.

Evaporation

When alcohol evaporates from the skin the liquid left behind feels cold. The liquid's molecules have a range of different speeds. At the surface, only the fast-moving molecules are able to break free of the bonds holding them to other molecules. The fast-moving molecules thus leave and become vapour. The slower (colder) molecules are left behind and the liquid cools.

Perspiration cools our bodies. The water evaporates by drawing heat from the body to facilitate the change of state from liquid to gas. Earthenware vessels keep liquids cool in a similar way.

Questions on Units 12 and 13

1 Describe an experiment to investigate the relationship between the volume and temperature of a fixed mass of gas, which is maintained at a constant pressure. Make clear how you would use your readings to establish the relationship.

A given mass of gas at atmospheric pressure occupies a volume of 200 cm³ at a temperature of 280 K. At what temperature would the volume become 250 cm³ if the pressure remained unaltered?

A sample of the same gas occupying 200 cm³ at atmospheric pressure of 760 mm Hg and 280 K, is heated to 350 K in a container, of which the volume remains constant during the heating. Calculate the pressure in the container at this higher temperature.

How does the kinetic theory of gases explain the pressure exerted on the walls of the container by a gas? Why does the pressure increase when the temperature is increased at a constant volume? (CAMB)

2 What do you understand by the terms **evaporation**, **diffusion** and **Brownian motion**? How may each of these phenomena be explained in terms of the kinetic theory? (CAMB)

3 a Use the kinetic theory to explain
   i why the rate of evaporation of water increases with temperature,
   ii why the pressure of a vessel containing air is the same on all parts of the walls of the vessel,
   iii why the pressure exerted by a given mass of gas increases when its temperature is raised, the volume being kept constant.
   b A metal cylinder containing gas is taken out of a refrigerated store maintained at −23 °C; the pressure in the cylinder was 5 atmospheres before it was moved. Calculate the pressure in the cylinder when the surrounding temperature rises to 27 °C, assuming that the cylinder itself does not expand. (CAMB)

4 The graph shows how the temperature of a certain quantity of a pure liquid varied when heated, at constant rate, by an electrical heater.

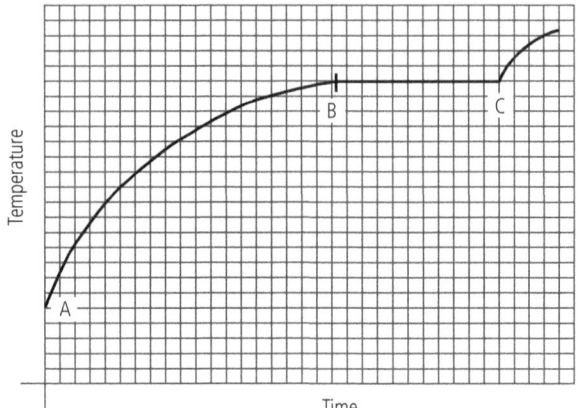

a Explain, on the basis of molecular theory, what changes occur in the molecular structure of the substance
  i over the region AB,
  ii over the region BC.
b Explain how the density of the liquid changes over the region AB. State clearly a reason for your answer.
c What effect would the following, separate, adjustments have on the length of the plateau region BC:
  i an increase in the power of the heater;
  ii repeating the experiment with half the mass of liquid? (WJEC, part question)

5 Distinguish between the solid, liquid and gaseous states in terms of spacing and motion of the molecules, and the effects of the forces acting between them. Explain why it is necessary to supply energy to a liquid in order to convert it into a gas without any increase in temperature. Describe an experiment to determine this quantity of energy for the conversion of unit mass of water into steam. (CAMB)

14 Transmission of thermal energy

[syllabus sections C4.1–4.6]

Thermal energy can be transferred from one place to another by three processes: conduction, convection and radiation.

14.1 Conduction

In solids

In solids, heat travels only by conduction. This is demonstrated as follows (Fig. 14.1).

We heat one end of the different materials. The small balls, attached with wax to the other ends, fall off when the wax melts. It melts owing to heat conducted along the bars. The copper bar conducts the heat effectively and the wax melts first on the copper bar.

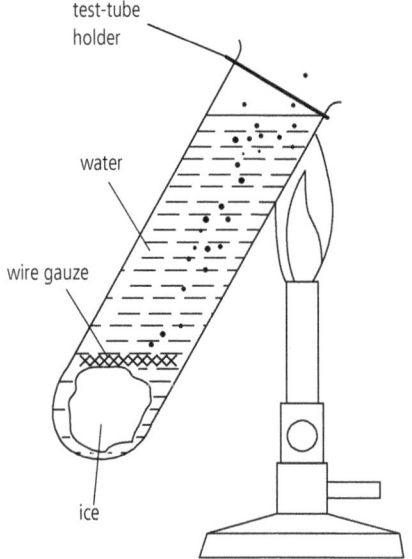

Fig. 14.2 *Conduction in liquids*

In gases

Air is a very poor conductor of heat. We use this property in materials where air is trapped, such as expanded polystyrene, which can be used to make containers to keep objects cool. Clothes trap pockets of air and this keeps us warm.

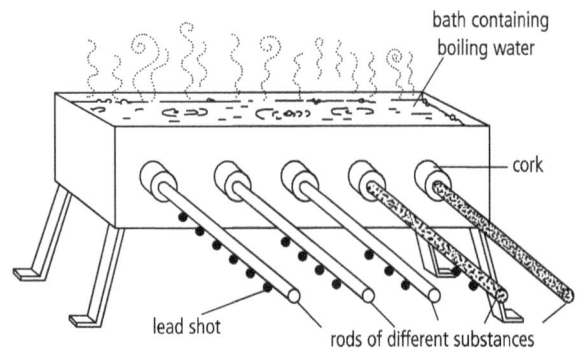

Fig. 14.1 *Conduction in solids*

All metals, for example copper and aluminium, conduct heat better than non-metals, for example plastic, glass and wood. Poor conductors of heat are **heat insulators**.

Handles of cooking pots are often made of a non-metal so that the heat is not conducted to us.

In liquids

We show that water is a poor conductor of heat using the apparatus in Fig. 14.2.

We heat the test-tube at the **top** and the water there boils. The water at the bottom of the test-tube stays cool.

In section 14.2 we see why, when heated at the **bottom, all** the water becomes hot.

14.2 Convection

Convection is the main process by which heat travels in liquids and gases (i.e. fluids).

We demonstrate convection using the apparatus in Fig. 14.3a and b.

In Fig. 14.3a we see water being heated at the bottom of a rectangular glass tube. We can see the purple colour of the crystals (potassium permanganate) rising as the hot water rises. We also see the cooler water falling down.

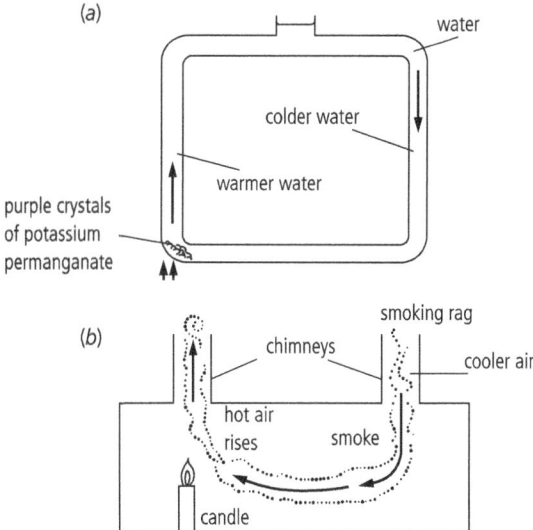

Fig. 14.3 *Demonstration of convection*

In Fig. 14.3b the hot air above the candle rises up the chimney. The smoke allows us to see the cool air flowing down the other chimney in the chamber. These movements of fluids are **convection currents**.

Land and sea breezes

On the coasts of islands of the Caribbean we often feel a sea breeze (from the sea to the land) during the day and a land breeze (from the land to the sea) at night. These are examples of convection currents.

During the day the land heats up more rapidly than the sea. The air above the land is heated, expands, becomes less dense and rises. Cool, denser air flows from the sea – a sea breeze.

At night the land cools very quickly. The warmer air now rises above the sea and the breeze is in the opposite direction.

Refrigerators and water heaters

The freezer section of a refrigerator is at the **top** of most refrigerators. The cooled air falls and the warmer air rises to be cooled.

However, the heating element in kettles and water heaters is placed at the **bottom**. The hot water rises and cooler water falls to be heated.

14.3 Radiation

In both conduction and convection a material is used to transfer the energy. No material is needed for heat transfer by radiation. There is a vacuum between the Earth and the Sun and the heat energy travels through space as invisible **infrared radiation** (see Unit 22).

Absorption and emission of radiation

Different surfaces at the same temperature absorb and emit radiation to different extents.

Absorption of radiation

In Fig. 14.4 we see two similar objects, A and B, with different surfaces. The same radiation falls on each. The black surface B absorbs more of the heat radiation and its temperature rises rapidly. The white surface A stays cool – it reflects the heat radiation. The wax on the dark surface melts more rapidly than on the white surface.

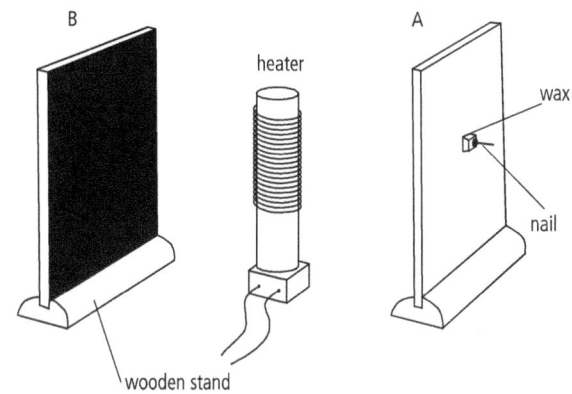

Fig. 14.4 *Absorption of radiation*

Light-coloured and silvery surfaces **reflect** most of the heat radiation. Dark, dull surfaces **absorb** heat radiation most efficiently.

In the Caribbean we often paint buildings a light colour to help to keep them cool. On the other hand we paint solar heat collectors a dull black to absorb the maximum amount of heat radiation.

Emission of radiation

To demonstrate this we use two equal-sized test-tubes. One is painted black and the other has a silver surface. We fill each with hot water at the same temperature. We measure the temperatures at regular intervals. The temperature of the black-painted test-tube falls more rapidly than the one with the silver surface.

A black surface **emits** radiation more rapidly than a silvery or light-coloured surface at the same temperature. Good **emitters** of heat radiation are also good **absorbers**.

14.4 Conduction, convection and radiation

In heat **conduction** the atoms or molecules are fixed and only **thermal energy** travels through the material. The thermal energy is, in part, passed on by vibrations down the line of molecules. Most of the energy is carried by **electrons** (see Unit 24). The electrons are heated, move down the bar and pass their energy to the fixed atoms further down the bar.

Convection occurs because the liquids and gases expand when heated. The density of the hot fluid becomes less and it rises. In convection the material moves from place to place.

No material is needed for the transfer of energy by **radiation**. Further properties of radiation are discussed in Unit 22.

Glasshouse effect

Most of the Sun's infrared radiation can pass through glass. However, when it is absorbed by objects and then re-emitted the nature of the radiation changes. It is now reflected by glass. This gives the glasshouse (or greenhouse) effect, where the temperature inside is much higher than outside.

Carbon dioxide has a similar effect on radiation. The temperature of the Earth's atmosphere has been gradually rising as more carbon dioxide is released into the air from industry.

Vacuum flask

A vacuum flask is designed to keep either hot liquids hot or cold liquids cold. It reduces the rate at which heat can pass in either direction, in or out.

A vacuum flask is shown in Fig. 14.5. Conduction and convection cannot occur across the vacuum. Radiant energy may cross the vacuum but is then reflected by the silver surfaces.

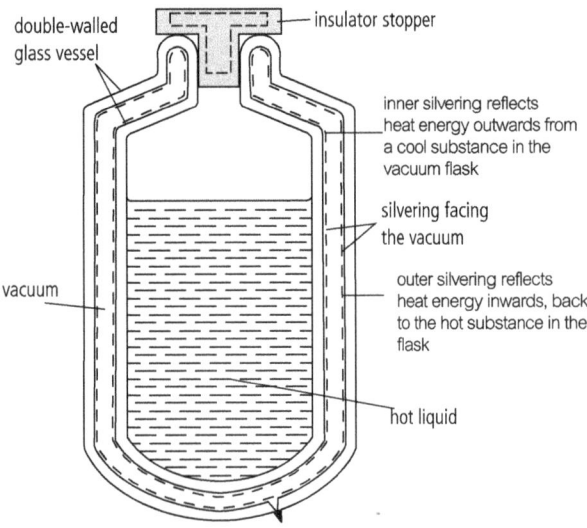

Fig. 14.5 *Vacuum flask*

15 Heat and temperature change

[syllabus sections C3.1–3.4]

The atoms or molecules of all substances are moving or vibrating. The temperature is a measure of the average kinetic energy of these particles. A **flow** of heat occurs when some of the internal energy of one object passes to another in contact with it.

Heat is a form of energy. Heat is energy **in transit** due to a temperature difference. The unit of heat is the **joule (J)**.

15.1 Specific heat capacity

When cooking we notice that equal masses of water and oil heated for the same time on the same source of heat do *not* reach the same temperature. The oil reaches a higher temperature than the water. The water has a higher specific heat capacity.

We define the specific heat capacity (SHC), c, of a substance as the quantity of heat required to raise the temperature of 1 kg of the substance by 1 K. The unit of SHC is $J\ kg^{-1}\ K^{-1}$.

Specific heat capacity of water

Water has a high SHC of $4200\ J\ kg^{-1}\ K^{-1}$. Most solids have an SHC which is smaller; e.g. copper ($380\ J\ kg^{-1}\ K^{-1}$), aluminium ($880\ J\ kg^{-1}\ K^{-1}$).

Water is used as a coolant in car engines. It can absorb a lot of thermal energy as a result of its high SHC.

Soil has an SHC of about $800\ J\ kg^{-1}\ K^{-1}$. This is why during the day the land heats up more rapidly than the sea. This leads to land and sea breezes (Unit 14).

Calculations on specific heat capacity

We calculate the heat required to raise the temperature of a mass m, of a substance of SHC c, by $\Delta\theta$ (delta theta – $\Delta\theta$ – as it is a **change** of temperature) using the following:

thermal energy = mass × SHC × temperature change
$$E_H = m \times c \times \Delta\theta$$

This is also the heat **given out** when a mass m, of SHC c, **cools** through a temperature change given out of $\Delta\theta$.

15.2 Heat capacity

The heat capacity, C, of an **object** is the heat required to raise the temperature of the object by 1 K.

We see that

heat capacity (C) = $m \times c$, where c is the specific heat capacity

15.3 Determination of the specific heat capacities of metals and liquids

Electrical methods

For both metals and liquids we supply a known amount of thermal energy and measure the temperature rise in a known mass. The apparatus used for a metal is shown in Fig. 15.1.

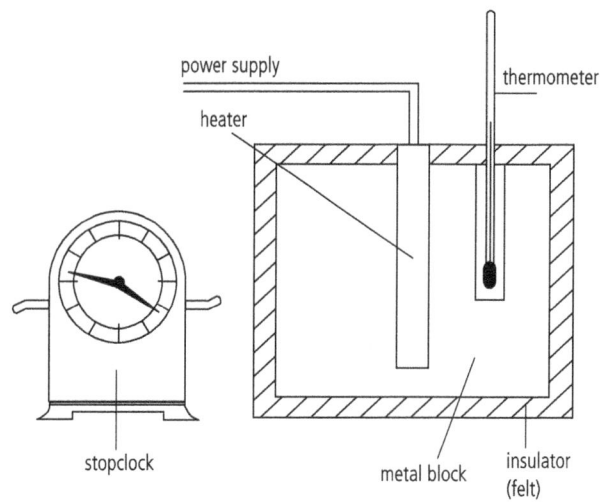

Fig. 15.1 *Determining the specific heat capacity of a metal*

The block has holes for the heater and the thermometer. We measure the initial temperature, T_1, and use the heater for, say, 5 minutes (300 seconds). If the heater has a power output P, in watts, then

energy supplied = time × power
$$E_H = 300\ P$$

The final temperature, T_2, is taken and the mass, m, of the block is measured. Thus
$$\Delta\theta = T_2 - T_1$$
As $\quad E_H = m \times c \times \Delta\theta$

Then $\quad c = \dfrac{300\ P}{m(T_2 - T_1)}$

For a liquid we use a known mass in a light insulating container, such as a polystyrene cup.

We can then ignore the small amount of energy absorbed by the container. The procedure is the same as for the metal.

We have to be careful to stir the liquid thoroughly to make sure that it is all at the same temperature. A few drops of oil should be added to the hole with the thermometer to ensure good thermal contact.

Method of mixtures

In your practical course you will also use the method of mixtures to find the SHC of liquids and solids.

We add a hot solid (or liquid) to a cold liquid and find the final temperature. All the heat from the hot substance goes to the cooler substance if we manage to reduce heat loss with insulation.

You might obtain the following results if you are finding the specific heat capacity of a solid using water.

Initial temperature of hot solid		= 100 °C
Final temperature of solid		= 36 °C
Temperature change	= 100 − 36	= 64 °C
Mass of solid		= 0.10 kg
Energy **lost** by hot solid, E_H	= $m \times c \times \Delta\theta$	
	= $0.1 \times c \times 64$	

Initial temperature of water		= 30 °C
Final temperature of water		= 36 °C
Temperature change	= 36 − 30	= 6 °C
Mass of water	= 80 g	= 0.080 kg
Energy **gained** by water, E_H	= $m \times c \times \Delta\theta$	
	= $0.080 \times 4200 \times 6$	

Energy gained by water = energy lost by solid
$$0.080 \times 4200 \times 6 = 0.1 \times c \times 64$$
$$c = 315 \text{ J kg}^{-1}\text{ K}^{-1}$$

Questions on Units 14 and 15

1. On a sunny day, the surface of the sea is much slower to heat up than the surface of the land. Suggest an explanation.

    How can you account for the fact that a breeze blowing from the land onto the sea may develop on a sunny day, which is otherwise calm? (CAMB)

2. It is found that 18000 J of heat are required to raise the temperature of a block of metal, of mass 0.80 kg, from 25 °C to 100 °C. What is the specific heat capacity of the metal?

3. The diagram shows the metal shade and bulb of an electric reading lamp.

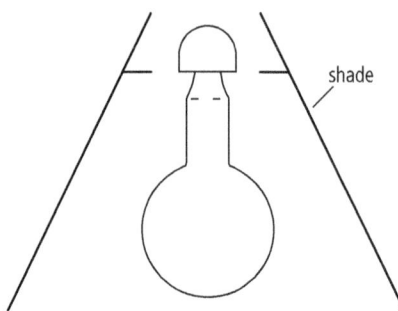

    On a simple copy of the diagram, draw arrows to indicate the convection currents in the air inside the shade when the lamp is in use. State the processes by which heat is transferred from the bulb filament to the shade. Why does the shade eventually reach a steady temperature? (CAMB)

4. A piece of iron of mass 0.20 kg is heated to 64 °C and then dropped into 0.15 kg of water at 16 °C. If the temperature of the mixture is 22 °C, find the specific heat capacity of the iron. (SHC of water = 4200 J kg^{-1} K^{-1})

5. On mixing 42 g of turpentine at 90 °C with 170 g of water at 13 °C, the final temperature is 20 °C. Find the specific heat capacity of the turpentine. (SHC of water = 4200 J kg^{-1} K^{-1})

6. Describe an experiment to determine the specific heat capacity of copper, and make clear how the result is calculated.

    In a storage heater, heat is used to raise the temperature of a block of material which subsequently re-emits heat as it cools down. In such a heater, what are the advantages of using a material which has (a) a higher capacity, (b) a high density?

    A liquid flows at the rate of 56 g (= 0.056 kg) per minute through a tube containing a heating element. If the heating element dissipates 6.3 W to the liquid and the liquid is uniformly heated, by how much will the temperature of the liquid rise as it passes through the tube? (SHC of the liquid = 600 J kg^{-1} K^{-1}) (CAMB)

7. A kettle of heat capacity 150 J K^{-1}, containing 0.5 kg of water at 20 °C, has an electric heater which supplies 2000 J each second. Assuming that no heat is lost to the surroundings, how long would it take the heater to raise the temperature of the water to 100 °C? (SHC of water = 4200 J kg^{-1} K^{-1}) (CAMB)

16 Heat and phase change

[syllabus sections C3.7–3.10]

16.1 Latent heat

When we heat water its temperature rises until it boils. Then, the temperature does not rise any more but the water changes to steam. The energy we supply to the boiling water is used to break the bonds between the molecules in the liquid. The molecules then move independently in the gas. The heat used to change a liquid to a gas is called the **latent heat of vaporisation**.

Similarly, we can heat a mixture of ice and water at 0 °C for a short while. We stir the contents to ensure an even temperature and the temperature is still 0 °C. Some of the ice melts but no temperature rise occurs. The energy that melts the ice is called the **latent heat of fusion**. This energy is used to break the bonds which hold the molecules in fixed positions in the solid state.

The **specific latent heat (SLH) of fusion**, l_F, of a substance is the quantity of heat required to convert 1 kg of the substance from the solid to the liquid state without a change in temperature.

For ice to water, at 0 °C, its value is
3.36×10^5 J kg^{-1}

The **specific latent heat (SLH) of vaporisation** of a substance is the quantity of heat required to convert 1 kg of the substance from the liquid to the vapour state without a change in temperature.

For water to steam, at 100 °C, its value is
2.26×10^6 J kg^{-1}

The unit for specific latent heat is J kg^{-1}.

Calculations on specific latent heat

If a mass m of a substance is converted from one phase to another and the SLH is l then the energy needed is given by

energy needed = $m \times l$

16.2 Condensing and freezing

When a substance changes from gas to liquid or from liquid to solid, heat is **given out**.

To make ice from water at 0 °C we **extract** the latent heat of fusion.

If steam condenses on the skin the burn is severe as the latent heat of vaporisation is given out. The water formed, at 100 °C, continues to burn the skin.

The energy given out is given by the same equation

energy given out = $m \times l$

16.3 Determination of the specific latent heat of fusion of water

We fill a funnel with dried ice (Fig. 16.1a). We use an electric heater to heat the ice for a few minutes (time, t). We collect the water formed and find its mass. This water is formed owing to heat from both the heater **and** the surroundings.

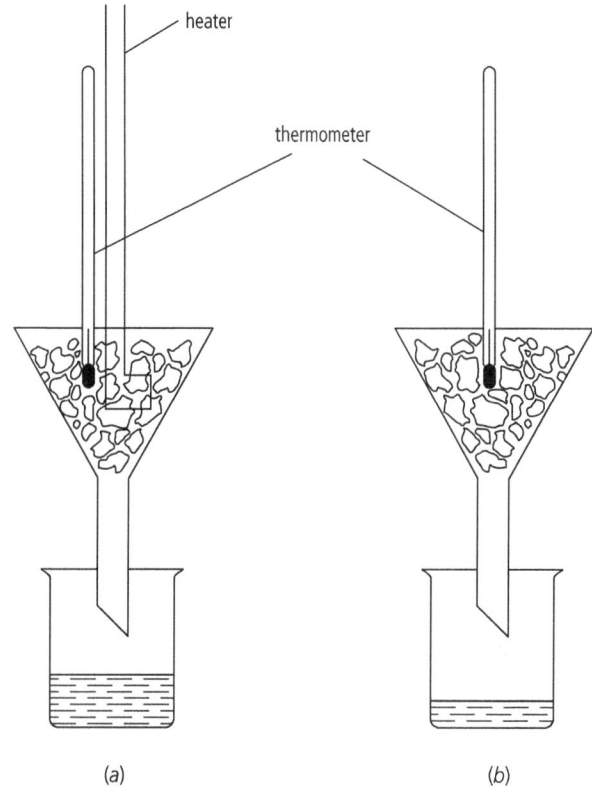

Fig. 16.1 *Determining the specific latent heat of water*

To find the mass of ice melted by heat **from the surroundings** we place a second identical funnel near the first, but without a heater (Fig. 16.1b). In the same time, t, some ice melts and we find the mass of the water formed. The **difference** in the mass of water in the two cases is the water melted by the heater, mass, m.

If the power output is P then we can calculate the energy output of the heater. (In Unit 25 we see how to measure the **power** output of an electric heater.)

energy supplied, E = power × time

If l_F is the SLH of fusion of ice then

energy needed to melt mass $m = m\, l_F$

Thus, $m\, l_F = Pt$

and $l_F = \dfrac{Pt}{m}$

16.4 Determination of the specific latent heat of vaporisation of water

We place a known mass of water and an electric heater, of power output P, in a well-insulated container. The water is heated to its boiling point, with a lid to prevent loss of vapour. As it starts to boil the lid is removed and a stopclock is started. The water is allowed to boil until a reasonable quantity has vaporised. We record the time taken, t, and replace the lid. We now measure the mass of water remaining and calculate the mass, m, that has evaporated. The energy supplied is Pt.

If the SLH of vaporisation is l_v, then

$m\, l_v = Pt$

and $l_v = \dfrac{Pt}{m}$

16.5 Evaporation and boiling

In both evaporation and boiling the process is one in which a liquid changes to a gas. However, there are important differences between them.

1. Evaporation only occurs at the surface of the liquid whereas boiling occurs throughout the liquid.
2. Evaporation occurs at all temperatures (but occurs more rapidly at higher temperatures). Boiling only occurs at a particular temperature for a particular liquid under normal conditions.
3. Evaporation is a spontaneous process but boiling normally only occurs with the continual addition of energy. Boiling occurs more rapidly with a greater **rate** of addition of energy.
4. Evaporation causes the liquid left behind to cool. In boiling the liquid and vapour are at the same temperature.

16.6 Cooling curve of naphthalene

We heat naphthalene in a test tube to 100 °C in a water bath. We then allow it to cool in air and take its temperature at regular intervals. We plot a graph of temperature against time (Fig. 16.2).

The temperature of the hot naphthalene falls quickly from 100 °C to 79 °C but then remains at 79 °C for quite a while. At 79 °C the molten (liquid) naphthalene is changing to the solid form. When all the liquid has changed to a solid, the temperature starts to fall again.

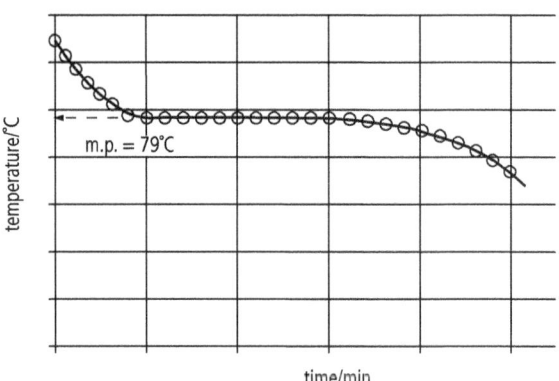

Fig. 16.2 *Measuring cooling in naphthalene*

The hot test-tube is losing heat all the time. At 79 °C the heat given off is the latent heat of fusion of the naphthalene as the naphthalene changes state.

Questions on Unit 16

1. a Distinguish between 'specific heat capacity' and 'specific latent heat'.
   b A beaker of crushed ice at −10 °C is heated by a bunsen burner in a laboratory where the pressure is normal. The temperature of the system is observed until the water has been boiling for some time. **Sketch and label fully** a temperature/time graph for the system over this period of time.
   c 1 kg masses of aluminium and copper are heated separately from 30 °C using the same source of heat over the same period. What is the specific heat capacity of aluminium if the temperatures of the two masses after heating are 50 °C and 75 °C respectively? (SHC of copper is 4×10^2 J kg^{-1} K^{-1})
   d If the same amount of heat as in (c) above is used to melt ice at 0 °C, how many grams of ice will be melted? (SLH of ice is 3.5×10^5 J kg^{-1} K^{-1})
   e Many people, when they first go for a swim in the sea at night, find it to be warmer than they expect. Explain why this is so. (CXC)

2. In sharpening a cutting tool on a grindstone, sparks are often seen flying in many directions from the stone. These sparks are hot; they are tiny particles of steel from the tool being sharpened. The particles cool and stop glowing in a very short time.
   a Name the main process by which the sparks cool. Justify your answer.

b The mass of one such tiny particle is 1.0×10^{-9} kg. If it cools through 800 K in 0.2 seconds, calculate its rate of loss of heat energy.
c Estimate how many such particles will have to cool in order that the total heat released may change 1 g of water, at its boiling point, completely to steam. SHC of steel = 500 J kg^{-1} K^{-1} and SLH of steam = 2.3×10^6 J kg^{-1} K^{-1}. (CXC)

17 Light

[syllabus sections D5.3 – 6.2]

Light is a form of radiation and is similar to heat radiation in several ways (see Unit 22).

Light is that particular kind of energy which we detect with our eyes. We see objects because either the objects **emit** light (e.g. the Sun and lamps) or they **reflect** other light.

We cannot see around corners. This is because **light travels in straight lines**.

Shadows, eclipses and the pinhole camera all depend upon this property.

17.1 Shadows

Point source of light

A small lamp illuminates an opaque object in front of a white screen (Fig. 17.1). The shadow, called an **umbra**, has sharp edges and no light is seen in the shadow.

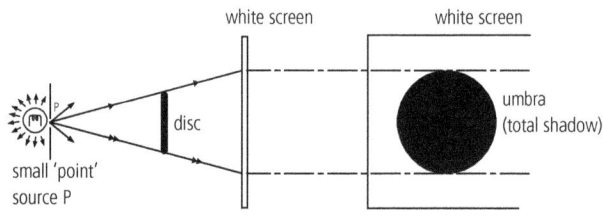

Fig. 17.1 *Umbra*

With a larger lamp (extended source), we obtain, around the umbra, an area called the **penumbra** (Fig. 17.2). In the penumbra the intensity of the shadow varies as some, but not all, of the light reaches the screen.

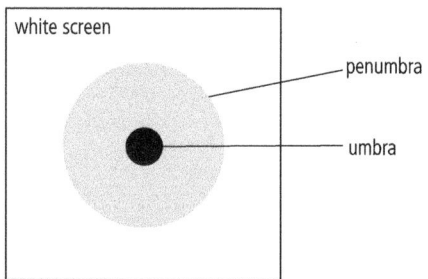

Fig. 17.2 *Umbra and penumbra*

The size of a shadow in a particular situation may be found by a scale diagram or calculation.

17.2 Pinhole camera

A pinhole camera can be made using a tin, such as a cocoa tin. One end is completely removed and replaced by some wax paper held on by tape or an elastic band. A small hole is made at the centre of the other end.

When we point the hole at a brightly lit window and look at the screen we see an inverted image of the window. The light can only enter the pinhole camera through the small hole and travels in straight lines (Fig. 17.3).

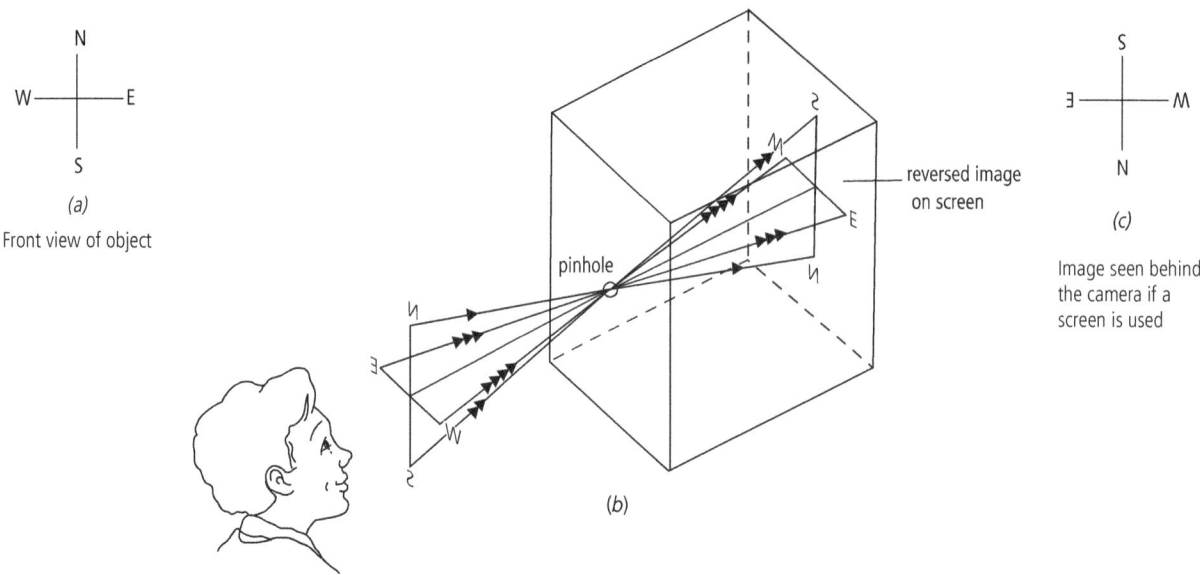

Fig. 17.3 *Pinhole camera*

If the camera is **longer** the image becomes **larger**. If the object is **nearer** to the same camera the image also becomes **larger**. Too large a pinhole creates a bright, blurry image because more light passes through and because a large pinhole acts as several tiny ones, each producing an overlapping image. You can draw diagrams, to scale, to prove these two points.

17.3 Eclipses

Eclipse of the Sun

Occasionally our view of the Sun is obscured as the Moon moves between the Sun and the Earth (Fig. 17.4).

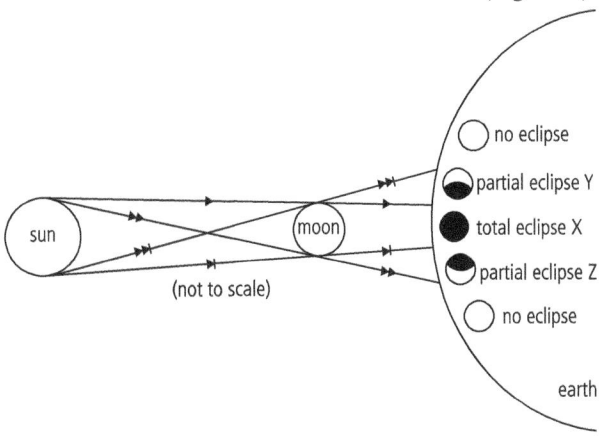

Fig. 17.4 *Eclipse of the Sun*

The region X experiences a **total** eclipse. It is in the **umbra** of the Moon's shadow. The regions Y and Z experience only a **partial** eclipse and are in the **penumbra** of the Moon's shadow.

Eclipse of the Moon

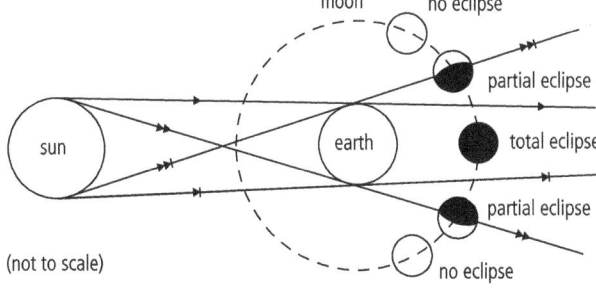

Fig. 17.5 *Eclipse of the Moon*

We see the Moon as it reflects the light of the Sun. An eclipse of the Moon occurs when the Moon moves into the shadow of the Earth. The Sun's light can no longer reach it and it cannot be seen (Fig. 17.5).

Total eclipses of the Moon occur more often than eclipses of the Sun because of the larger size of the Earth's shadow compared to that of the Moon.

17.4 Reflection from a plane mirror

A ray of light from a raybox shines on a plane mirror (Fig. 17.6). We mark the path of the ray of light and the position of the mirror. We remove the mirror and add a line called the **normal**.

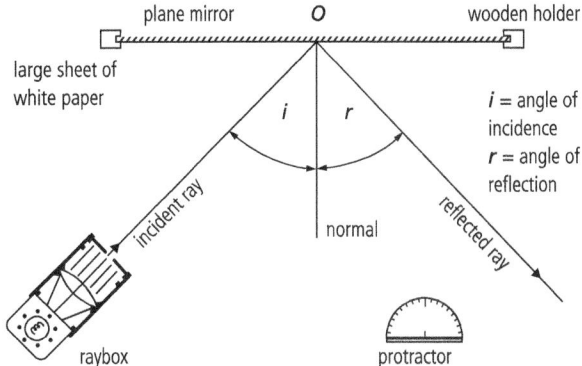

Fig. 17.6 *Angle of incidence and angle of reflection*

The normal is a line drawn at 90° to the surface of the mirror at the point where the rays of light meet the mirror.

The ray initially falling on the mirror is called the **incident ray**. The ray leaving the mirror after reflection is the **reflected ray**.

The angle between the incident ray and the normal is called the **incident angle** or angle of incidence (i).

The angle between the reflected ray and the normal is called the **angle of reflection** (r).

We measure the angles marked i and r and find that they are always **equal** to each other.

Laws of reflection

1. The angle of incidence is equal to the angle of reflection.
2. The incident ray, the reflected ray and the normal are all in the same plane.

Formation and properties of the image in a plane mirror

The formation of the image in a plane mirror of a point object is shown in Fig. 17.7. We can see the image because after reflection the light rays appear to come from a point behind the mirror. This is a **virtual image**; i.e. an image where the light does not actually pass through the image but appears to come from the image. A virtual image cannot be shown on a screen.

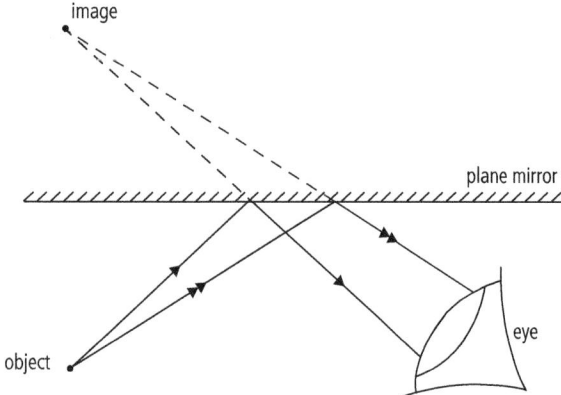

Fig. 17.7 *The image in a plane mirror*

Method of no-parallax

We use the method of no-parallax to find the **position** of the image in a plane mirror. The mirror and an object pin, with a small flag, are set up as in Fig. 17.8. A second pin is now placed behind the mirror so that it can be seen over the mirror.

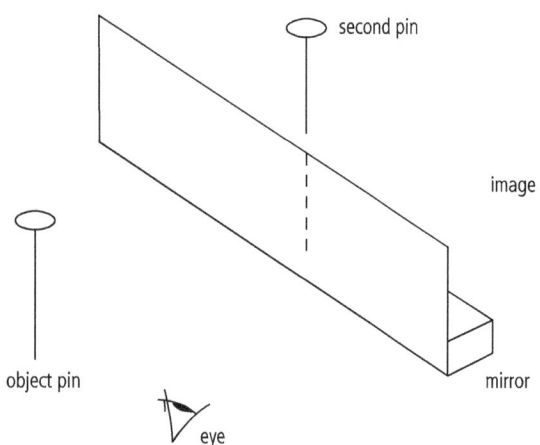

Fig. 17.8 *No-parallax*

When we move our head from side to side the image and the second pin usually appear to move relative to each other. This movement is known as **parallax**. When the search pin is in the same position as the image there is **no** relative movement – a position of **no-parallax**.

We find that the perpendicular distance from the mirror to both the image and the object is the same. A final property of an image in a plane mirror is that it is **laterally inverted**. This means that looking in a mirror our left hand appears to be our right hand.

Summary of the properties of the image in a plane mirror

The image in a plane mirror is:
1 virtual
2 the same size as the object
3 laterally inverted
4 the same distance behind the mirror as the object is in front of the mirror.

Questions on Unit 17

1 What is meant by a ray of light?
   Copy the diagram below and complete, using rays of light, to show the shadow of the object formed on the screen with the aid of the source AB. Also indicate the darkest part of the shadow.

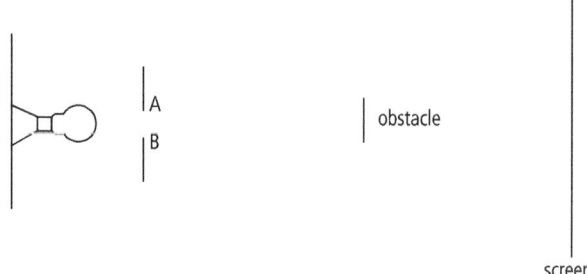

Draw
   i a simple diagram to show the appearance of the Moon when it is partially eclipsed; and
   ii a further diagram to show how an eclipse of the Moon occurs, making sure that the position of the Moon corresponds with its appearance as you have drawn it.
   Why does an eclipse of the Moon only last a few hours at the most? (CAMB)

2 A small lamp L hangs above a sheet of white paper, AB, as shown in the diagram.

With the aid of rays drawn on a copy of the diagram, explain briefly why the paper around P appears brighter when a plane mirror M is placed above, in the position shown. Why does the appearance of the paper around A remain unchanged when the mirror is introduced? (CAMB)

3 Two plane mirrors are placed at right angles to each other. A point object is placed between the mirrors and the same distance from each. Draw a diagram to show the mirrors and the object and add the positions of the three images that are formed.

18 Refraction

[syllabus sections D6.3–6.8]

Figure 18.1 shows the refraction of light. We notice that the direction of the light ray changes as it **enters** the glass block **and** as it **leaves** the block.

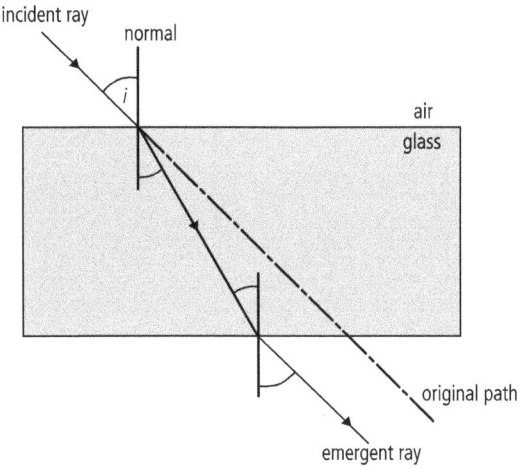

Fig. 18.1 *Refraction through a glass block*

Refraction is the change of direction of light as it travels from one material into another.

We mark normals to the surface at the points where the light enters and leaves. The **angle of incidence** (i) and the **angle of refraction** (r) are labelled at the first face.

When light passes from **air into glass** it is refracted **towards** the normal.

At the other face, as the light passes from **glass into air**, it bends **away from** the normal. Transparent liquids also refract light in a similar way.

When we use parallel-sided blocks, or rectangular tanks of liquid, we see that the light usually emerges parallel to the original ray but is **displaced** to one side.

No change of direction occurs when the incident ray travels along the normal (Fig. 18.2).

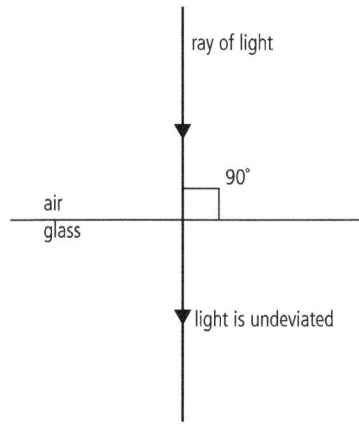

Fig. 18.2 *Incident ray along the normal ray of light*

We use glass prisms to deviate light (Fig. 18.3).

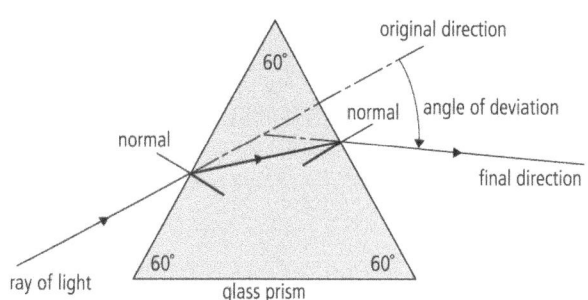

Fig. 18.3 *Angle of deviation*

18.1 Laws of refraction

We find the laws of refraction by experiment.

We place a piece of paper below the glass block in Fig. 18.1 and mark the path of the light ray and position of the block. We remove the block, draw the normal and measure the angles of incidence (i) and refraction (r). We repeat this several times, with different angles of incidence, and obtain a set of pairs of these angles. We also calculate $\sin i$ and $\sin r$. Typical results are as in Table 18.1.

Table 18.1

Angle of incidence i/degree	Angle of refraction r/degree	$\sin i$	$\sin r$	$n = \dfrac{\sin i}{\sin r}$
45	28	0.707	0.469	1.51
50	31	0.777	0.515	1.51
60	35	0.866	0.574	1.50
70	39	0.940	0.629	1.49
80	41	0.985	0.656	1.50

The results show that the ratio $\sin i : \sin r$ is a constant for the block. This is known as **Snell's law**. The two laws of refraction are as follows.

Law 1 The incident ray and the refracted ray are on opposite sides of the normal at the point of incidence and all three lie in the same plane.

Law 2 (Snell's law) The ratio of the sine of the angle of incidence to the sine of the angle of refraction is a constant for a particular medium.

We call the constant in Snell's law the **refractive index** of the material. In the section on the refraction of waves (Unit 20), we learn that refraction occurs owing to a change of speed as the light passes from one material to the next.

Snell's law leads to the equation:

$$\frac{\sin i}{\sin r} = \text{constant (refractive index)}$$

The refractive index has no unit – it is a ratio.

We use the symbol n for refractive index with subscripts to indicate the materials and direction of travel, e.g. $_a n_g$ is the refractive index as light passes from air to glass.

18.2 Examples of refraction

When we have a straight stick, such as a pencil, partially immersed in water it appears bent at the water surface (Fig. 18.4).

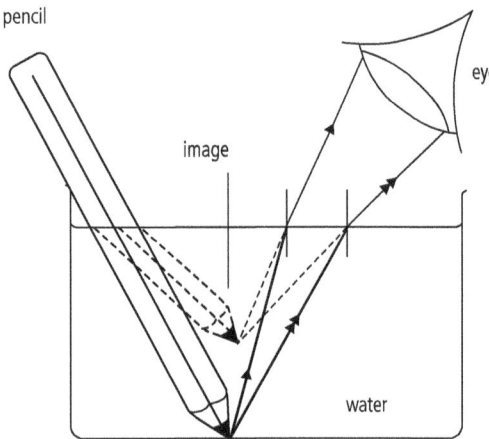

Fig. 18.4 *Pencil seen in water*

The light from the stick refracts as it reaches the surface and appears to come from points higher than the actual stick. We see the image shown in the diagram: a virtual image.

Swimming pools and rivers look shallower than they are. The light from the bottom refracts as it enters the air and so the bottom appears above its actual position.

18.3 Total internal reflection

When we see a light ray passing through a block we notice that as the light leaves the block some is reflected back into the glass. Under certain conditions **all** the light is reflected within the glass and none enters the air. We use a semi-circular glass (or perspex) block to investigate this (Fig. 18.5).

The light ray is not deviated at the circular face as it travels along the normal. It bends away from the normal at the face AB (Fig. 18.5a).

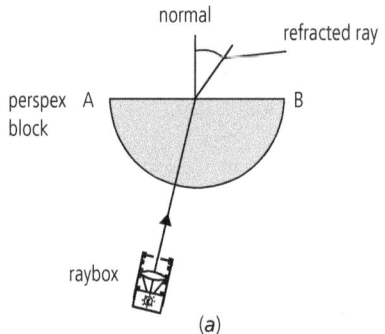

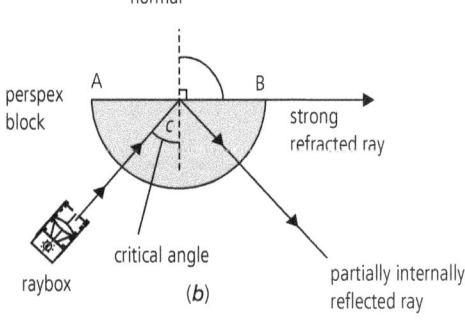

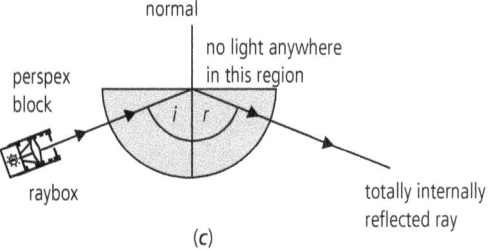

Fig. 18.5 *Total internal reflection*

We increase the angle at which the light meets AB, i.e. the angle of incidence in the glass. At a certain angle of incidence, the critical angle, the refracted ray emerges at 90° to the normal (Fig. 18.5b).

The **critical angle** c is that angle of incidence in the glass for which the angle of refraction in the air is 90°.

When the angle of incidence is **greater** than the critical angle, no light emerges from side AB (Fig. 18.5c). It is all reflected and the rays obey the usual law of reflection. We call this **total internal reflection**.

18.4 Relation between refractive index and critical angle

We can show that the relationship between the refractive index and the critical angle is

$$\sin c = \frac{1}{_a n_g}$$

We can measure the critical angle for the block in Fig. 18.5b and find the refractive index.

Total internal reflection only takes place when the ray of light is in the glass or perspex (a denser medium).

Also, the angle of incidence at the glass/air boundary has to be greater than the critical angle.

18.5 Applications of total internal reflection

Periscope
A periscope allows us to see over an obstacle and produces an image which is the same way up as the original object (Fig. 18.6a).

Binoculars
Binoculars also use two prisms (Fig. 18.6b).

Light pipes (optic fibres)
When we shine light into one end of a glass rod the light travels along the rod, without coming out of the sides, and all the light emerges at the far end. The light is totally internally reflected at the sides of the rod.

Light pipes are now used in hospitals to examine people internally. They can be quite thin and flexible and allow direct observation of internal cavities.

Optic fibres are replacing copper wires as the means of transmission of telephone calls. Internet connections are greatly enhanced by their superior transmission rates of data.

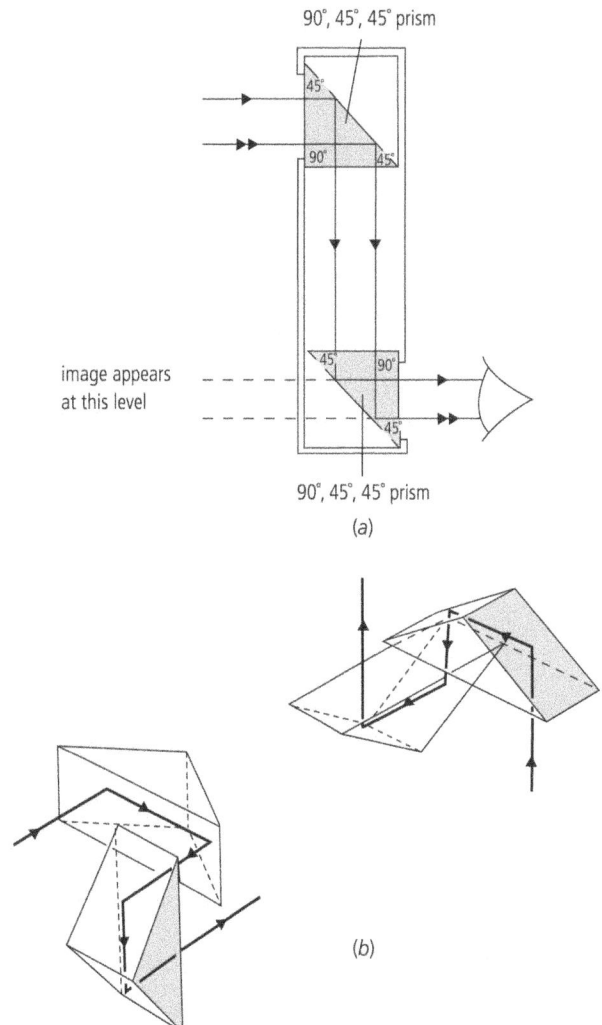

Fig. 18.6 *(a) Prism periscope (b) Prism binoculars*

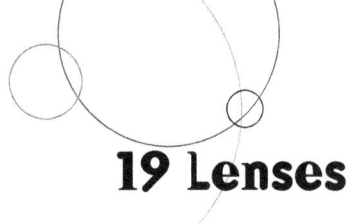

19 Lenses

[syllabus sections D.6.9 –7.7]

The refraction of light is applied very usefully in lenses.

19.1 Converging and diverging lenses

We use two kinds of lens: converging and diverging. We can shine parallel light rays on to these lenses (Fig. 19.1).

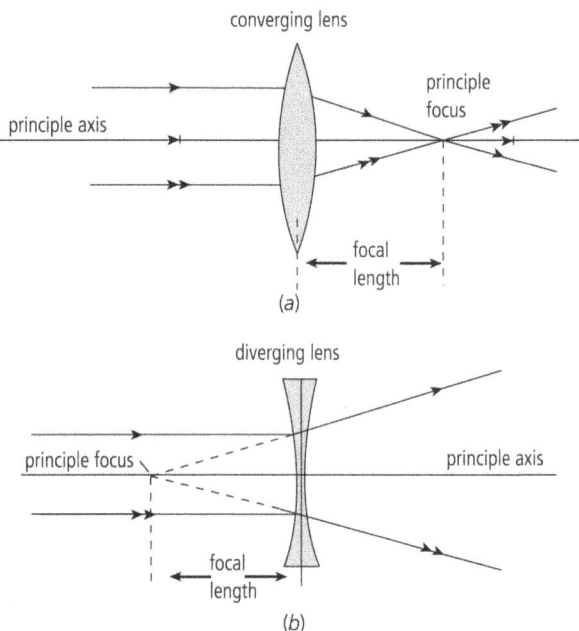

Fig. 19.1 (a) Converging lens (b) Diverging lens

A **converging lens** is thicker in the centre than at its sides. A **diverging lens** has a centre that is thinner than its sides.

The **principal axis** of a lens is the line joining the centres of curvature of the surfaces. This line goes through the centre, or optical centre, of the lens.

The **principal focus** of a lens is that point on the principal axis to which all rays, which are originally parallel to the axis, converge, or from which they appear to diverge, after passage through the lens. Each lens has two principal foci, one on each side.

The **focal length** of a lens is the distance between the centre of the lens and the principal focus. The **focal plane** is the plane in which a sharp image is formed by the lens of an object that is far away. The focal plane is at 90° to the principal axis and includes the focus.

The light is refracted at each surface. It is as if a lens were a set of prisms (Fig. 19.2).

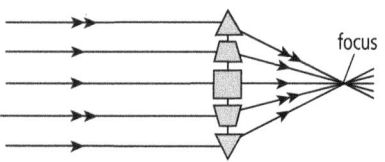

Fig.19.2 *Convex lens as a series of prisms*

19.2 Image formation in lenses

We can use the same converging lens in different ways to form different images.

In a **magnifying glass** (Fig. 19.3a) the lens is close to the object (for example the writing on this page). We obtain a magnified image, which is the **same way up** as the actual writing.

In a **camera** (Fig 19.3b) the object is far from the lens. We obtain an image that is much smaller than the object and that is **inverted**.

In a **projector**, such as those used in cinemas (Fig. 19.3c), the object (the film) is just outside the focal length. We obtain an image that is much larger than the film and that is **inverted**.

Figure 19.3 shows the formation of these three types of image.

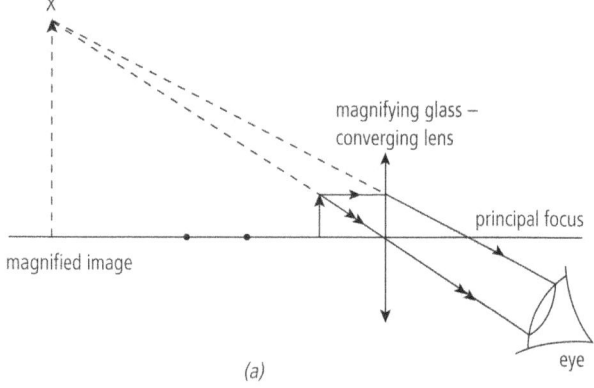

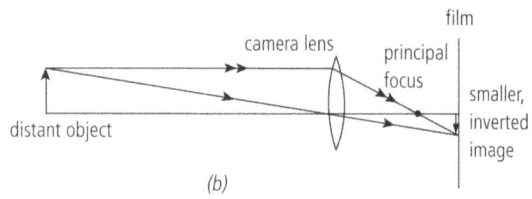

Fig. 19.3 *Image formation in lenses (a) Magnifying glass (b) Camera*

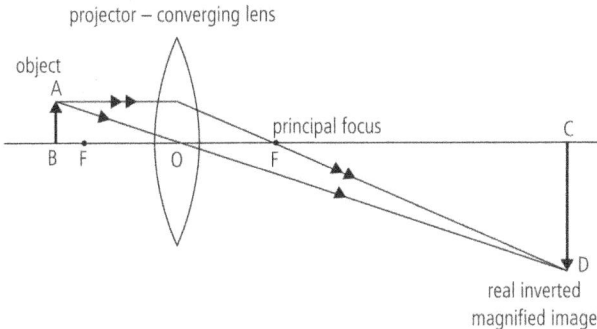

Fig. 19.3 *Image formation in lenses (c) Lens projector*

19.3 Ray diagrams

We can understand these uses of lenses by drawing ray diagrams. The rules for drawing ray diagrams can be found using light rays and lenses in the laboratory.

1. All light rays that are travelling **parallel** to the principal axis on hitting the lens are deviated through the principal focus.
2. Any light ray passing through the principal focus **before** hitting the lens emerges parallel to the principal axis.
3. Any light ray passing through the **centre** of the lens is **undeviated**.

19.4 Real and virtual images

In the camera and the projector we see that light actually passes **through** the image. These are **real images** and can be shown on a screen (or they fall on a camera film). In our diagrams we draw real images, and light rays, as solid lines.

In the case of the magnifying glass we obtain a **virtual image**. The light appears to come from the image but does not pass through the image. We draw virtual images, and construction lines, as dotted lines.

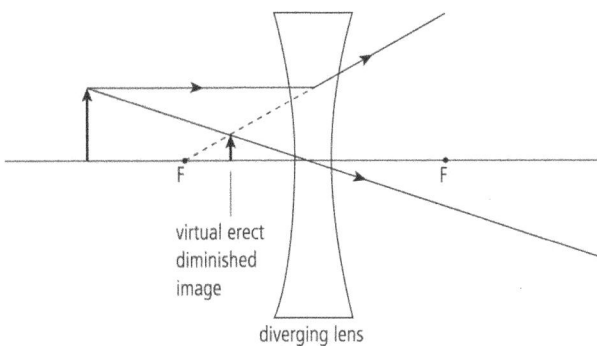

Fig. 19.4 *Using a diverging lens*

You will use a converging lens to form real images in your practical course. A diverging lens produces an image that is always smaller than the object (Fig. 19.4).

19.5 Scale diagrams

To solve numerical problems we need to draw the ray diagrams accurately to scale.

We represent the lens as a vertical line and choose a suitable scale.

19.6 Magnification

The linear magnification(m) is defined as the ratio of the height of the image to the height of the object:

$$m = \frac{\text{height of image}}{\text{height of object}}$$

In Fig. 19.3c, the triangles OAB and OCD are **similar** – all angles are equal to the equivalent one in the other triangle. Therefore:

$$\frac{\text{height of object}}{\text{distance of object from lens}} = \frac{\text{height of image}}{\text{distance of image from lens}}$$

or

$$\frac{\text{height of image}}{\text{height of object}} = \frac{\text{image distance}}{\text{object distance}}$$

$$m = \frac{\text{distance of image from lens }(v)}{\text{distance of object from lens }(u)}$$

19.7 The eye

The main parts in the human eye are shown in Fig. 19.5.

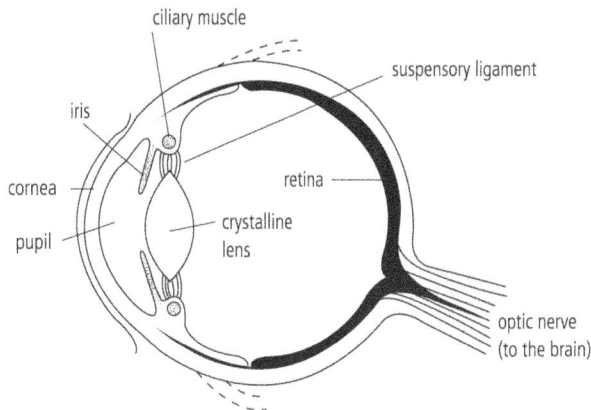

Fig. 19.5 *Human eye*

Refraction occurs at the boundaries of the cornea and the lens. An inverted image is formed on the **retina**. The information is then sent along the optic nerve to the brain. The eye is optically similar to the camera.

To focus upon objects that are at different distances from the eye, the **shape** of the lens is altered using the **ciliary muscles**. This alters the focal length of the lens. This process is called **accommodation**.

The **pupil** is the hole that allows light into the eye. The coloured part of the eye, the iris, changes its **size** to vary the size of the pupil and thus the amount of light that is allowed into the eye.

Eye defects

Short sightedness is when a person is unable to see clearly objects that are far away. It is due to the eyeball being too long. The image is formed **in front of** the retina. Short sightedness is corrected using a diverging lens (Fig. 19.6).

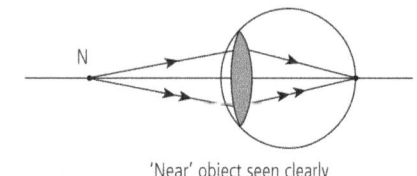

'Near' object seen clearly

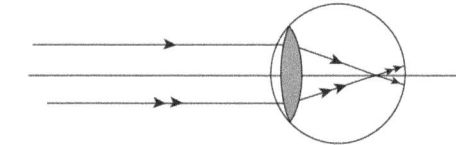

Object between the near point and infinity cannot be focused

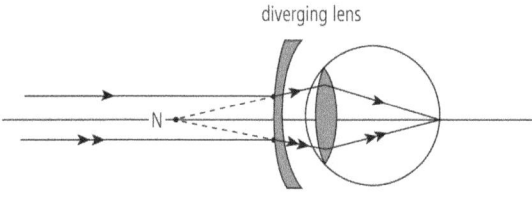

Parallel light is refracted by the lens so that it appears to come from N

Fig. 19.6 *Short sightedness and its correction*

Long sightedness occurs when a person is unable to see clearly objects close to the eye. This happens because the eyeball is too short. The image of the object is formed **behind** the retina. Long sightedness is corrected with a converging lens (Fig. 19.7).

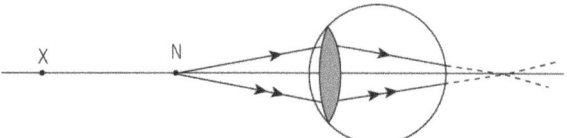

Objects between X and the near point N cannot be focused

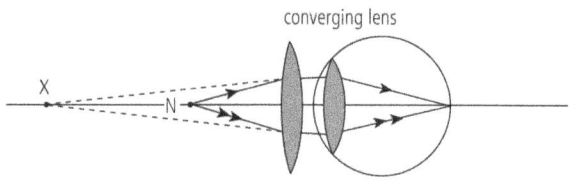

Light from N is refracted by the lens so that it appears to come from X

Fig. 19.7 *Long sightedness and its correction*

19.8 Dispersion

White light can be separated into colours using a triangular prism (Fig. 19.8).

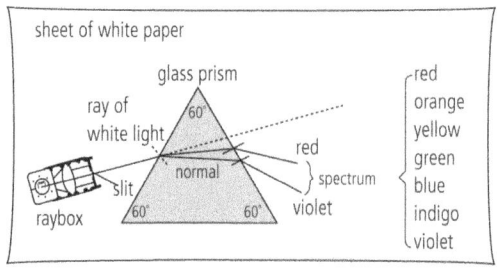

Fig. 19.8 *Dispersion of white light*

This splitting of light into its component colours is known as dispersion.

Dispersion occurs because the different colours have different refractive indices and thus are deviated by different amounts.

If we use just one colour, **monochromatic light**, we cannot disperse it; it is just deviated. Monochromatic light has just one wavelength (see Unit 22). Newton first performed this experiment in 1666. We discuss this experiment in Unit 35, as it is an example of the development of more modern scientific methods.

Questions on Units 18 and 19

1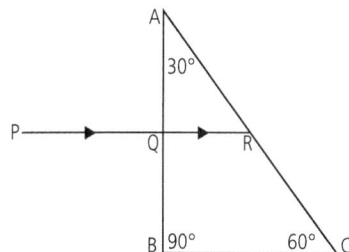

The diagram above shows a ray of light, PQ, passing normally across the face, AB, of a 90°–60°–30° glass prism. On a copy of this diagram:
a Sketch the path of the ray emerging into the air at R. Label this ray 'Ray 1'.
b Show where the eye could be placed to view the image of a pin placed at P.

It is possible for some of the light travelling along QR to be reflected at R and then to emerge from the prism.

c Sketch, on the same diagram, the path of such a ray. Label this 'Ray 2'.
d Explain whether the image produced by rays such as 'Ray 1' above is real. (CXC)

2 Draw separate diagrams showing a converging lens being used as
a a magnifying glass, to produce a magnified image,
b a camera lens to produce a diminished image.

A normal eye viewing a distant object adjusts to focus on an object a short distance away. State the change that takes place in the eye. What adjustment can be made to a camera in order to take clearly focused photographs of objects at widely different distances?

A converging lens is used to project an image of a slide on to a screen 1000 mm away from the lens, which has a focal length of 200 mm. The size of the image is 250 mm square. By means of a scale drawing determine
  i the distance of the slide from the lens,
  ii the size of the slide. (CAMB)

3

The diagrams above illustrate two converging lenses made from the same glass. State which lens has the shorter focal length. Use your answer to explain the process of **accommodation** in the human eye. Describe a laboratory method of measuring the focal length of a converging lens, making clear how you would obtain the result.

A brightly illuminated slide, 60 mm square, is placed 340 mm from a converging lens of focal length 200 mm. Determine, by means of a scale drawing, the position and size of the image focused on a screen by the lens.

Explain, with the aid of your diagram, why a slide must be placed both upside down and laterally inverted in a projector, to produce a correct image. (CAMB)

20 Waves

[syllabus sections D1.1–1.4, 2.1–2.6]

In your practical course you will see waves on a ripple tank or in springs ('slinkies'). Other examples of waves we find are those in rope, sound waves and electromagnetic waves (light and radio waves).

20.1 Types of waves

A **pulse** is a single disturbance that moves through a medium. Continuous disturbances create waves.

We can produce two kinds of waves on a slinky: transverse and longitudinal waves.

In a **transverse wave**, such as a water or electromagnetic wave, the vibration is at right angles (90°) to the direction of travel of the wave (Fig. 20.1a).

In a **longitudinal wave**, such as a sound wave, the vibration is in the same direction as the direction of travel of the wave (Fig. 20.1b).

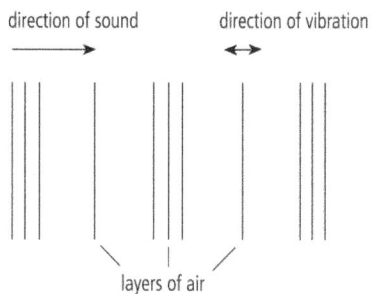

(b) *Longitudinal waves*

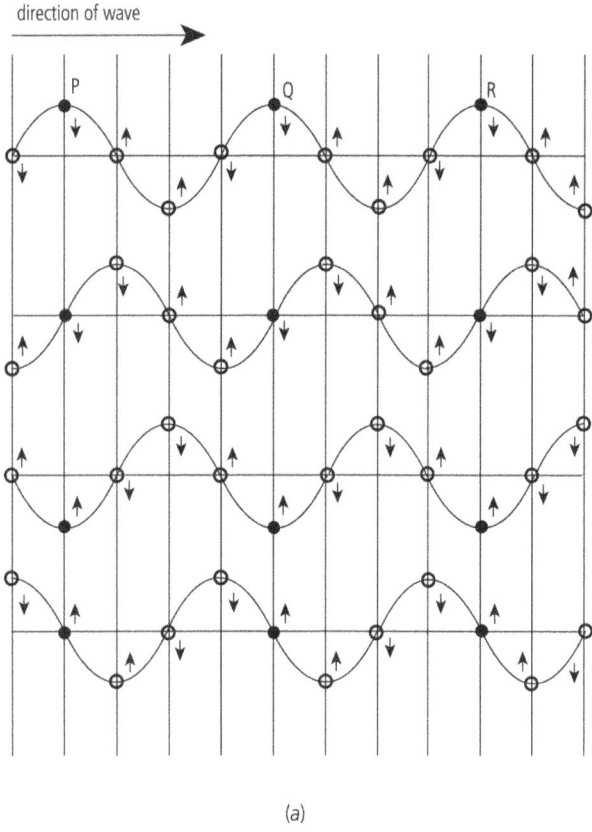

Fig. 20.1 (a) *Transverse waves*

Progressive and standing waves

A **progressive wave** is one in which energy is transferred along the wave. The waveform (wave profile) moves in the direction of energy transfer. Both transverse and longitudinal progressive waves can be formed in a slinky spring.

A **standing wave** (or stationary wave) is one in which the waveform does not move along. Energy is not transferred along the wave.

A standing wave can also be formed in a slinky spring. One end is fixed and the other end is moved from side to side, setting up transverse waves. They are reflected from the fixed end. At a certain rate of vibration the slinky vibrates in large loops that do not move along.

20.2 Describing waves

We can represent a transverse wave in a displacement/distance graph at a particular moment (Fig. 20.2).

The **amplitude**, a, of the wave is the maximum displacement of a particle from its rest position.

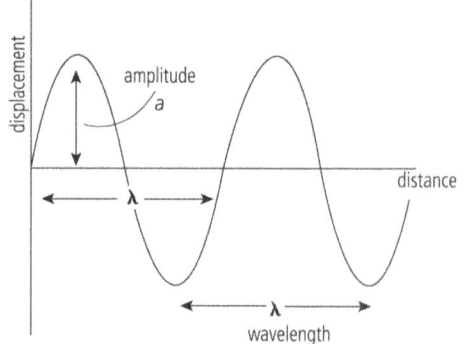

Fig. 20.2 *Displacement/distance graph*

The **wavelength**, λ (lambda), is the distance between two successive particles which are at the same point in their paths, and which are moving in the same direction. These particles are said to be **in phase**. Two particles that are ½ apart are exactly **out of phase**. Generally, phase refers to the relationship between two oscillations.

A **wavefront** is a line of particles that are vibrating in phase.

The **period**, *T*, of an oscillation is the time taken to make one oscillation.

The **frequency**, *f*, of a wave, is the number of complete oscillations made in one second. Thus

$$f = \frac{1}{T}$$

The unit of frequency is the **hertz**, Hz (or s^{-1}).
The **speed**, *v*, of a wave is the speed at which the wave profile moves along. It can be shown that the relationship between the speed, frequency and wavelength is

speed = frequency × wavelength
or $v = f \times \lambda$

We can also represent a transverse wave by a displacement/time graph (Fig. 20.3). In this case we consider the vibration of **one particle at a point** at different times. In Fig. 20.3 the wave moves forward ½ in 0.4 seconds. The graph is similar in shape to the displacement/distance graph.

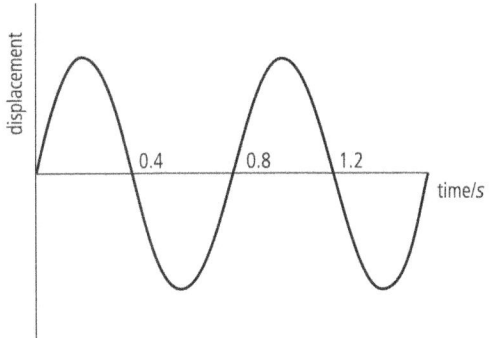

Fig. 20.3 *Displacement/time graph*

20.3 Properties of waves

All waves have the properties of reflection, refraction and diffraction.

Reflection

A wave pulse can be reflected on a slinky if one end is fixed (see above).

A **ripple tank** is used to demonstrate the properties of water waves. This is a shallow tank of water through which light shines. A small motor with an off-centre weight on a rod suspended above the tank makes the rod vibrate. This vibration is used to set up waves that move across the surface of the water. The wave pattern can be observed on a sheet of white paper below the tank (Fig. 20.4).

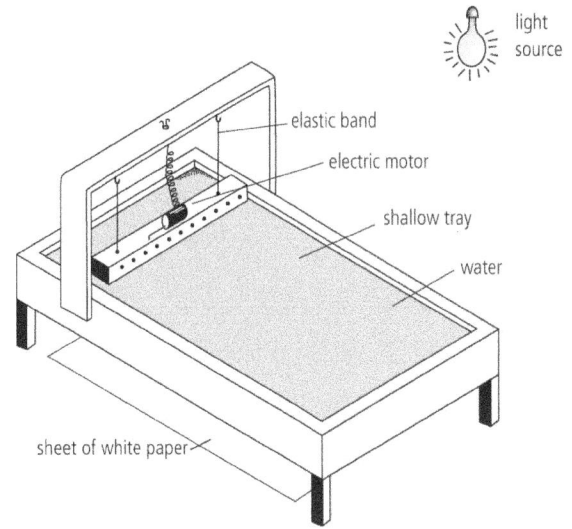

Fig. 20.4 *Ripple tank*

Plane water waves
The result of reflection of plane water waves is shown in Fig. 20.5.

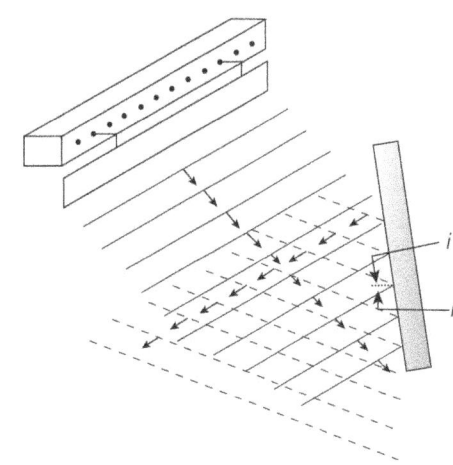

Fig. 20.5 *Plane waves*

The laws of reflection are the same as those discussed in Unit 17 for light. The angle of incidence *i* equals the angle of reflection *r*.

Circular waves
The result of reflecting circular waves at a plane barrier is shown in Fig. 20.6.

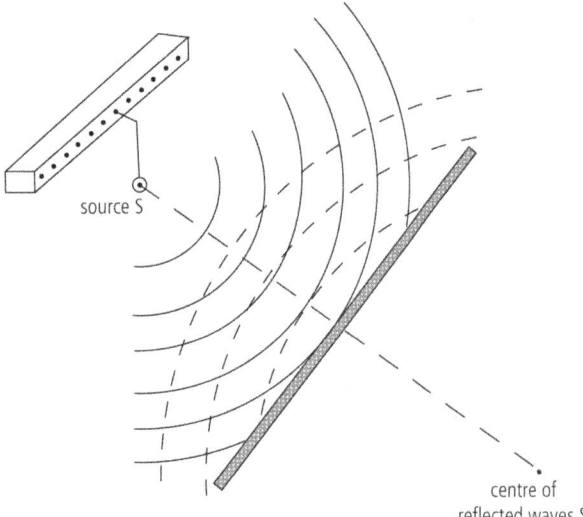

Fig. 20.6 *Reflection of circular waves*

Refraction

A water wave refracts, i.e. changes its direction, as it moves from one depth of water to another. We see the pattern in Fig. 20.7.

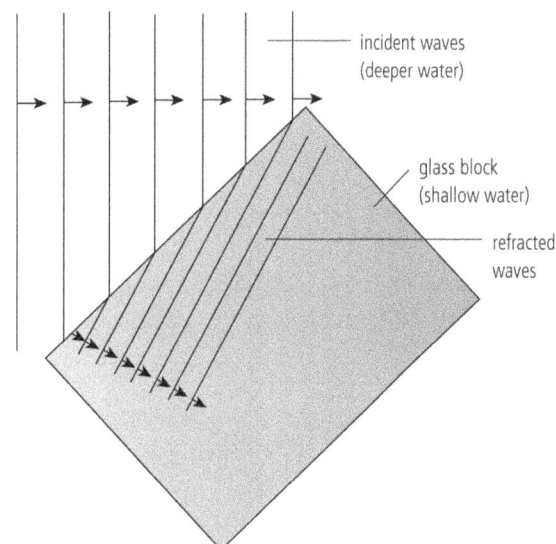

Fig. 20.7 *Reflection of plane waves*

Refraction occurs because the wave changes speed as it crosses the boundary. The frequency remains unchanged during refraction but the **velocity** and **wavelength** change.

Snell's Law is

$$_1n_2 = \frac{\sin\theta_1}{\sin\theta_2}$$

It can also be written as

$$_1n_2 = \frac{v_1}{v_2}$$

where v_1 is the speed in the first medium and v_2 the speed in the second medium. As

$$v_1 = \lambda_1 f \quad \text{and} \quad v_2 = \lambda_2 f$$

then $\quad \dfrac{v_1}{v_2} = \dfrac{\lambda_1 f}{\lambda_2 f} \quad$ and $\quad \dfrac{\lambda_1}{\lambda_2} = {_1n_2}$

Diffraction

Waves spread after passing through gaps between obstacles. This spreading effect is known as **diffraction**.

We show the diffraction of water waves using a ripple tank (Fig. 20.8).

Plane waves generate circular waves in the shadow of an obstacle (Fig. *20.8a*).

When the width of the gap is much larger than the wavelength, we see diffraction at each edge (Fig. 20.8*b*).

When a **gap** is approximately equal to the wavelength, we obtain circular waves (Fig. 20.8*c*).

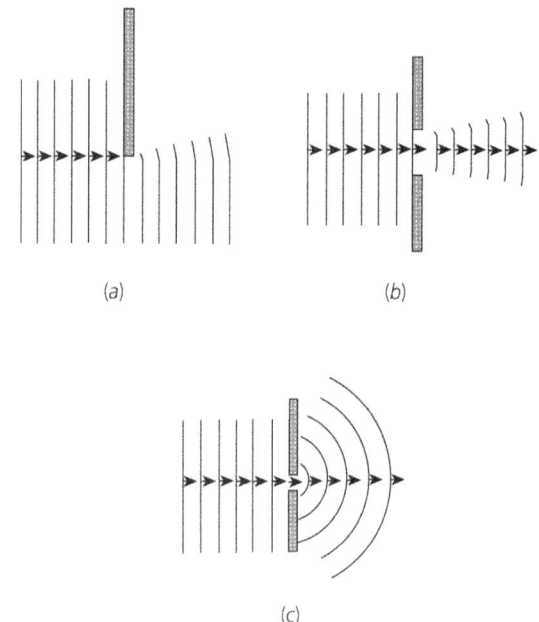

Fig. 20.8 *Diffraction of waves in a ripple tank*

We obtain greater diffraction either by decreasing the size of the gap *or* by increasing the wavelength of the incident waves.

20.4 Superposition and interference

When two waves meet they **superpose**. The net displacement is the sum of the original displacements of the two waves.

We use a slinky spring to show that when two similar wave pulses meet, the disturbance at the meeting point can be larger. This is known as **constructive interference** (Fig. 20.9a).

If two waves originally have displacements in the opposite directions and if the amplitudes are the same, they cancel out when they meet, resulting in 0 displacement. This is called **destructive interference** (Fig. 20.9b).

20.5 Interference of water waves

We use two point sources of waves in a ripple tank. The two sets of waves are vibrating in phase and overlap (Fig. 20.10).

We see lines along which there is no disturbance. At all points along this line we obtain destructive interference. The two waves arrive **out of phase**. A trough falls on a crest and makes a flat water surface.

Along other lines large troughs and crests are created as we obtain constructive interference. The waves meeting at points along these lines are **in phase**. A crest falls on a crest (or a trough on a trough) and a large disturbance is the result.

The same effect can be obtained using plane waves that are incident at two small gaps. Circular waves are formed at the gaps (diffraction) and interference then occurs as a result of the overlap of these circular waves.

If the slit spacing is **increased** then the lines of interference come **closer together**. If the **wavelength** of the waves is increased the lines of interference move **further apart**.

The interference of light is discussed in Unit 21 and that of sound in Unit 23.

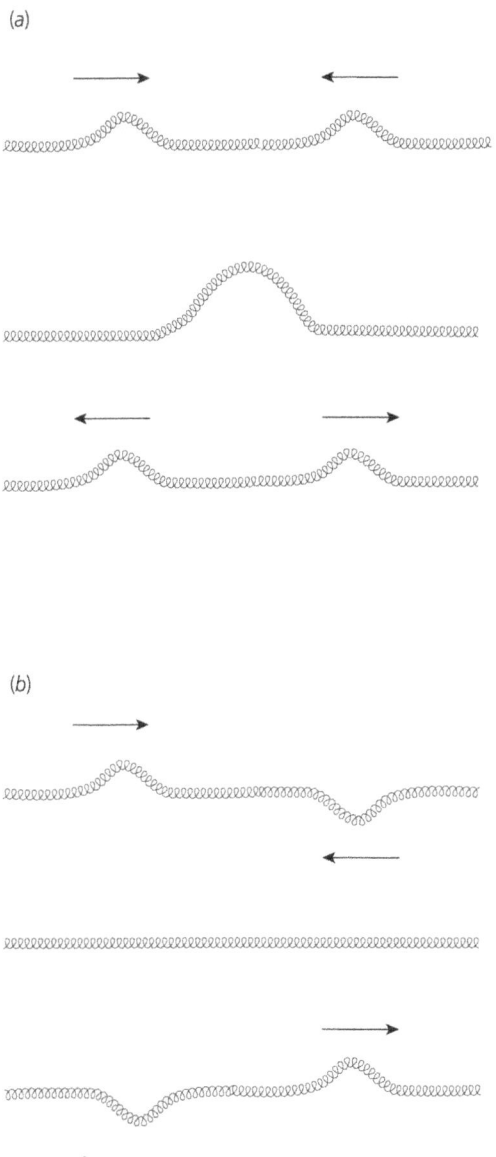

Fig. 20.9 *(a) Constructive interference (b) Destructive interference*

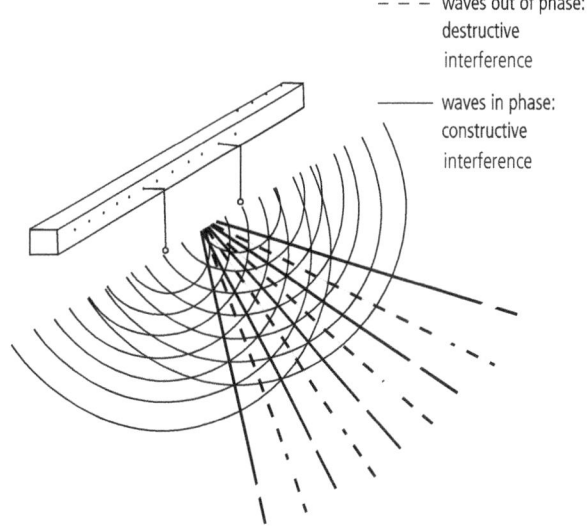

Fig. 20.10 *Interference in a ripple tank*

21 Theories of the nature of light

[syllabus sections D2.7, 5.1]

It was suggested by Newton that light consists of a stream of moving particles. This could explain the reflection of light (compare the reflection of a ball from a wall). Also, forces at the surface of glass might cause the change of direction as the light enters (refraction).

A Dutch man, Huygens, suggested that light is a form of wave motion. Waves reflect and refract and thus explain those properties of light. Young's experiment, performed in 1801, strongly supports a wave theory of light. It is hard to explain Young's experiment with a particle theory of light.

21.1 Young's slits experiment

The laboratory demonstration of the Young's slits experiment is shown in Fig. 21.1. The double slits near the lamp produce two beams of light which overlap. On the screen bright and dark lines (fringes) are observed.

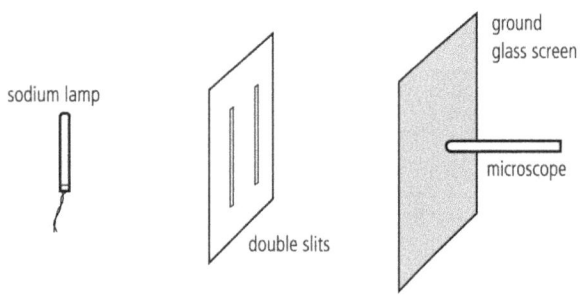

Fig. 21.1 *Young's slits experiment*

At the dark lines **destructive interference** between the two light beams is occurring. At the bright lines **constructive interference** is occurring.

This result cannot be explained using a particle theory as it is difficult to see how two particles can add to give zero.

If the slits are made closer together the separation of the lines increases. If the wavelength of the light is increased, e.g. by changing from yellow to red (see Unit 22), then the separation of the lines also increases.

21.2 Foucault's experiment

If light is a **wave** then the refraction of light suggests that the speed of light in glass should be **less** than that in air.

If light is a **particle** then refraction of light suggests that the speed of light in glass should be **greater** than that in air.

In an important experiment Foucault showed that the speed of light in glass is **less** than in air. This provided further strong support for the wave theory of light.

21.3 Diffraction of light

The different colours of light have different wavelengths. They range from 4×10^{-7} m (violet) to 7×10^{-7} m (red) (see Unit 22).

Diffraction of light is not usually observed, as openings are always many thousand times larger than the wavelength of the light. Diffraction around obstacles is also too small to be noticed. This leads to the fact that light travels in straight lines. Diffraction and interference effects are only observable, with light, with very small openings.

X-rays are diffracted by crystals. As they have smaller wavelengths than light (see Unit 22), diffraction only occurs with smaller apertures. The inter-atomic spacing in crystals is the correct size for X-ray diffraction.

21.4 Wave-particle duality

During the twentieth century several experiments have suggested that light has both a particle and a wave nature. Both models are necessary to explain fully the behaviour of light and we use one or the other, as is useful.

It has been shown that particles have certain wave-like properties. Electron diffraction has been observed. A beam of electrons is diffracted by a crystal and the results are similar to the diffraction of electromagnetic radiation.

In fact, equations used to describe the properties of atomic particles contain a mixture of quantities that apply to waves and particles. The 'wavelength' of a particle depends on its speed.

22 Electromagnetic spectrum

[syllabus sections D4.1–4.3]

Heat radiation and visible light are part of the spectrum of radiation known as the electromagnetic spectrum. This consists of radio waves, infrared radiation (IR or heat radiation), visible light, ultraviolet radiation (UV), X-rays and gamma rays (γ-rays).

22.1 Properties of electromagnetic waves

In a vacuum the velocity of **all** these radiations is the same: 3×10^8 m s^{-1}. They are a form of **transverse waves** and each has a particular range of wavelengths and frequencies. The relation between the velocity, frequency and wavelength is, as for all waves, $v = f \times \lambda$.

The higher-frequency radiations carry more energy. The particular characteristics of the radiations are outlined below. We start with the low frequency, long-wavelength radiation – radio waves – and look at the radiations in order of increasing frequency (decreasing wavelength).

Radio waves

Radio waves include the radiations used in radio, television and microwaves. Radio waves have wavelengths from about 10 km to 1 mm, i.e. 10^4 m to 10^{-3} m.

We use radio and TV waves for communication and detect them with a radio or TV receiver. Microwaves are very short wavelength radio waves used in radar. We use radar at sea and at airports for the security and control of ships and aircraft.

Infrared radiation

All objects emit infrared (IR) radiation (heat radiation). The amount emitted increases as the temperature rises. IR radiation has wavelengths that range from approximately 10^{-4} m to 7×10^{-7} m.

We detect IR radiation just beyond the red end of the visible spectrum (obtained by dispersing the light – and heat – from a filament lamp: see Unit 18). One detector is a mercury thermometer with a blackened bulb. When IR radiation falls on the bulb, the mercury rises.

We can use a converging lens to focus the Sun's heat and light. In an eclipse of the Sun the heat and light are cut off at the same time. This suggests that the IR radiation and light travel at the same speed.

Visible light

Hot objects, i.e. those above about 600 °C, are the main source of visible light. It has a small range of wavelengths: 7×10^{-7} m (red) to 4×10^{-7} m (blue). The properties of visible light have already been outlined. Visible light is important to plants. It is used in the making of food (photosynthesis).

Ultraviolet radiation

Ultraviolet (UV) radiation is emitted, in small quantities, by the hot filament in a light bulb. It is then mainly absorbed by the glass. Hotter objects emit more UV radiation. Most of the Sun's UV radiation is absorbed by the atmosphere and does not reach the Earth's surface.

UV radiation has a range of wavelengths from 4×10^{-7} m to about 10^{-9} m and is just outside the violet end of the visible spectrum. We detect UV radiation using photographic film.

Certain materials emit visible light when UV radiation falls upon them. This is called **fluorescence**. Paraffin oils are an example (we can use Vaseline on paper). A fluorescent lighting tube develops most of its light in this way. The UV radiation created inside the tube falls on the coating. The coating then emits visible light. UV radiation also causes darkening of the skin.

X-rays

X-rays are produced when high-speed electrons hit a metal target. X-rays have wavelengths in the range 10^{-9} m to 10^{-12} m.

X-rays are absorbed by different materials to different extents and also affect photographic film. We use these two properties in medicine and industry. We pass X-rays through a person's body and onto a photographic film. Bones, or foreign objects, are clearly visible on the negative obtained. A very large dose of X-rays can have harmful effects on living tissue.

Gamma rays (γ-rays)

Gamma rays are emitted from the nuclei of certain atoms (see Unit 34).

Gamma rays have very small wavelengths, 10^{-10} m or smaller and very high frequencies. They are very dangerous and are one product of an atomic bomb explosion. They are detected by a Geiger-Müller tube (Unit 34).

23 Sound

[syllabus sections D3.1–3.5]

Sound is produced by **vibrating** systems, e.g. a stretched string that is plucked, a column of air or a tuning fork.

Sound is transmitted as **progressive longitudinal wave**. The layers of air vibrate backwards and forwards in the same energy. This results in compressions and rarefactions in the air.

In a **compression** the layers of air are closer together than usual and the pressure at the point is higher than usual. In a **rarefaction** the layers of air are further apart than usual and the pressure is lower than normal (Fig. 23.1).

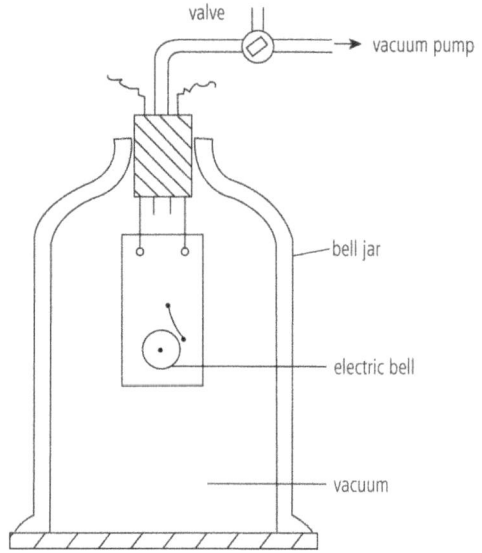

Fig. 23.2 *Sound waves do not pass through a vacuum*

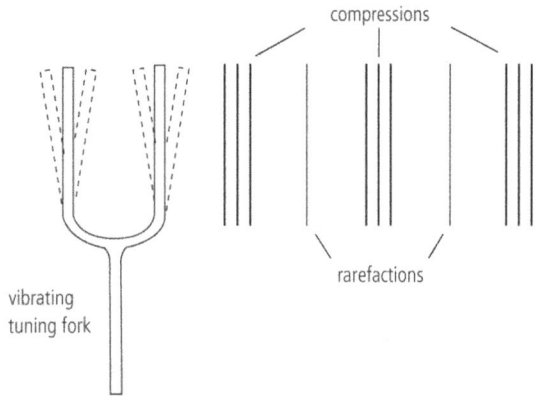

Fig. 23.1 *Vibration of a tuning fork*

The wavelength of the sound wave is the distance between successive compressions or rarefactions.

23.1 Transmission of sound

Sound cannot travel through a vacuum. The apparatus used to demonstrate this is shown in Fig. 23.2.

At first we can both see and hear the bell ringing. We use the vacuum pump to extract the air from the bell jar. The ringing slowly dies down to a weak hum. Some sound is still conducted through the suspensions for the bell.

23.2 Properties of sound

We can show that sound, like other waves, has the properties of reflection, refraction, diffraction and interference.

Reflection

Hard, flat surfaces are best for the reflection of sound. We can use the apparatus shown in Fig. 23.3.

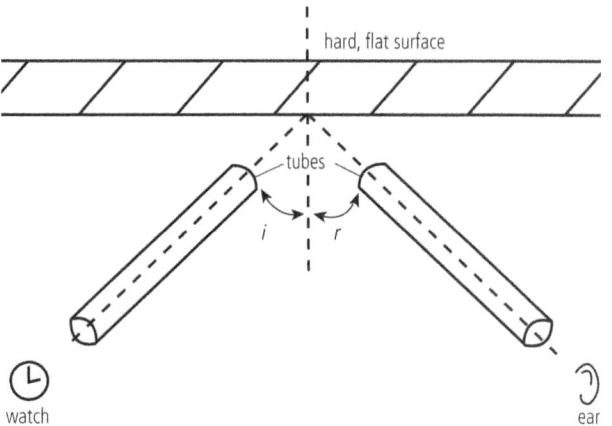

Fig. 23.3 *Reflection of sound*

A quietly ticking clock or watch is the source of sound. It can be heard clearly at the end of the other tube if the tubes are placed at the appropriate angles. The incident and reflected sounds obey the law of reflection – the angles of incidence and reflection are equal ($i = r$)

Refraction

On cool evenings, with no wind, a sound can be heard quite clearly some distance away. This is a result of the refraction of sound.

The air higher above the ground is warmer than the air lower down. The sound travels faster in the warmer air. As the sound travels from the cooler to the warmer air it bends continuously and is refracted back towards the ground (Fig. 23.4).

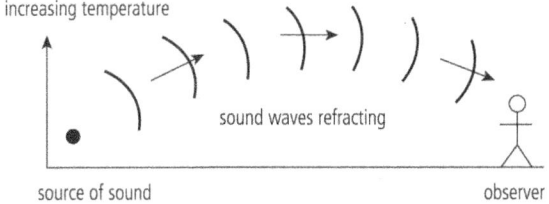

Fig. 23.4 *Refraction of sound*

Diffraction

Diffraction of sound occurs frequently. We can hear people speaking around a corner even when we cannot see them. The frequency of human speech is on average about 160 Hz. This means it has a wavelength of about 2 m. Doorways produce diffraction and the diffraction around obstacles is considerable. Higher-frequency sounds, with shorter wavelengths, diffract much less.

Interference

We demonstrate interference of sound using two loudspeakers attached to the same audio-frequency generator (Fig. 23.5).

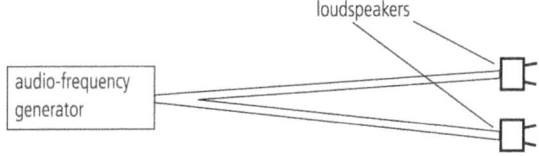

Fig. 23.5 *Interference of sound waves*

In front of the speakers there are places where the sound is loud and other places where it is hard to hear.

Constructive interference occurs when a compression meets a compression and a large amplitude results. Two rarefactions also add up to give a large amplitude. Destructive interference occurs when a compression meets a rarefaction and the amplitude becomes zero, if the two amplitudes are equal.

23.3 Speed of sound

To measure the speed of sound we stand about 100 m from a large flat wall. We use two pieces of wood to make a large clap. We hear the echo and then clap in time with the successive echoes.

We time ten claps. This is the time for the sound to travel to the wall and back ten times. We calculate the time, t, for one journey. If the distance between the wall and us is d then the total distance travelled is $2d$.

The speed of sound, v, is given by

$$v = \frac{2d}{t}$$

The speed of sound in air is about 330 m s^{-1} but varies if the temperature changes. Sound travels quicker in liquids and solids than in air. Sound obeys the wave equation $v = f\lambda$.

Applications of the speed of sound

When we are timing a race we start our stopwatch according to the **sight** of the gun firing. If we wait for the **sound** of the gun we will start our watches late, as the sound travels quite slowly.

Thunder is often heard some time after the lightning is seen, although both occur simultaneously in a storm. This is because the light travels very fast and reaches our eyes almost immediately. The sound often takes a few seconds to reach us.

23.4 Pitch, loudness and quality

The **frequency**, f, of a sound wave is the number of oscillations made in one second. A high-pitched note has a high frequency. The human ear can hear a range of frequencies from about 20 Hz to about 16 000 Hz. Younger people may hear up to 20 000 Hz.

The **loudness** of sound depends on the **amplitude** of the vibration. A louder sound has a greater amplitude.

In an orchestra the instruments sound different even when playing the same note. We say that the **quality** of the note is different. The notes produced in musical instruments are not pure notes but have other notes, called **overtones**, mixed in with the basic note. The sweet sound of pan is primarily due to its laminar (sheet-like) nature; striking any note causes vibrations in the notes adjacent on either side. This causes the mixing of notes and the unique sound of pan.

23.5 Noise pollution

Loud noises can be uncomfortable and harm our health and hearing. Common sources of excessive noise are aircraft, motor vehicles, factory machines and amplified music. There are several ways of reducing these problems.

Houses in the flight path near airports can have double-glazed windows.

Exhausts in motor vehicles can have improved design and vehicles can have better shock absorbers to absorb vibrations and reduce noise.

Greater use can be made of sound-absorbing materials in buildings and greater recognition of the problem may lead to better design.

In factories, airports and other situations where the noise level is high, workers should be issued with earplugs or similar protectors.

Questions on Units 20 to 23

1. a Describe how you could use a ripple tank to illustrate the **interference** of waves on the surface of water. With the aid of a diagram, make clear the effects you would expect to observe.
   b Calculate the **wavelength** in air of the light from a monochromatic source, given that the **speed** of light in air is 3.00×10^8 m s^{-1} and the **frequency** of the light is 6.25×10^{14} Hz.
   c Describe briefly a simple experiment to demonstrate the wave nature of light. Make clear the effects you observe which indicate the wave-like properties.
   (CAMB)

2. a Explain the difference between longitudinal and transverse waves.
   The diagram represents a continuous train of longitudinal waves travelling along a 'slinky' spring.

   If the distance AB is 7 m, what is the wavelength of the wave?

   b

γ-rays		ultra violet waves		micro waves	radio waves

   i Copy the above diagram of the electromagnetic wave spectrum, and label, in their correct position, the three parts omitted.
   ii State how each of the missing parts may be detected.
   iii State one use for microwaves.
   iv Assuming the speed of electromagnetic waves in free space to be 3×10^8 m s^{-1}, calculate the frequency of the radio waves broadcast with a wavelength of 1500 m.   (WJEC)

3. Outline the Young's slits experiment. Explain how it supports a wave theory of light.
   Briefly discuss the importance of Foucault's experiment to the development of our understanding of the nature of light.

4. In the diagram below, a powerful source of sound is at A, 60 m above the flat surface of water in a swimming pool. The bed of the pool is level and is a good reflecting surface.
   The source gives out a single sharp note of frequency 10^4 Hz. The velocity of sound in air may be taken to be 330 m s^{-1} and, in water, as four times this value. An observer is at B, 160 m from A and the same distance as A above the water surface. He hears three notes at separate times.

   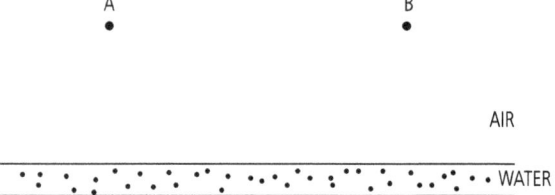

   a Copy the above diagram and sketch rays between A and B for each of the notes heard. Label each ray distinctly as x, y and z and give any other information on the diagram you think necessary.
   b Would there be any difference in (i) the pitch and (ii) the loudness of the three notes heard by the observer? Explain your answer in **each** case.
   c How much later would the observer hear the second note after he hears the first?
   d What is the wavelength of the sound waves in water?
   e If at A there were a light source instead of a sound source, would the person at B be able to detect the time differences among the corresponding three rays of light? Give the reason for your answer.   (CXC)

24 Static electricity

[syllabus sections E1.1–1.5]

When we rub certain materials, for example plastic, with cloth, small pieces of paper can be attracted towards the material. The material is now electrically charged with static electricity.

If we rub two strips of polythene with a dry woollen cloth and then suspend one strip and bring the second strip near to the first, the suspended one moves away. It is **repelled**.

If we rub pieces of ebonite or cellulose acetate with cloth we find that they **attract** the polythene strip.

24.1 Basic structure of atoms

To understand these experiments we must consider the particles in the atoms of the material. The atoms consist of a central fixed mass, the **nucleus**. The nucleus contains **protons**, which are electrically **positively-charged**, and **neutrons**, which have **no charge**.

Electrons are moving in orbits around the nucleus. The electrons are **negatively-charged**.

There are equal numbers of protons and electrons in a neutral atom (Fig. 24.1). (See also Unit 33, Structure of atoms.)

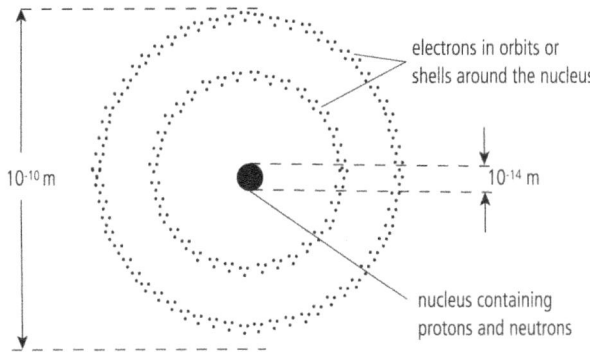

Fig. 24.1 *Structure of the atom*

24.2 Explanation of experiments

In the above experiments some of the electrons from the cloth have been transferred, by friction, to the polythene strips. The strips are then negatively-charged (leaving the cloth equally positively-charged). The electrons **repel** each other leading to the mutual repulsion of the polythene strips.

The protons are fixed. The ebonite or cellulose acetate **loses** electrons to the cloth and, as there is now more positive charge than negative charge, becomes positively-charged.

Positive charge **attracts** negative charge and the positively-charged ebonite thus attracts the negatively-charged polythene.

Generally,
  Like charges repel,
  Unlike charges attract.

The materials used above are all electrical **insulators**. They do not conduct electricity so the charge does not flow away along these materials.

24.3 Attraction of uncharged objects

When we bring a positively-charged rod near an object with **no** net charge, **attraction** occurs.

The electrons in the uncharged object move towards the positive charge making one side of the uncharged material negative and leaving the other side positive (Fig. 24.2).

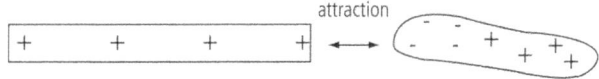

Fig. 24.2 *Attraction of an uncharged object*

24.4 Gold-leaf electroscope

A gold-leaf electroscope, used to test charges on objects, is shown in Fig. 24.3. The metal rod has a metal plate at one end and a metal cap at the other. Attached to the plate is a thin piece of gold foil. The rod is separated, by an insulator, from the metal case.

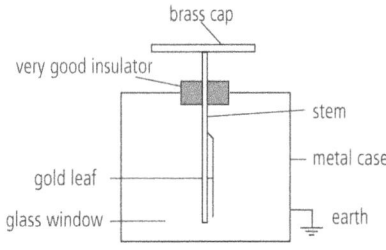

Fig. 24.3 *Gold-leaf electroscope*

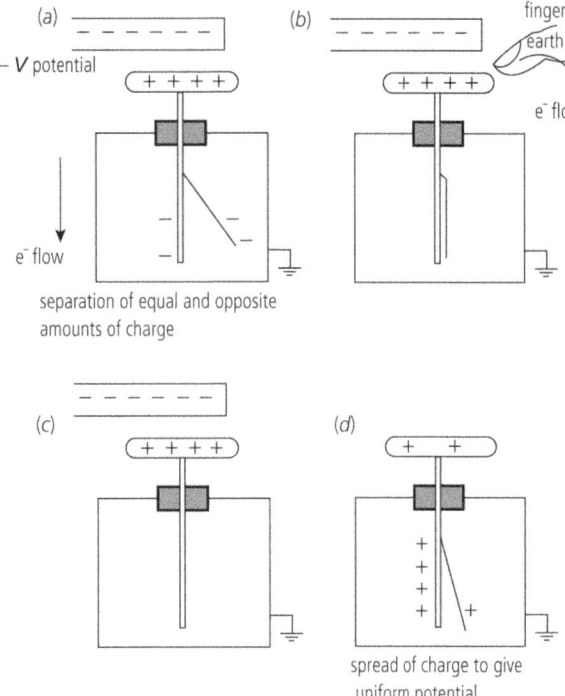

Fig. 24.4 *Charging an electroscope by induction*

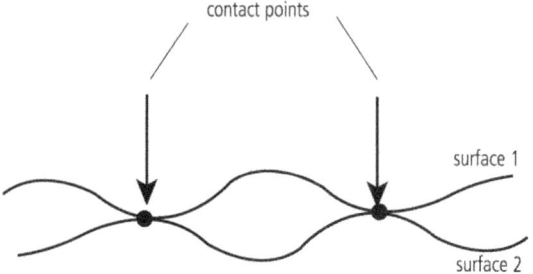

Fig. 24.5 *Rubbing two surfaces together on a microscopic level*

Charging an electroscope by induction

When we bring a negatively-charged rod near the cap, the gold leaf moves. The electrons in the cap are repelled down the rod and onto both the gold lead **and** the plate. These now repel each other and the leaf diverges (Fig. 24.4a).

We earth the cap by touching it with a finger (Fig. 24.4b). The gold leaf falls as the electrons flow to earth. We remove the rod and the electroscope is **positively-charged** (Fig. 24.4c). Charging a conductor in this way is called charging **by induction**. The charge on the original rod is unchanged.

With a positively-charged electroscope we can test unknown charges. A positively-charged rod near the cap causes the gold leaf to diverge more (repulsion). A negatively-charged rod causes the leaf divergence to fall. An uncharged rod also causes a drop in the leaf divergence. Repulsion is the only true test of the sign of a charge.

Charging an electroscope by conduction

When a negatively-charged rod is rubbed on the cap of an uncharged electroscope, electrons flow from the rod to the electroscope. Rubbing the two surfaces together increases the contact area between them. On a microscopic level no two surfaces are completely smooth and so contact only occurs at a few points.

It is for this reason that conduction is an inefficient process. It occurs slowly and the actual quantity of charge transferred is difficult to gauge.

24.5 Electric fields

We define an electric field as a region in which a charge experiences a force.

We represent electric fields as a set of lines: **electric field lines**. Charges would move along these lines. The strength of the field is represented by the number of lines (Fig. 24.6).

We define the **direction** of an electric field as the direction that positive charge would move.

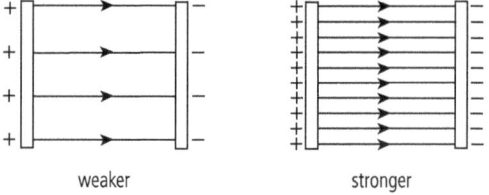

Fig. 24.6 *Electric field lines*

The electric field lines start on a positive charge and end on a negative charge.

24.6 Charge, potential and potential difference

The unit of electric charge is the **coulomb** (C). The symbol for electric charge is Q.

The **potential at a point** in an electric field is the work done in bringing one coulomb of positive charge from earth to that point. The unit of potential is the **volt** (V). One volt is the potential at a point when one joule of work is done in bringing one coulomb of positive charge from earth to that point.

The earth is taken as the zero of potential. All earthed objects are at zero potential.

Potential difference

The potential difference (V) between two points A and B is the work done in moving one coulomb of positive charge from B to A.

The work done on the charge is stored as **electrostatic potential energy**.

A positive charge can lose this potential energy and gain kinetic energy if it moves to a position of lower potential.

The energy stored, E, when a charge Q moves through a potential difference V is given by

$$\text{energy} = \text{charge} \times \text{potential difference}$$
$$E = Q \times V$$

24.7 Conduction in gases

Normally gases are **electrical insulators**, i.e. they do not allow electricity to pass through them. If we have a strong electric field a gas molecule may be **ionised**.

When a gas is ionised, one or more electrons leave the molecule. The molecule now has a net positive charge. It is called a **positive ion**. Lightning can be the result of this process.

Lightning and lightning conductors

A rain cloud becomes charged in a storm and an electric field is set up between the cloud and the Earth. If the electric field is strong enough it **ionises** the air and the electric current is then conducted to earth. We see the burst of current as a flash of lightning.

The electrons move in one direction (to the ground) and the positively-charged ions in the other direction.

A lightning conductor is a strip of metal on a building that extends into the ground from above the highest point of the building. A lightning conductor has two uses:
1. It causes continuous ionisation of the air above its pointed end. The positively-charged ions move up to the cloud and tend to neutralise the cloud and prevent lightning from occurring. Electrons flow to earth – the Earth acts as a large reservoir for electric charge.
2. It conducts the lightning to earth if lightning strikes.

In a storm it is best not to seek shelter under a large tree as it may be hit by lightning. A television aerial can act as a lightning conductor and this can have disastrous effects. Aerials should be disconnected in storms.

24.8 Connection between electrostatics and electric current

Using a high-voltage supply we charge two metal plates (insulated from each other), one with positive charge and one with negative charge. We then discharge the plates by connecting them through a sensitive meter. A short burst of current is registered.

This shows that the charge responsible for electrostatic effects is also the charge that moves in an electric current.

25 Direct current

[syllabus sections E2.1–2.4, 4.1–4.15]

In metals some of the electrons are not firmly attached to an atom. These 'free' electrons can easily move through the metal.

We find that all metals are conductors of electricity.

In a metal, current consists of these negatively-charged electrons flowing towards a region of more positive potential. However, we consider **conventional current** as flowing from **positive** to **negative**. (This is important for several rules in electromagnetism.)

The unit of electric current (I) is the **ampere** (A). This is a base unit in the SI system and electric current is a fundamental quantity.

25.1 Current and charge

The unit of electric charge, the coulomb, is the charge that passes one point in one second when a current of one ampere is flowing:

1 coulomb = 1 ampere-second

More generally, charge = current × time
Or, $Q = I \times t$

25.2 Symbols in electrical circuits

The following symbols will be used in electrical circuits in your course (Fig. 25.1).

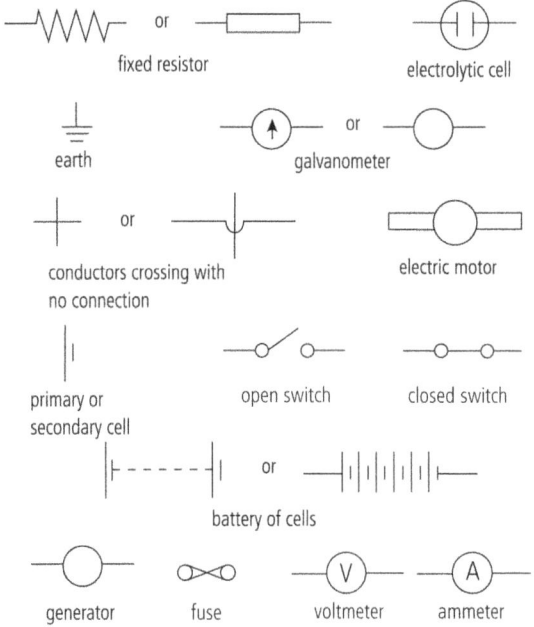
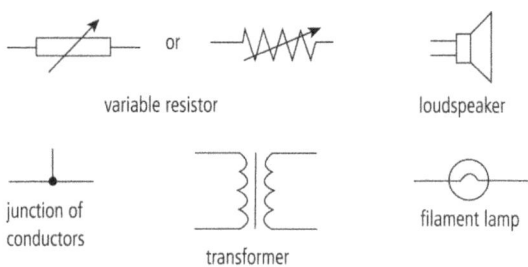

Fig. 25.1 *Electrical symbols*

25.3 Electromotive force and potential difference

The **electromotive force** (e.m.f.), in volts, of a source of electricity in a circuit is defined as the energy in joules converted per coulomb of charge flowing round the circuit.

To drive electric current through a component, a **potential difference** (p.d.) is needed across the component. This is created by the cell or other source (see below).

25.4 Resistance and Ohm's law

All metal wires conduct electricity but some materials conduct less easily than others. We say that the wires have a **resistance** to the flow of electricity.

We use the circuit in Fig. 25.2 to investigate the relationship between the potential difference across a metallic conductor and the current through it.

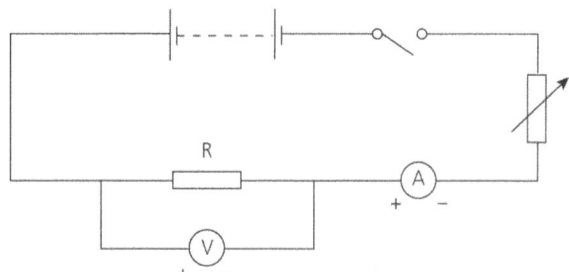

Fig. 25.2 *Circuit to check Ohm's law*

Note that the ammeter is used in line, or **in series**, with the resistance wire, and the voltmeter is used **in parallel** with the wire.

We use the **variable resistor** (rheostat) to change the current flowing. If the variable resistance is high, the current is low.

We take a set of pairs of readings of the potential difference (V) and the current (I) and plot a graph of V against I. A typical graph is a straight line through the origin (Fig. 25.3).

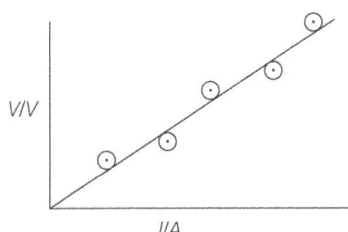

Fig. 25.3 *Voltage-current graph*

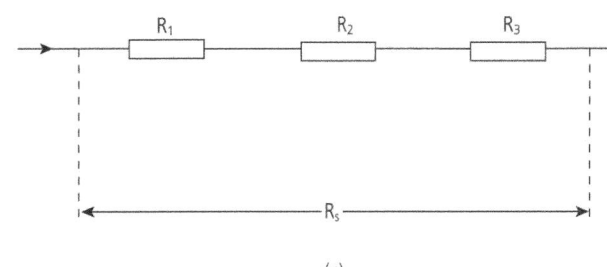

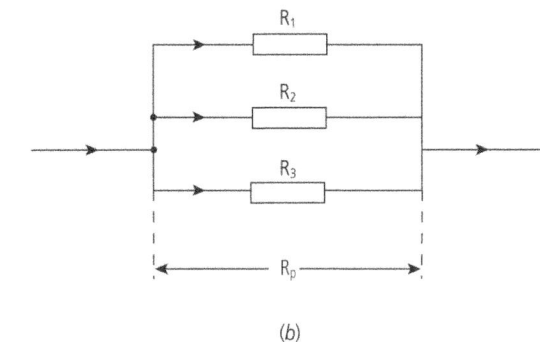

Fig. 25.4 *(a) Resistors in series (b) Resistors in parallel*

From this we obtain **Ohm's law**. For a metallic conductor at a constant temperature the current flowing is proportional to the potential difference applied across the conductor.

We also notice that the ratio, V/I, is a constant and equals the gradient of the graph.

$$\frac{V}{I} = \text{constant}$$

The constant is called the **resistance**, R, of the wire. The unit of resistance is the **ohm**, Ω. We obtain

$$\frac{V}{I} = R$$

One ohm is that resistance of a conductor that allows a current of 1 A to flow if a p.d. of 1 V is applied across the conductor.

25.5 Series and parallel circuits

We can arrange components in several ways: in series, in parallel, or in some combination of the two arrangements.

In your practical course you should show that
1. in a **series circuit** the current is the same in all components
2. with components **in parallel** the total current is equal to the sum of the currents in the different branches.

You can also show that
3. the potential differences across the individual components **in series**, add to give the total potential difference
4. the potential difference for components **in parallel** is the same for each component.

25.6 Series and parallel resistors

The total resistance, R_S, of a set of resistors **in series**, is the sum of the individual resistances (Fig. 25.4a)

$$R_S = R_1 + R_2 + R_3$$

If the resistors are **in parallel** (Fig. 25.4b), the total resistance, R_P, is given by

$$\frac{1}{R_P} = \frac{1}{R_1} + \frac{1}{R_2} + \frac{1}{R_3}$$

In the special case of two resistors, R_1 and R_2 in parallel, we have

$$\text{Total resistance in parallel, } R_P = \frac{R_1 R_2}{R_1 + R_1} \quad \frac{\text{(product)}}{\text{sum}}$$

You should note that the overall resistance is
a **increased** when resistors are placed in series with each other
b **reduced** when resistors are placed in parallel with each other.

25.7 Ammeters and voltmeters

We can now see that an ammeter, which is placed in series with a component, needs a low resistance. This is so that the ammeter does not reduce the current by any significant amount.

We place voltmeters in parallel with the component. The resistance of a voltmeter is very high to ensure that it takes little current from the circuit.

25.8 Resistance of wires

We can use the Ohm's law circuit (Fig. 25.2) and replace the fixed resistance wire by a series of wires of differing length, diameter and material.

The results we obtain are as follows:
1. The **longer** the wire the **greater** its resistance.
2. The **smaller** the diameter (or cross-sectional area) of the wire the **greater** its resistance.
3. For wires of the same dimensions different materials have different resistances.

Nichrome, an alloy of nickel and chromium, and constantan are two materials commonly used to make resistance wires.

25.9 Power in electrical circuits

In an electrical circuit electrical energy is often transformed into thermal energy.

The power of a component is the rate of change of energy from one form into another.

The power output, P, of a component with a p.d. of V across it, carrying a current, I, is given by

power = p.d. × current

or $\boxed{P = VI}$

If the component is used for a time t then the energy converted is

$E = Pt$

or $E = VIt$

If the component obeys Ohm's law then $V = IR$

so $P = IV = I \times IR$

and $\boxed{P = I^2R}$

also $P = IV = \dfrac{V}{R} \times V$

and $\boxed{P = \dfrac{V^2}{R}}$

25.10 Cells and accumulators

We obtain direct current from chemical cells and accumulators.

Dry cell

The cross-section of a dry cell is shown in Fig. 25.5. The carbon rod is the positive terminal and the zinc container the negative terminal. Hydrogen is formed in the reaction between the zinc and ammonium chloride. The manganese (IV) oxide converts this hydrogen into water. The carbon mixed with the manganese (IV) oxide helps current flow (reduces the internal resistance – see below).

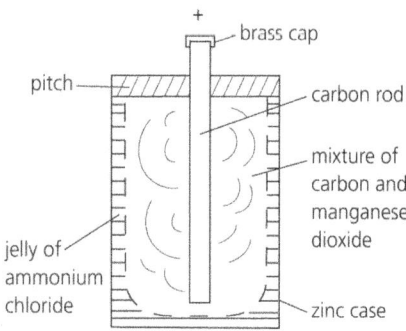

Fig. 25.5 *Dry cell*

A dry cell is a **primary** cell. When the chemical energy has been converted to electrical energy, the changes in the cell cannot be reversed. The cell cannot be recharged and is thrown away.

The dry cell has quite a high internal resistance of about 0.5 Ω. Large currents cannot be obtained. However, a dry cell is convenient and is used in many situations that require a portable source of electricity.

E.m.f., p.d. and internal resistance

When we buy a dry cell we often see '1.5 V' marked on the cell. This is the **e.m.f.** of the cell.

When we place the cell in a circuit the total potential difference measured across the components of the circuit is always **less** than 1.5 V. Some of the e.m.f. is used to drive the current through the cell itself against the internal resistance of the cell.

Energy is converted into heat inside the cell.

You can demonstrate this 'loss' of e.m.f. in your practical course.

Lead-acid cell

The basic structure of a lead-acid cell is shown in Fig. 25.6. We first pass electricity through the cell, that is, we **charge** the cell. This causes chemical changes that store energy. When the terminals are connected, electrical energy is obtained.

When we have used the cell for a while we can **recharge** it. Cells that can be recharged are called **secondary** cells.

Six lead-acid cells are used, in series, in a car battery. A lead-acid cell has a very small internal resistance of about 0.01 Ω.

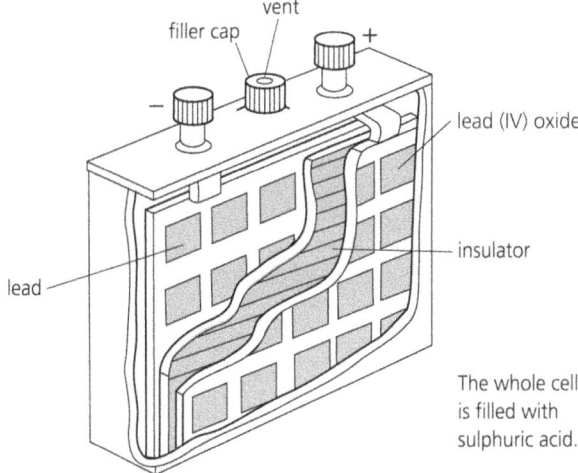

Fig. 25.6 *Lead-acid cell or accumulator*

Recharging secondary cells

The circuit used to recharge a lead-acid cell or battery is shown in Fig. 25.7. Note that the positive terminal of the supply is connected to the positive terminal of the battery. The **variable resistor** limits and varies the current and the **ammeter** measures the charging current used. Low charging currents are more efficient.

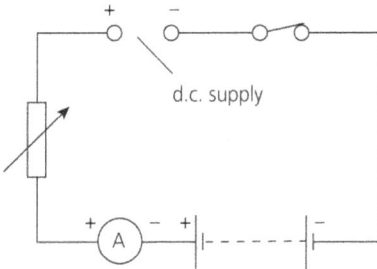

Fig. 25.7 *Charging circuit for a lead-acid cell*

Care of accumulators

To maintain a lead-acid cell, distilled water is added occasionally as evaporation occurs.

The terminals of an accumulator must never be connected directly as a high, damaging current results.

The accumulator should not be left discharged for a long time. The level of charge can be checked by measuring the density. A fully-charged accumulator has acid of density of 1.25 g cm^{-3}.

25.11 Electrolysis

When we pass electricity through a liquid, chemical changes often occur in the liquid. This process is called electrolysis. The liquid that conducts the electricity is called the **electrolyte**.

Two metal plates, the **electrodes**, conduct the electricity in and out of the liquid. They are the cathode and the anode. The **cathode** is attached to the **negative** terminal of the electricity supply and the **anode** to the **positive** terminal.

The electric current is carried in the liquid by both positively- and negatively-charged **ions** moving in opposite directions.

Electrolysis of copper sulphate solution

We dissolve blue copper sulphate in water. We use copper plates for both the anode and the cathode (Fig. 25.8).

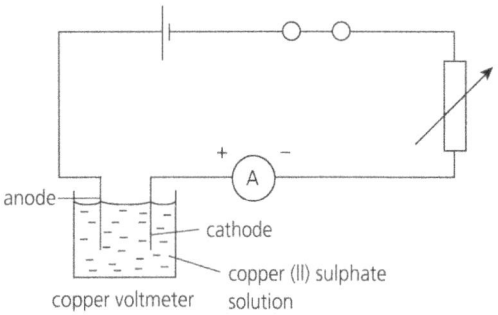

Fig. 25.8 *Electrolysis of copper sulphate solution*

When current flows the cathode becomes coated with a layer of copper. We can also show that the copper anode starts to dissolve. Any conducting material used as the cathode is covered with copper. This process is called **electroplating**.

Theory of electrolysis of copper sulphate

In the solution we have copper ions, which have lost two electrons and are therefore positively charged. They move towards the negative cathode, receive two electrons and are deposited on the cathode as neutral copper atoms.

The atoms of copper at the anode give up two electrons and move into solution. The electrons move away through the wire attached to the anode.

Relationship between p.d. and current for copper sulphate solution

We use the same circuit as for Ohm's law (Fig. 25.2), but substitute a solution of copper sulphate for the fixed resistor.

Platinum electrodes are used and the anode does not dissolve. We obtain a set of pairs of values of V and I by varying the rheostat. We also change the direction of the p.d. and plot a graph of current against p.d. (Fig. 25.9).

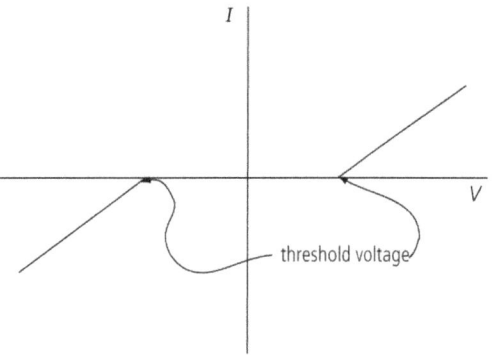

Fig. 25.9 *Graph of current against p.d. for copper sulphate solution with platinum electrodes*

The platinium electrodes create a potential difference that opposes the battery voltage (depending on the type of electrode used). A certain threshold voltage in either direction needs to be achieved before current flows. In Fig. 25.9 above, V is **related to** I (after the threshold voltage). V is **not proportional to** I (since the graph does not pass through the origin).

The difficulties that Faraday might have had with his experiments on electrolysis are discussed in Unit 35.

26 Electricity in the home

[syllabus sections E4.16–4.21]

When we wire a home for electricity, safety is a very important consideration. Layouts of typical wiring systems are shown in Fig. 26.1.

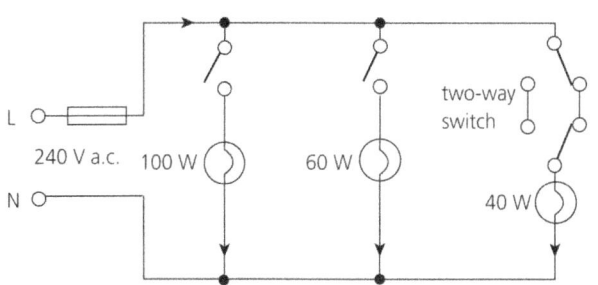

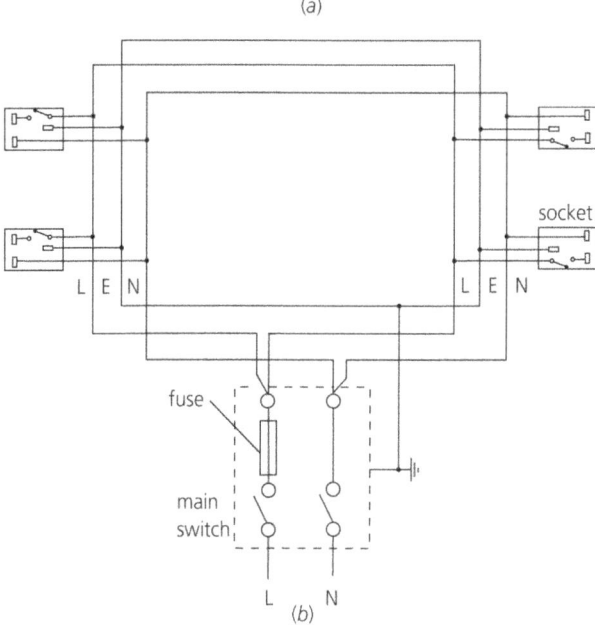

Fig. 26.1 *Wiring systems (a) Lighting circuit (b) Power circuit*

The supply enters through the meter which measures the **energy** used.

26.1 Live, neutral and earth wires

There are three wires leading to the plugs and appliances. These are the **live** wire (with brown insulation), the **neutral** wire (blue) and the **earth** wire (green and yellow stripes).

The live wire is usually at a potential of 110 V in the Caribbean (sometimes 220 V). The neutral wire is at zero (earth) potential.

The earth wire connects the casing of the appliance to earth for safety. If there is a fault and the casing becomes live then the current goes to earth via the earth wire.

26.2 Power and lighting circuits

All plugs, lights and appliances are arranged in **parallel** so we can use each independently.

The lighting circuit uses a small current as the power consumption of lights is quite low. However, the circuit with the power outputs uses much more power. The wires in the power circuit are thicker to allow greater currents to pass safely.

26.3 Wiring a plug

You will wire plugs in your practical course. A three-pin plug is shown in Fig. 26.2.

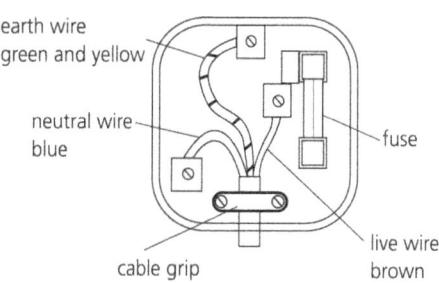

Fig. 26.2 *Wiring a plug*

26.4 Switches, fuses and circuit breakers

We place switches in the **live** wire so when the switch is open the appliance is at the zero potential of the neutral wire.

Fuses and circuit breakers are safety devices. They break the circuit, in the live wire, if the current is too high. Fuses and breakers are rated to carry a certain current and break the circuit for any greater current. A kettle of 1 kW working at 110 V uses 9.1 A:

$$I = \frac{P}{V}, \frac{1\,000}{110} = 9.1 \text{ A}$$

A suitable fuse would be 13 A. A fuse melts and needs to be replaced. A circuit beaker can be reset. If the case becomes live, a high current flows down the earth wire. This causes a break in the circuit.

26.5 Incorrect voltages

If we connect an electrical appliance to an incorrect voltage supply it is likely we will damage it – in $P = IV$, if P remains constant and V decreases, I must increase, so an appliance may overheat. Damage is also likely with fluctuating supplies.

26.6 Costs of electrical energy

We know that

energy output = power output × time

or E = P × t

If a 1000 W heater is used for 30 minutes (1800 seconds) it uses 1 800 000 J of energy.

With more appliances the number of joules of energy used becomes very high. For convenience we use a different unit of energy, the **kilowatt hour** (kW h), on commercial electricity bills.

We express the power in **kilowatts** and the time in **hours**. In our example,

$P = 1$ kW, $t = ½$ hour so $E = Pt$
$E = 1 \times ½ = ½$ kW h

The energy used is either 1 800 000 J or ½ kW h.

Commercially, electrical energy is priced in units of KW h, e.g. 80c per kW h. Here the cost would be 40c.

Example

Three lamps, each of power 100 W, are used for 4 hours. A water heater, rated at 2.5 kW, is used for 2 hours. Calculate (a) the total energy used, in kW h, and (b) the cost of this electricity if 1 kW h costs 60 cents.

a 100W = 0.1 kW
   Therefore energy
   used by lamps   = 3 × 0.1 kW × 4 h = 1.2 kW h
   Energy used by
   heater   = 2.5 × 2   = 5.0 kW h
                                        ─────────
                          Total   = 6.2 kW h

b Cost at 60c/kW h = 6.2 × 60c
                    = $3.72

Questions on Units 24 to 26

1. How much work is done when 10^{-6} C of charge is moved through a potential difference of 5×10^5 V?

2.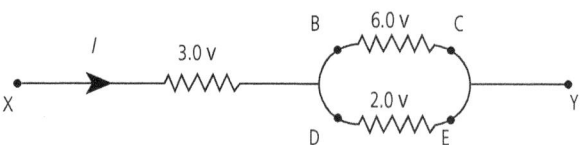

The arrangement of resistors shown in the diagram is included in a circuit through which a current I is flowing. The current in DE is 3.0 A. Find (a) the current in BC, (b) the current I, (c) the total resistance between X and Y. (CAMB)

3.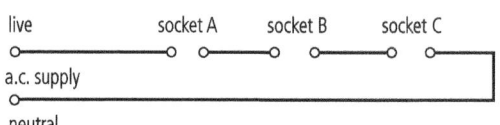

The diagram shows an **incorrect** attempt to wire three sockets A, B and C to the mains supply. When a mains electric heater is plugged into any one of the three sockets, no current flows in the circuit. When similar mains heaters are plugged into **each** of the sockets simultaneously, a current flows in the circuit but the heaters give out much less heat than they were designed to do.

Explain these observations.

Draw a circuit diagram to show the three sockets correctly wired to the mains supply so that the three heaters can operate normally. Include (a) a fuse, (b) an earth wire, in your circuit diagram.

Explain clearly why a fuse and an earth wire are used in a mains wiring circuit.

Draw a labelled diagram of the structure of one type of fuse.

A 3 kW heater is fitted with a 35 W indicator lamp and a 15 W fan.

These three components of the appliance are connected directly to the 250 V mains and switch on and off together.

When the appliance is operating, calculate
 i the total power
 ii the total current
 iii the energy used in 4 hours.
(CAMB)

4. a i Explain the difference between 'electromotive force' and 'terminal potential difference' as applied to a cell.
   ii If the terminals of a dry cell are short-circuited (connected by a wire of negligible resistance), its terminal potential is

practically zero. Why is this so?

    iii What is the function of a fuse in a circuit and what factors should be taken into consideration when selecting fuses?

b Draw a diagram of the circuit you would use to charge a 12 V lead-acid battery using a d.c. supply of 50 V. State clearly (i) the purpose of each component used in the circuit and (ii) **two** precautions you would take during the charging process.

c An electric kettle rated at 1000 W, 200 V, is plugged into 200 V mains using leads of resistance 10 Ω.

    i What is the effective power transferred by the kettle under these conditions?

    ii What voltage must be used if the kettle were to transfer energy at the intended rate with the 10 Ω leads still attached to it?

(CXC)

5. a Describe, with the aid of a circuit diagram, how you would investigate the relationship between the current, I, in a filament lamp and the potential difference, V, applied between its terminals.

  b i Sketch the graph you would expect to obtain from this investigation if V were plotted against I.

    ii Sketch, also, the graphs that would be obtained if the lamp were replaced by (a) a metallic conductor maintained at constant temperature (b) a semi-conductor diode.

    iii What conclusions could be drawn from these graphs about the resistance of **each** of the three components mentioned above?

c A sealed box, with two terminals on the outside, contains two components, one of which is known to be a resistor of high value. When these terminals are connected through a fuse to a 6 V dry battery in one way, the fuse remains intact but, when the battery is reversed, it blows.

    i Suggest the nature of the other component in the box.

    ii Draw a circuit diagram showing the arrangement of the two components in the box.

    iii Explain, with the aid of the diagram you drew in (c) (ii) above, why the fuse blows with one arrangement of the battery, but not with the other.

(CXC)

27 Magnetism

[syllabus sections E6.1–6.10]

Magnets are used in electric motors, dynamos and generators, loudspeakers and microphones.

Magnets were made exclusively from steel until relatively recently. Alloys of several metals are now used to produce stronger magnets.

27.1 Properties of magnets

Magnets only attract a very small number of common materials: iron, steel, nickel and cobalt. These are called **magnetic materials**. Most metals and all non-metals are not attracted by a magnet.

The points on a magnet where the magnetism is strongest are called the **poles** of the magnet. If a magnet is dipped in iron filings, the filings cluster around the poles near the end of the magnet.

When we suspend a bar magnet by a thin thread it always lines up in a north-south direction. The end of the magnet that points in a northerly direction is called the **north pole** of the magnet. The other end is the **south pole**. This property is used in a compass.

When we bring a north pole of one magnet near to the north pole of a suspended magnet they repel each other. Two south poles also repel but a north pole attracts a south pole.

In general

Like poles repel,
Unlike poles attract.

This is sometimes known as the First Law of Magnetism.

If we increase the distance between two magnets the force between them becomes less.

27.2 Magnetisation

Using a permanent magnet

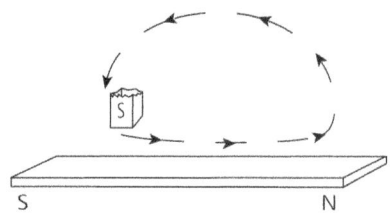

Fig. 27.1 *Magnetisation by stroking*

We can use a permanent magnet to magnetise a bar of steel. We stroke the bar around 20 times in one direction with one end of the permanent magnet (Fig. 27.1). Care must be taken to lift the magnet high above the bar in a circular direction.

The steel bar becomes magnetised with the poles marked in the diagram. Note that where the stroke finishes, the pole is the opposite to that of the permanent magnet.

Using a solenoid

We can use a coil of insulated wire, a **solenoid**, to magnetise a steel bar. We place the bar inside and pass **direct current** through the wire for a couple of seconds. The bar is magnetised by the magnetic field around the solenoid (see Unit 28).

The poles of the magnet depend on the direction of current (Fig. 27.2).

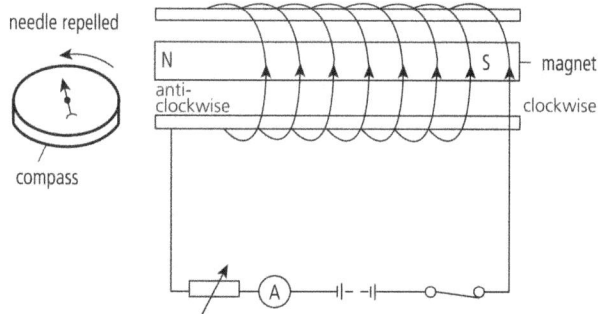

Fig. 27.2 *Using a solenoid to make a magnet*

One way of remembering the polarity of the coil, and the polarity of the magnet made, is to look at the ends of the coil. Where the current is travelling **clockwise** as we look at the end, we obtain a **south** pole. Where the current is **anti-clockwise**, we obtain a **north** pole.

27.3 Demagnetisation

We can demagnetise a magnet using a solenoid and **alternating current** (a.c.) (see Unit 30). In a.c. the direction of the current changes regularly. The electric current in our homes, offices and factories, the **mains supply**, is a.c.

The varying current in a.c. produces a varying magnetic field around the solenoid. This causes regular reversals of the magnetism in the bar. If we slowly withdraw the magnet we find that it is demagnetised (Fig. 27.3).

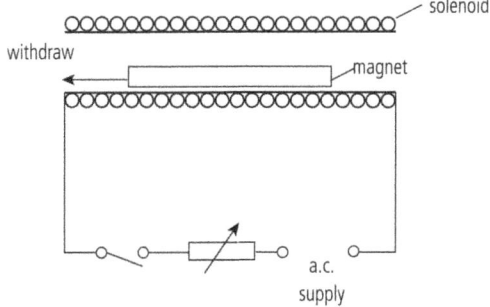

Fig. 27.3 *Demagnetisation*

If a magnet is hammered strongly or heated in a N–S direction to red heat it loses much of its magnetism.

27.4 Magnetic domains

In iron and steel, the constituent atoms have magnetic properties. When two or more atoms have the same magnetic alignment in the same physical area, that area is called a **domain**.

However, in unmagnetised steel or iron the domains are arranged at random and their effects cancel out (Fig. 27.4a).

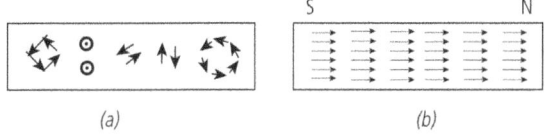

Fig. 27.4 *Magnetic domains (a) Unmagnetised (b) Magnetised*

When we magnetise a bar we line up the dipoles in the domains so that they all point in the same direction (Fig. 27.4b).

When we demagnetise the bar in any way the dipoles in the domains return to their original random arrangement.

27.5 Magnetic induction

When a magnet is brought close to unmagnetised iron the iron becomes magnetised – the dipoles in the domains line up. It is then attracted towards the permanent magnet. This method of magnetisation is known as magnetic induction. The pole induced near to the south pole of a permanent magnet is a north pole.

Iron and steel

We can induce magnetism in a chain of small steel pins and in a chain of small iron nails using the same magnet. The iron chain is found to be rather longer than the steel chain. When the magnet is removed we find that the iron chain splits up but the steel chain stays together.

The iron loses its magnetism immediately – its magnetism is **temporary**, but stronger. The steel retains its magnetism for a considerable time – its magnetism is **permanent**, but weaker.

Iron and metal are said to be 'soft' magnetic materials – they lose and gain magnetism easily. Steel and magnador ore are 'hard' magnetic materials – they are somewhat hard to magnetise but keep their magnetism for a long time.

27.6 Magnetic fields

A magnetic field is a region in which a magnetic force is experienced by a magnetic material.

Michael Faraday visualised a magnetic field as a set of **lines of force**. A magnetic field line (or flux line) indicates the direction of the magnetic force acting on a north pole. The number of lines gives us an idea of the strength of the magnetic field.

Plotting magnetic fields

Using iron filings

We place a bar magnet under a thin sheet of cardboard. We sprinkle iron filings onto the cardboard and then tap the cardboard. The iron filings take up the shape of the magnetic field (Fig. 27.5).

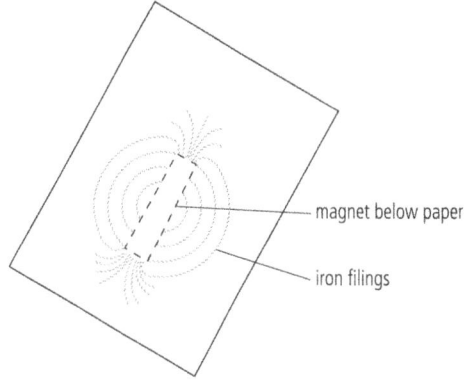

Fig. 27.5 *Demonstrating the magnetic field with iron filings*

Using a plotting compass

A plotting compass is a small compass used to investigate magnetic fields. When we place a plotting compass in a magnetic field it takes up the direction of the magnetic field at that point.

We start at a point near the magnet and mark two dots to show the position of the ends of the compass.

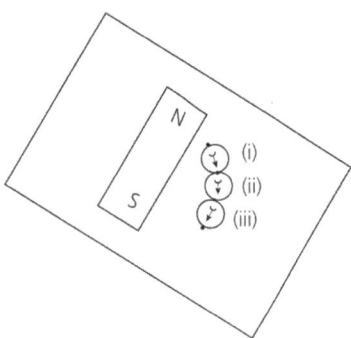

Fig. 27.6 *Plotting the lines of force with a compass*

We move it forward and mark its new direction (Fig. 27.6).

We can plot complete field lines in this way. They lead from one pole to the other pole of the magnet. By starting at other points the overall pattern of the magnetic field may be drawn.

Magnetic field patterns

In Fig. 27.7 we see the magnetic fields due to two bar magnets close together. In Fig. 27.7*a* the adjoining poles are **like** poles and in Fig. 27.7*b* the adjoining poles are **unlike** poles.

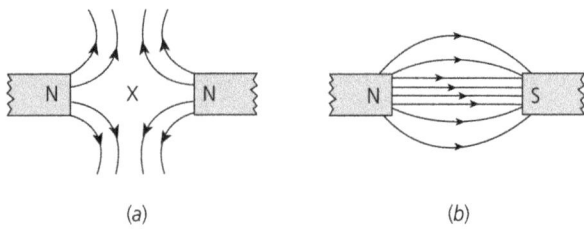

Fig. 27.7 *Magnetic field patterns (a) Like poles (b) Unlike poles*

X is a neutral point – the two fields cancel out. An approximately uniform field may be made using a horseshoe magnet (Fig. 27.8).

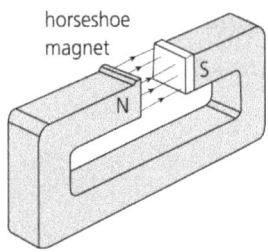

Fig. 27.8 *Horseshoe magnet*

Magnetic screening

An iron ring placed in a magnetic field prevents the magnetism from entering the ring. This is known as magnetic screening (Fig. 27.9).

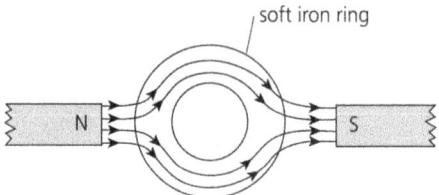

Fig. 27.9 *Magnetic screening*

Delicate measuring instruments can be surrounded by an iron mesh to prevent magnetic fields from interfering with their operation.

The iron concentrates the magnetic field lines in itself. This property is used in transformers and motors (see Units 29 and 30).

28 Magnetic effect of an electric current

[syllabus sections E7.1–7.4]

We have discussed the use of direct current in a solenoid to magnetise a steel rod (Unit 27). We now look at the magnetic fields created by electric currents in various situations.

28.1 Straight wire

We can use a single, thick straight copper wire, aligned in a north-south direction, and a plotting compass. The compass is placed above the wire. When current flows the compass deflects approximately east-west. If the compass is below the wire is deflects in the opposite direction (west-east). The magnetic field around the wire causes these deflections. This experiment was first performed by Oersted.

We can use the apparatus shown in Fig. 28.1 to find the precise shape and direction of the magnetic field around a straight wire.

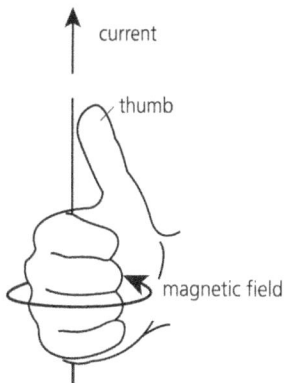

Fig. 28.2 *Right-hand grip rule*

Field pattern around two parallel conductors

The field pattern around two straight, parallel conductors depends on whether the currents are in the same or opposite directions (Fig. 28.3)

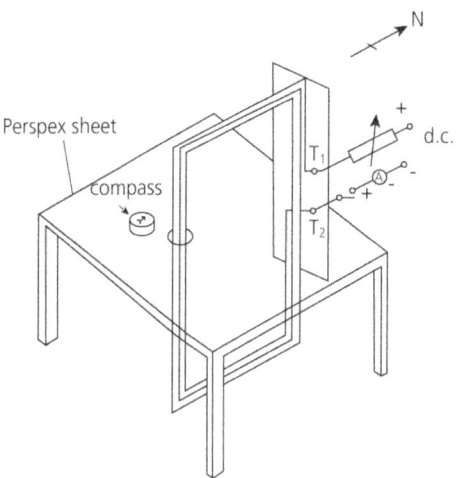

Fig. 28.1 *Magnetic field in a straight wire*

We shake iron filings onto the sheet and pass current through the wire. (Remember that current flows from positive to negative.) The iron filings take up a circular pattern when the sheet is lightly tapped.

We find the direction of the magnetic field using a plotting compass. The magnetic field is circular and reverses its direction if the current is reversed. The strength of the magnetic field is greater if the current is increased.

Right-hand grip rule

If the wire is grasped by the right hand with the thumb pointing along the wire in the direction of current, the direction of the fingers gives the direction of the magnetic field (Fig. 28.2).

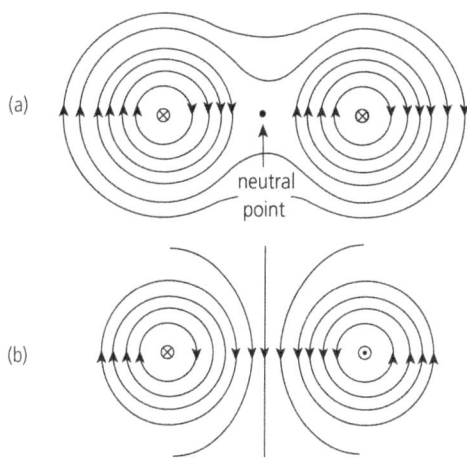

Fig. 28.3 *Field pattern around two parallel conductors*
(a) Currents in same direction, fields oppose
(b) Currents in opposite directions, fields reinforce

28.2 Magnetic fields due to coils

Short-circuit coil

A short coil has a magnetic field, which is the sum of the fields from the two wires (Fig. 28.4).

A compass or iron filings are used to plot the field and to find its direction.

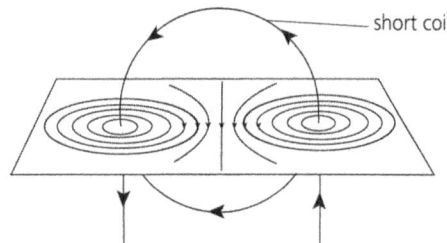

Fig. 28.4 *Short circular coil*

Solenoid

We find a strong and uniform field inside a solenoid with current flowing. Outside the solenoid the field is similar to that of a bar magnet (Fig. 28.5).

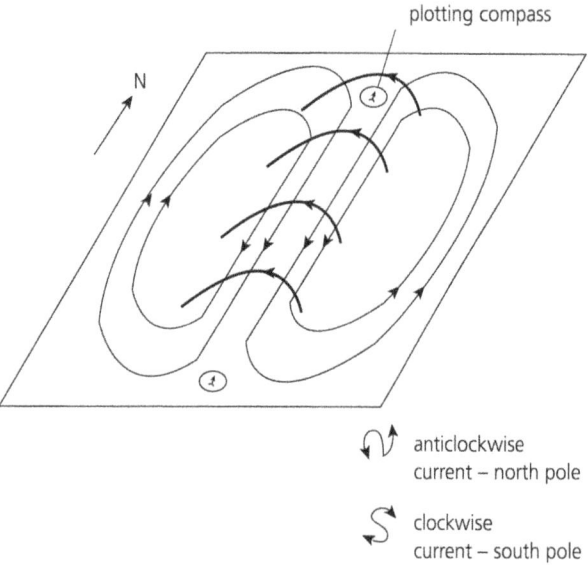

Fig. 28.5 *Magnetic field due to solenoid*

We use a compass to find which end of the solenoid acts as a north pole.

If the current appears to be travelling **clockwise**, looking at the end of the solenoid, we obtain a **south** pole. A **north** pole is associated with an **anti-clockwise** current.

28.3 Electromagnet

An electromagnet is shown in Fig. 28.6. The iron core becomes magnetised when the current flows in the wire wrapped around it. The magnetic field created by the current lines up the domains in the iron.

The magnetism is lost immediately when the current stops flowing.

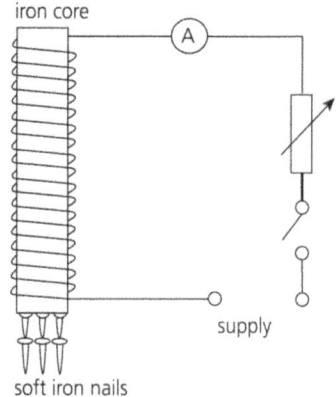

Fig. 28.6 *Electromagnet*

The polarity of the electromagnet can be predicted in the same way as for the solenoid.

Electromagnets are found in electric bells, magnetic relays and in industry.

We can use larger electromagnets to lift heavy steel castings and also to sort iron and steel from a mixture of metals.

Electric bell

Figure 28.7 shows an electric bell. With the switch closed, current flows and creates a magnetic field around the electromagnet. This attracts the iron armature that moves and sounds the bell once. The flow of current is now broken as contact is lost at C. The armature is pulled back to its original position by the spring. Current flows again and the process is repeated.

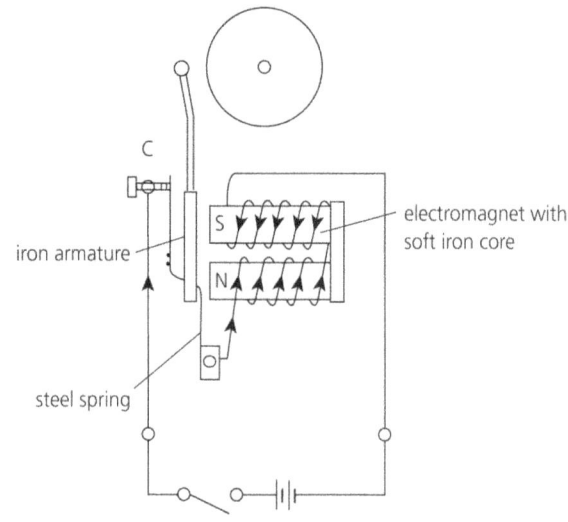

Fig. 28.7 *Electric bell*

Magnetic relay

Relays are used for switching on motors of elevators and in starter-motors in cars. A telephone exchange is a set of relays.

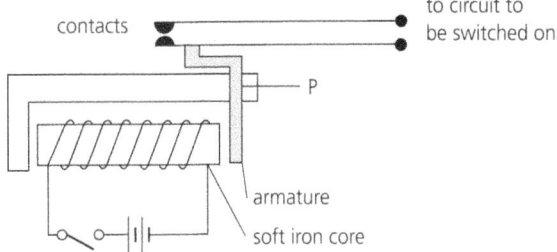

Fig. 28.8 *Magnetic relay*

A relay is a switch that is operated by an electromagnet. The electromagnet uses a low voltage supply and, via the relay, can switch on appliances that use high voltages and high power. A relay is shown in Fig. 28.8. When current flows through the coil the iron core is magnetised and attracts the armature. This pivots at P and causes the contacts to close. This turns on the second circuit.

Starter-motor

A starter-motor in a car uses large currents.
When we close the starter switch the relay closes the switch in the motor circuit (Fig. 28.9).

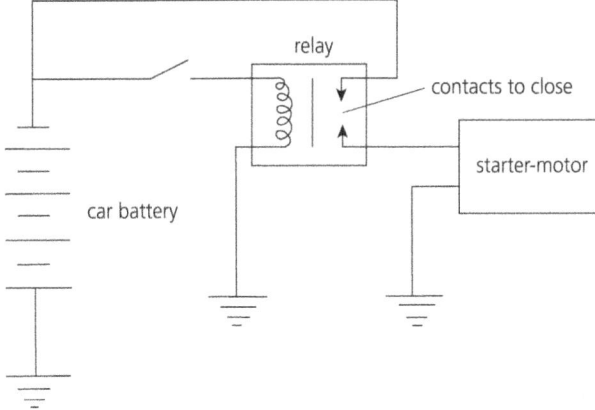

Fig. 28.9 *Starter-motor*

29 Force on a conductor in a magnetic field

[syllabus sections E7.5–7.10]

We place a wire in a magnetic field. When current flows the wire moves (Fig. 29.1). The current in the wire creates a magnetic field that interacts with the field of the permanent magnet. The resulting motion is at right angles to both the direction of the electric current and the magnetic field. This experiment leads to Fleming's left-hand rule (the motor rule).

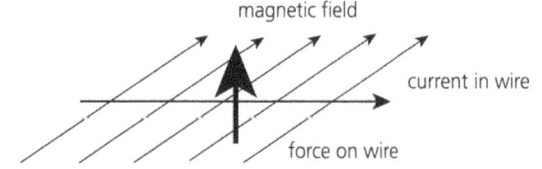

Fig. 29.1 *Force on a current-carrying conductor*

29.1 Fleming's left-hand rule

Spread out the thumb and the first two fingers of the **left** hand at 90° to each other. Point the first finger in the direction of the field and the second finger in the direction of the current. The thumb indicates the direction of the force (Fig. 29.2).

The wire has to be at right angles (90°) to the field for maximum force. If the wire is **parallel** to the field there is no force created.

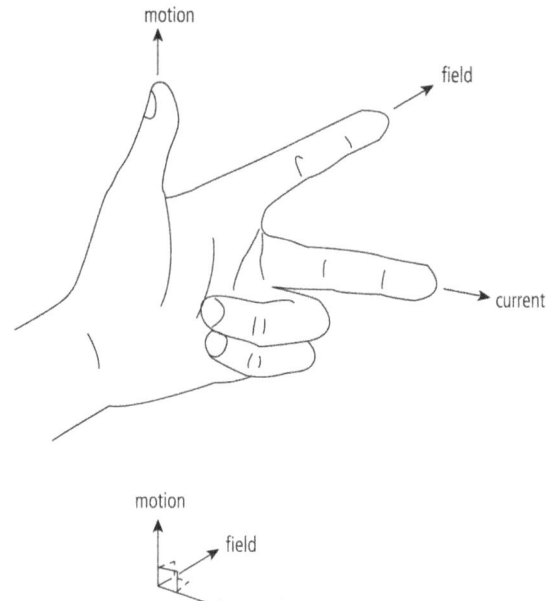

Fig. 29.2 *Fleming's left-hand rule*

29.2 Magnetic fields and the motor rule

We can understand the motor rule from the addition of the two magnetic fields – the circular field due to the wire and the uniform field due to the permanent magnet (Fig. 29.3). The force on the wire will **increase** if

1. the magnetic field is increased
2. the current increases.

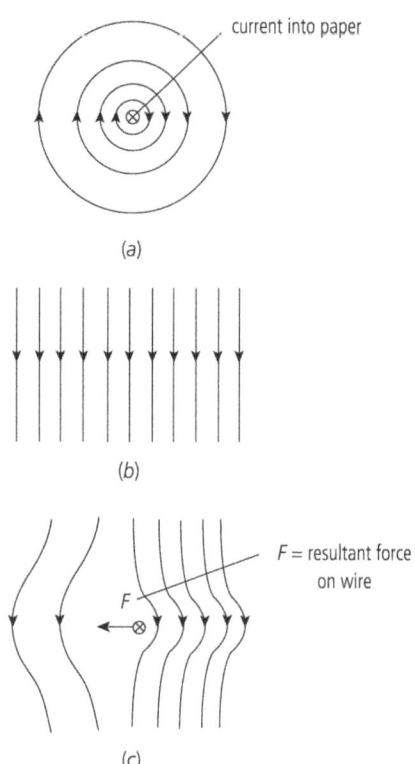

Fig. 29.3 *Force on a current-carrying conductor in a magnetic field (a) Field due to electric current alone (b) Uniform magnetic field (c) Combined field*

29.3 Coils in a magnetic field

Electric motors, loudspeakers and electric meters all have coils of wire in magnetic fields.

29.4 Direct current motor

Figure 29.4 shows the construction of a simple electric motor you could make. The two sides AB and CD are at 90° to the magnetic field. They both experience forces but in opposite directions. The direction of these forces can be found using the left-hand rule.

This pair of equal, but oppositely directed forces

separated by a distance is called a **couple**. The couple provides a torque and causes the coil to turn.

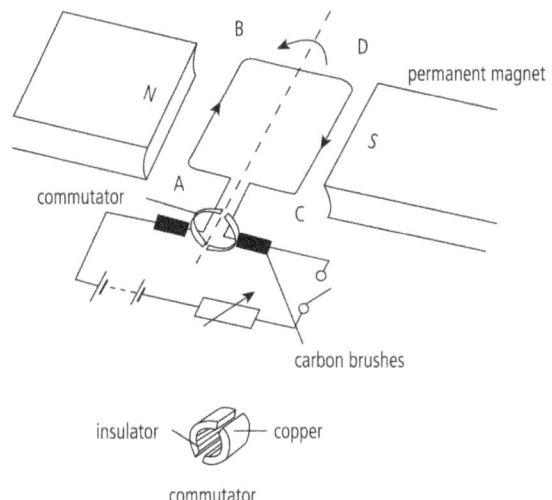

Fig. 29.4 *D.C. electric motor*

When current enters the coil from A to B, it experiences a force according to Fleming's left-hand rule, i.e. downwards.

When the coil is vertical, sides AB and CD are moving parallel to the field and experience no force. The coil continues to turn because of its inertia. If AB were still connected to the positive end of the battery, AB would now want to move upwards. This would cause the coil to stick in a vertical position. This is solved by using a commutator.

When the coil has turned through 180° the brushes, which are not moving, now make contact with the other sides of the split-ring commutator. The current in the coil now reverses.

This means that the couple continues to act in the **same direction**. The coil continues to turn.

29.5 Efficiency of commercial motors

Motors are made more powerful by winding several coils, equally spaced, around a laminated, soft-iron cylinder. A larger couple is obtained.

The magnetic poles are shaped to improve the field or an electromagnet can be used to provide the field.

The bearings are also well made to reduce friction and increase efficiency.

29.6 Loudspeaker

A moving-coil loudspeaker is shown in Fig. 29.5. The coil is in the magnetic field and from the left-hand rule, the force will be at 90° to the coil – it causes it to move in and out of the magnetic field. As the coil moves, the attached paper cone sends sound waves out into the air.

The direction and magnitude of the current in the loudspeaker changes. This causes similar changes in the movement of the paper cone. We then hear sound waves of different frequencies and intensities.

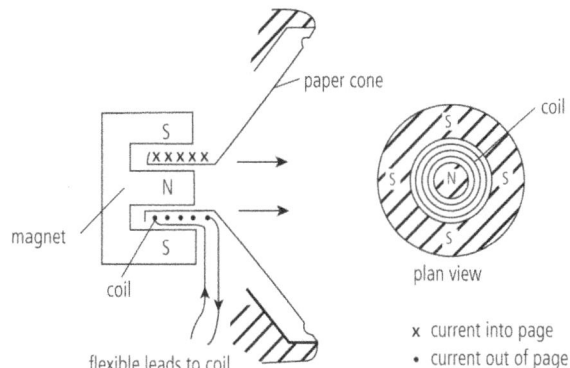

Fig. 29.5 *Moving-coil loudspeaker*

Apply Fleming's left-hand rule to the above diagram. The cone is pushed outwards.

29.7 Galvanometer

A **moving-coil galvanometer** is a sensitive current-measuring device. It is also the basis for ammeters and voltmeters (see below). Its structure is shown in Fig. 29.6.

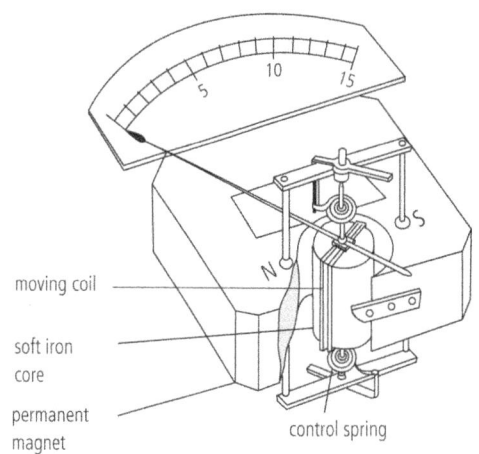

Fig. 29.6 *Moving-coil galvanometer*

When current flows the coil experiences a torque and turns. This twists the control spring, which provides an opposing torque.

When the torque due to the spring **equals** the torque due to the current, the coil comes to rest. The pointer attached to the coil indicates the reading on the calibrated scale. A moving-coil galvanometer detects currents of the order of milliamperes **or** p.d.s. of a few millivolts.

29.8 Ammeter

We can convert a moving-coil galvanometer into an ammeter suitable for larger currents.

We use a **shunt resistor**, of low resistance, perhaps 0.01 Ω, placed in **parallel** with the coil. Most of the current now passes through the shunt. A known proportion passes through the coil. The scale is now recalibrated so that it indicates the **total** current flowing through the shunt and the coil.

29.9 Voltmeter

We convert a moving-coil galvanometer into a voltmeter, suitable for larger p.d.s. using a high-value resistor placed in **series** with the coil. This resistor is known as a **multiplier**.

Most of the applied p.d. is used across the multiplier. The calibration is changed so that it reads the total p.d. across the multiplier and coil. The multiplier may have a resistance of 1000 Ω or more.

29.10 Force between current-carrying wires

We demonstrate the force between two conductors carrying current using the apparatus in Fig. 29.7. When the current is flowing in the **same** direction in the two wires there is a force of **attraction**. When the currents are in **opposite** directions there is a **repulsive** force. The forces are a result of the two magnetic fields adding together (see Fig. 28.3).

When the currents are in the **same** direction the magnetic fields cancel out at a point in between the wires, creating a **neutral point**. The resulting field tends to pull the wires together – an attractive force.

The field that results from currents in the opposite directions is stronger in between the two wires. The wires are repelled.

The ampere is actually defined in terms of the force between two current-carrying wires. An exact definition is not needed.

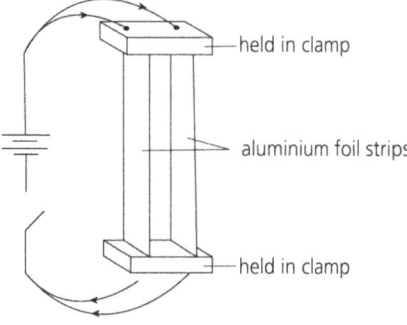

Fig. 29.7 *Force between current-carrying wires*

30 Electromagnetic induction

[syllabus sections E7.11–7.18]

We move a straight wire AB, connected to a galvanometer, at 90° to a magnetic field (Fig. 30.1). We notice a short burst of current. This is an **induced** current.

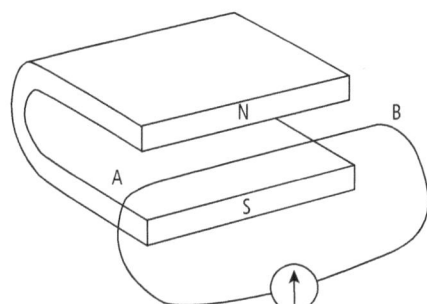

Fig. 30.1 *Induced e.m.f. in a wire*

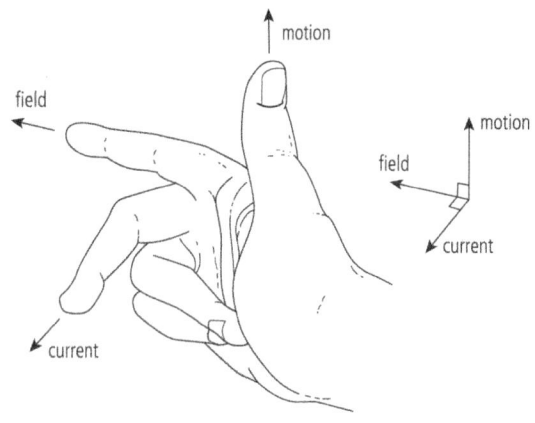

Fig. 30.2 *Right-hand rule*

If we reverse **either** the direction of movement **or** the direction of the magnetic field, then the direction of the induced current also reverses.

However, if we leave the wire **stationary** in the magnetic field, **no** current is induced. We also obtain no current if we move the wire *along* the field from one magnetic pole to another.

Michael Faraday suggested the idea of **flux linkage**. When the magnetic field or flux lines cut the wire they are **linked** with the wire (see Unit 35 for more on Faraday's contribution).

30.1 Faraday's laws of electromagnetic induction

Whenever there is a change in the magnetic flux linked with a conductor, an electromotive force, e.m.f., is induced in the conductor.

The size of the e.m.f. is proportional to the **rate of change of flux linkage** with the conductor.

Right-hand rule

For a straight wire the relation between the directions of the magnetic field, movement and induced current is given by the right-hand rule.

The thumb, first and second finger of the right hand are extended at 90° to each other. If the first finger represents the direction of the field and the thumb the direction of motion, then the direction of the induced current is given by the second finger (Fig. 30.2).

Experimental verification of Faraday's laws

We use a coil and a magnet to verify the laws of electromagnetic induction (Fig. 30.3).

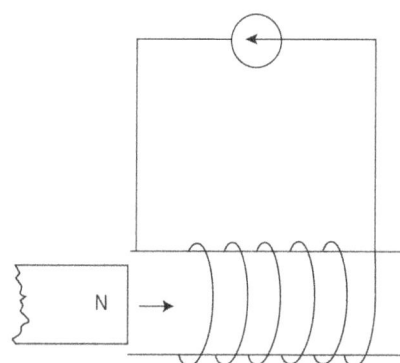

Fig. 30.3 *Induced e.m.f. in a coil*

We move the magnet in and out of the coil and note the effect on the galvanometer.

The e.m.f. induced **increases** if we increase
1. the number of turns on the coil
2. the strength of the magnet
3. the speed of movement of the magnet.

The e.m.f. can also be increased by placing an iron core in the coil.

Factors (1) and (2), and the iron core, increase the **flux linkage**.

Factor (3) increases the **rate of change** of flux linkage. All these changes lead to a greater e.m.f.

30.2 Lenz's law

Lenz's law states that the induced e.m.f. is always in

such a direction to **oppose** the change producing it. We use the apparatus in Fig. 30.4 to demonstrate Lenz's law.

The current that flows in the coil because of the induced e.m.f. creates a magnetic field. When a north pole is moved **towards** the coil the induced current creates a magnetic field with a **north** pole near the moving magnet. Thus the magnetic field repels the approaching magnet, opposing the change (Fig. 30.4).

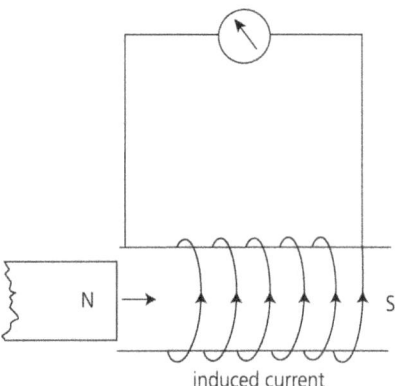

Fig. 30.4 *Demonstrating Lenz's law*

If a north pole is **withdrawn** from the coil a south pole is created by the induced current again tending to oppose the motion of the magnet. It attracts the magnet.

30.3 A.C. generator

A simple a.c. generator is shown in Fig. 30.5. We spin the coil within the magnetic field and a current is induced. The slip rings conduct the current, via the stationary brushes, to the external circuit. Slip ring 1 is in constant contact with side AB and Slip ring 2 is in constant contact with side CD.

The current induced in the coil reverses its direction each half rotation (180°). The graph of the output of the a.c. generator is shown in Fig. 30.6. The orientation of the coil at certain times is shown below the graph.

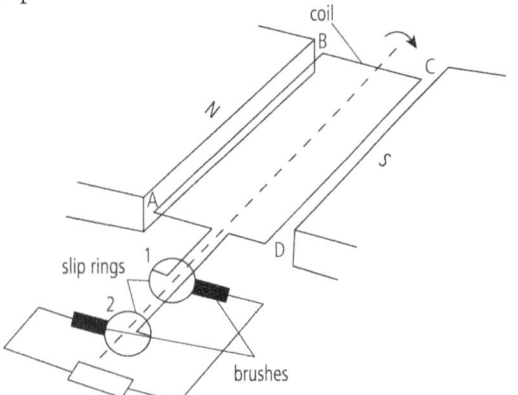

Fig. 30.5 *A.C. generator*

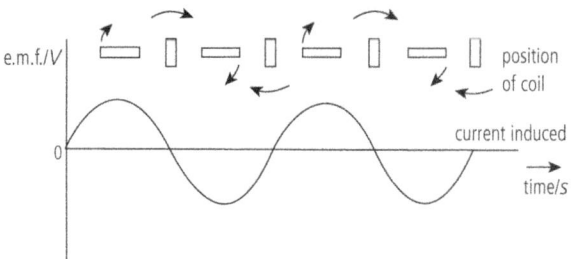

Fig. 30.6 *Positions of coil relating to induced e.m.f.*

The heating effect of a.c. is less than that of d.c. of the same peak value, just as the 'average' value of a.c. is less than the peak value of a.c.

Commercial A.C. generator

We can increase the output of a generator by
1. rotating at a higher speed
2. having a larger magnetic field
3. having several coils set at different angles on the same core
4. having a larger number of turns on the coils
5. using a soft iron core.

30.4 D.C. generator

To make a d.c. generator we replace the slip rings in an a.c. generator by a split-ring commutator. It is then identical in construction to the d.c. motor (see Fig. 29.4).

The commutator has a **rectifying** effect, i.e. it changes a.c. to d.c. When the coil rotates through 180° the stationary brushes change the side of the split ring that they touch. Thus one brush remains positive throughout the rotation and the other negative. The graph of output is shown in Fig. 30.7.

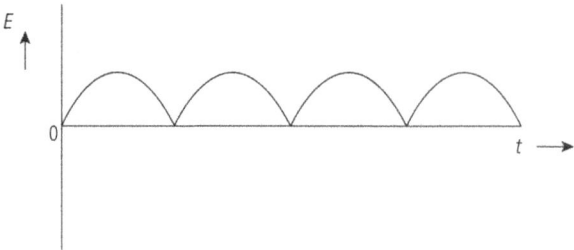

Fig. 30.7 *E.m.f./time graph for a d.c. generator*

30.5 Moving-coil microphone

A moving-coil microphone is similar to a loudspeaker. The paper cone is replaced by a diaphragm. The diaphragm vibrates when sound strikes and a coil attached to the diaphragm vibrates in a magnetic field. A current of varying magnitude and direction is induced.

A microphone changes sound into electrical energy but a loudspeaker changes electrical energy into sound.

30.6 Transformer

A transformer is made from two coils of wire, wound on an iron core (Fig. 30.8). We supply a.c. to the primary coil. Due to the changing current in the primary coil we have a changing magnetic field. This changing magnetic field is linked with the secondary coil. The flux linkage is increased by the iron core. An e.m.f. is induced in the secondary coil by the changing flux linkage.

A transformer does not work with d.c. as there is no change of magnetic flux linkage.

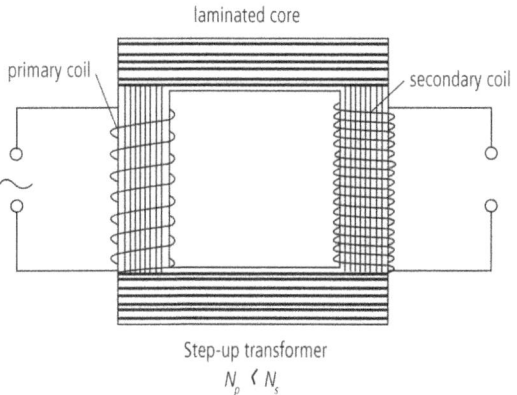

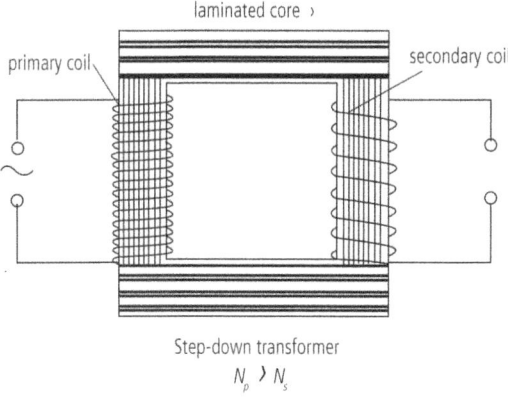

Fig. 30.8 *Transformers*

Step-up and step-down transformers

The e.m.f. induced in the secondary coil, E_s, depends on the strength of the e.m.f. in the primary coil, E_p. It also depends on the number of turns on the coils, N_s and N_p respectively. We can show that

$$E_s \propto N_s \text{ and } E_p \propto N_p \Rightarrow \frac{E_s}{E_p} = \frac{N_s}{N_p}$$

If N_s is greater than N_p then the e.m.f. induced in the secondary is greater than that supplied to the primary coil. This is called a **step-up transformer**.

If N_s is less than N_p, then the e.m.f. in the secondary coil is less than that in the primary coil and we have a **step-down transformer**.

Power in a transformer

Although the e.m.f. can be greater in the secondary coil than in the primary, a transformer cannot increase the **power** available.

In an ideal transformer all the energy supplied to the primary coil is transferred to the secondary coil. The power taken in is equal to the power given out.

As the power is given by $P = VI$ then

$$V_p I_p = V_s I_s$$

Where I_p is the primary current and I_s is the secondary current. If the e.m.f. increases in the secondary, the current must decrease.

$$\frac{V_s}{V_p} = \frac{I_p}{I_s}$$

In summary

$$\frac{N_s}{N_p} = \frac{V_s}{V_p} = \frac{I_p}{I_s}$$

Experimental verification

We can verify the relationships outlined previously in a school laboratory. The alternating input and output p.d.s. are measured. We also measure the currents in the primary and secondary circuits. The number of turns on the coils is varied.

The power in the secondary coil will be rather less than in the primary coil due to energy losses.

Efficiency of transformers

Transformers waste some of the energy supplied. The following points help to reduce the energy lost.

1. The core is designed so that all the magnetic flux is linked with the secondary coil.
2. The core is **laminated**, i.e. made of sheets of soft iron separated by an insulator. This reduces the eddy currents in the core, which occur due to the varying flux linkage.
3. The wire of the coils is reasonably thick so that the resistance is low and the energy wasted as heat is small.

Advantage of A.C.

A.C. is produced in power stations and then transformed to high voltages, 13.8 kV or 69 kV, for transmission across the country. This reduces energy losses in the wires carrying the power. The current is less at the higher voltage and the heating effect is smaller ($P = I^2R$). (The current is squared in the formula and has a larger effect on power used than resistance.)

The a.c. is then transformed down to the appropriate voltage for supply to consumers by using a series of step-down transformers.

Questions on Units 27 to 30

1. a Suppose you are provided with the following list of equipment:
   12 V lead accumulator, insulated copper wire, cardboard tube, rheostat, stiff cardboard sheet, iron filings and a key.
   Describe, with a diagram, how you would use this apparatus to investigate the magnetic field inside a solenoid. Draw a diagram showing the results you would expect.
   b A step-down transformer is used to operate an electric bell from the domestic mains.
     i Explain why a step-down transformer is necessary.
     ii Would the secondary winding of such a transformer consist of thicker or thinner wire than the primary winding? Explain your answer.
   c i Draw a circuit diagram of the arrangement you would use to operate the electric bell in (b) above from the mains.
     ii Explain briefly why the length of the connecting wire between the transformer and the bell should be as short as possible.
   (CXC)

2. a A rectangular metal coil is supported with its rectangular plane perpendicular to the ground and the coil carries a strong current. Describe how you would use a magnetic needle to explore the magnetic field round each of the arms of the coil and say what you would expect to observe. **Diagrams are essential**.
   b The source of current is replaced by a centre-zero milliammeter and the coil is then placed with its rectangular plane horizontal in a vertical, uniform magnetic field. Describe what will be observed on the milliammeter if the coil is moved (i) vertically (parallel to the field) and (ii) horizontally, in and out of the field. Explain these observations.
   c The coil is moved from left to right and back in a horizontal plane (i) quickly and (ii) slowly, in and out of the magnetic field. Describe what will be observed on the milliammeter in **each** case.
   d Discuss the beliefs and reasoning that led Faraday to the discovery of the effect at (b) above.

3.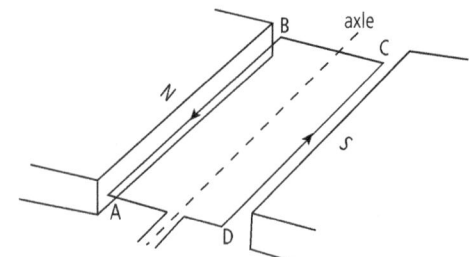

   The diagram shows a coil of wire ABCD mounted on an axle, which is free to rotate between the poles of a permanent magnet. A current flows in the direction shown by the arrows.
   a Which of the four conductors, AB, BC, CD and DA, have forces acting on them when the coil is in the position shown?
   Make clear, either in words or on a diagram, the directions of these forces.
   b Show, by a labelled addition to a copy of the diagram, how you would pass a current from a battery to the coil, so that the coil operates continuously, i.e. the device operates as a simple d.c. motor.
   (CAMB)

4. Describe experiments to demonstrate
   a the pattern of the magnetic field produced by a long straight wire which is carrying a current, ignoring the effect of the Earth's magnetic field;
   b the behaviour of a wire supported perpendicular to the lines of force (field lines) of a magnetic field, so that it is free to move when a current is passed through the wire.
   (CAMB)

31 Electronics

[syllabus sections E5.1–5.3]

31.1 Electron beam in a magnetic field

When a magnet is brought near to the beam of electrons the beam is deflected. The direction of force on the electron beam can be found using Fleming's left-hand rule. (Note that the direction of current is in the opposite direction to the direction of motion of the electrons.)

31.2 Semiconductors

In modern electronics we use transistors and diodes extensively. They are usually made of silicon or germanium. Silicon and germanium are semi-conductors. They are conductors of electricity but have a resistance greater than metals.

In a semiconductor, current is carried by both negatively-charged carriers (**electrons**) and positively-charged carriers (**holes**).

A small amount of impurity can be added to silicon so that the resistance decreases. This is called **doped silicon**. Depending on the impurity added, current in doped silicon is carried mainly by **either** electrons **or** holes:

n-type silicon is doped so that the impurity provides **extra electrons**
p-type silicon is doped so that the impurity provides **extra holes**.

Semiconductor diode

A semiconductor diode is made from two small pieces of silicon, one n-type silicon and one p-type silicon. It is a p-n junction and is shown, along with the symbol, in Fig. 31.1.

Fig. 31.1 *Semiconductor diode*

V/I relation for a diode

We can investigate the relation between the p.d. across a diode and the current through the diode using the circuit shown in Fig. 31.2.

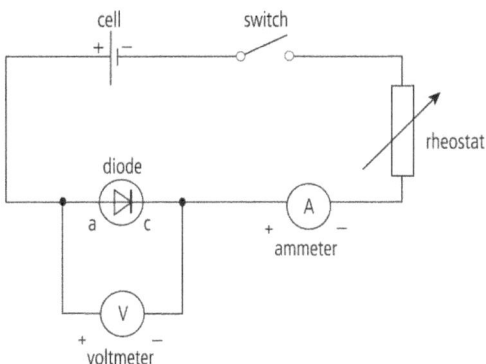

Fig. 31.2 *Semiconductor diode circuit*

With the positive terminal of the supply connected to the anode of the diode (**forward biased**), we obtain a current flow. It does not increase linearly and is typically 50 mA for 1.5 V.

When we reverse the diode (**reverse biased**) the current obtained is extremely small (a few micro-amperes, 10^{-6} A). Using our results we can plot the graph shown in Fig. 31.3.

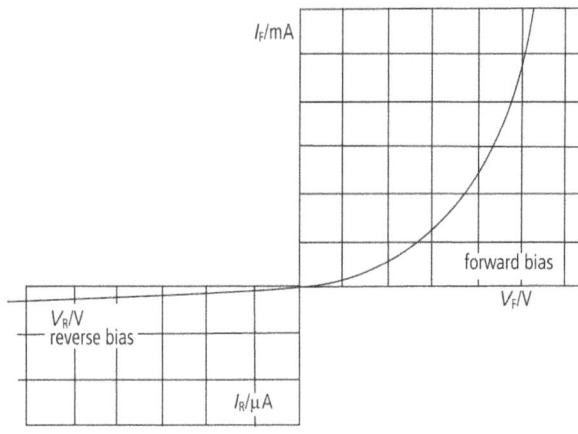

Fig. 31.3 *Characteristic curve for a silicon diode*

Conduction in a p-n junction

When the **anode** of the p-n junction is connected to the **positive** terminal of the supply, the holes in the p-type material move into the n-type material. The electrons in the n-type material move into the p-type material and current flows.

When the connections are reversed the electrons move towards the positive terminal and the holes towards the negative terminal. No current flows across the junction.

A defective diode will allow similar currents in both directions.

Rectification

A diode can be used to convert alternating current to direct current. This is called rectification and the diode is a rectifier.

We demonstrate this using the apparatus in Fig. 31.4. The p.d. across the resistor is examined using a CRO. With the diode in the circuit we obtain the waveform shown in Fig. 31.5. When the supply p.d. reverses, no current flows. This form of rectification is known as **half-wave rectification**.

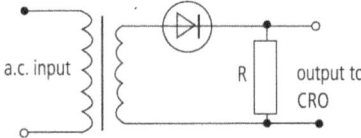

Fig. 31.4 *Rectification*

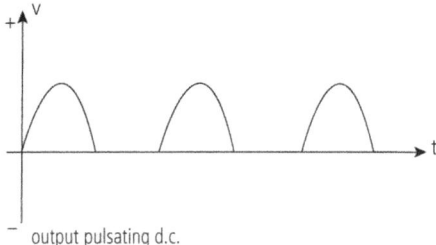

Fig. 31.5 *Half-wave rectification*

The p.d./time graph for a battery should be compared with the half-wave rectified a.c. (Fig. 31.6). With no diode the waveform is a full wave.

Fig. 31. 6 *Output of car battery*

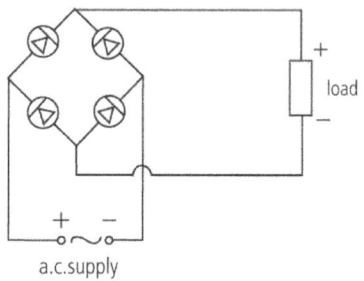

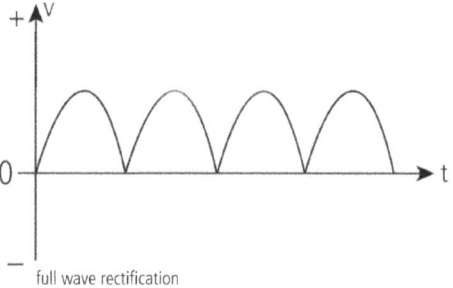

Fig. 31.7 *Full-wave rectification*

This circuit ensures that one end of the load is always positive, i.e. the negative parts of the a.c. supply are inverted.

31.3 Transistors and integrated circuits

Transistors are used to amplify currents and voltages. A transistor consists of three pieces of doped silicon, either n-p-n, or p-n-p.

An integrated circuit, known as a **silicon chip**, contains many thousand transistors, diodes and resistors on a small piece of silicon. They are central to the operation of pocket calculators, digital watches and computers.

32 Logic gates

[syllabus sections E5.4–E5.6]

There are five logic gates at this level: NOT, AND, NAND, OR and NOR. In Fig. 32.1 we see these gate symbols.

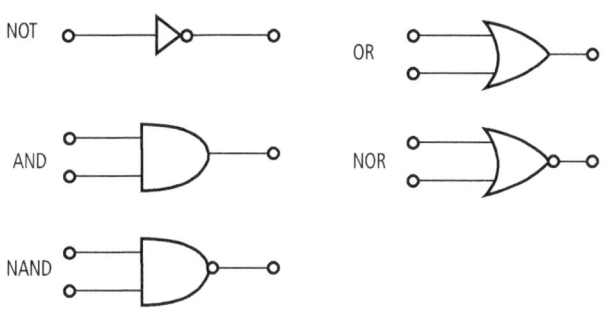

Fig. 32.1 *Logic gates*

32.1 The NOT gate

The NOT gate is a one-input, one-output device. The other gates are two-input, one-output devices.

Gates are two-state devices, either on or off. A low voltage is interpreted as a 0 state. A high voltage is interpreted as a 1 state.

A NOT gate inverts the input. In Fig. 32.2 we see its truth table.

input	output
A	B
0	1
1	0

Fig. 32.2 *The truth table for a NOT gate*

32.2 The AND gate

An AND gate is only activated when both inputs are high. It is very much like two bulbs in series, if one or both of the bulbs 'blow', then both bulbs remain off. In Fig. 32.3 we see its truth table.

inputs		output
A	B	C
0	0	0
0	1	0
1	0	0
1	1	1

Fig. 32.3 *The truth table for an AND gate*

32.3 The NAND gate

A NAND gate is a NOT gate in series with an AND gate. Once a low input (zero) is provided, a high output is achieved. In Fig. 32.4 we see its truth table.

A	B	C
0	0	1
0	1	1
1	0	1
1	1	0

Fig. 32.4 *The truth table for a NAND gate*

Combinations of NAND gates can be used to form any other gate (see the example at the end of this unit).

32.4 The OR gate

The OR gate has an action such that at least one high input produces a high output. In Fig. 32.5 we see its truth table.

A	B	C
0	0	0
0	1	1
1	0	1
1	1	1

Fig. 32.5 *The truth table for an OR gate*

This gate behaves like two bulbs in parallel. If one 'blows' the other continues to give light.

32.5 The NOR gate

The NOR gate is an OR gate in series with a NOT gate. A high (one) output is only achieved when both inputs are low (zero). In Fig. 32.6 we see its truth table.

A	B	C
0	0	1
0	1	0
1	0	0
1	1	0

Fig. 32.6 *The truth table for a NOR gate*

32.6 Uses of logic gates

Logic gates are used in alarm systems. A large jewel in a glass cup may be placed on a push switch. The switch is then in the ON position. The NOT gate inverts this to a 0. If the jewel is stolen, the switch goes to 1, a current flows and the alarm sounds. Fig. 32.7 shows the circuit involved:

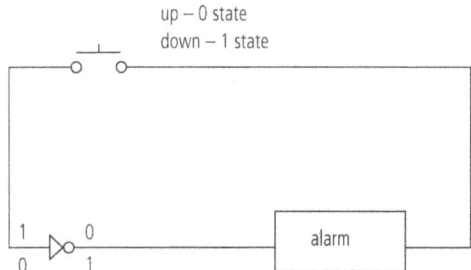

Fig. 32.7 *An alarm circuit*

32.7 Combining logic gates

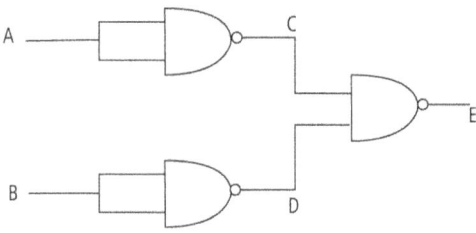

A	B	C	D	E
0	0	1	1	0
0	1	1	0	1
1	0	0	1	1
1	1	0	0	1

Fig. 32.8 *Combining logic gates*

This is the same truth table as that for the OR gate.

33 Structure of atoms

[syllabus sections F1.2–2.6]

Atoms are not hard, solid balls, as was once thought. We already know two of the particles that make up atoms: the **electron** and the **proton**.

An important experiment, performed by Geiger and Marsden, used thin gold foil and positively-charged **alpha (α) particles** (these are discussed in Unit 34).

The experiment was carried out in a vacuum. A stream of α-particles hit the gold foil. Nearly all the α-particles passed straight through the foil without being affected (or affecting the foil). A few α-particles were deflected and only a very small number was reflected in the opposite direction (Fig. 33.1).

Ernest Rutherford suggested that all the positive charge (and nearly all the mass) is concentrated in a very small volume at the centre of the atom; the **nucleus**. The electrons move in orbits around the nucleus.

Most of the α-particles pass **straight through**, as most of an atom is empty space.

The α-particles passing close to the nucleus are **deflected**. The positively-charged nucleus repels the positively-charged α-particles. Only if they meet the nucleus 'head-on' are they reflected. Because the nucleus is very small this does not happen often.

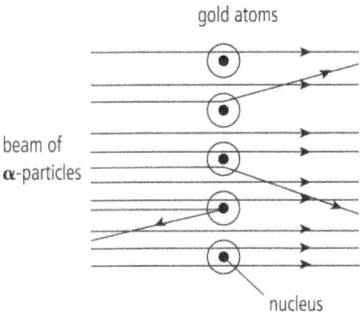

Fig. 33.1 *Alpha particles passing through gold foil*

Later it was shown that with the protons in the nucleus there are **uncharged** particles, of about the same mass, called **neutrons**. Protons or neutrons have about 1840 times the mass of electrons. The mass of a proton is 1.67×10^{-27} kg.

33.1 A typical atom: the carbon atom

A carbon atom with six protons, six neutrons and six electrons is shown in Fig. 33.2.

Usually we have equal numbers of protons and electrons in an atom. The charges on protons and electrons are equal, but opposite, so they cancel out and the atom is electrically neutral. The size of the charge on a proton (+) or electron (-) is $\pm 1.6 \times 10^{-19}$ C.

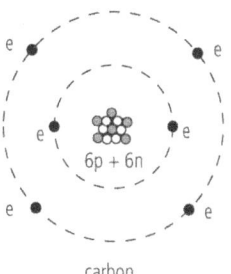

Fig. 33.2 *Structure of the carbon atom*

33.2 Nuclear symbols

The number of protons in an atom is the **atomic number** or **proton number**, Z.

The **neutron number** is symbolised by N.

The total number of protons and neutrons (nucleons) is called the **mass number**, or **nucleon number**, A. Therefore

$$A = Z + N$$

We represent the carbon, C, nuclide in Fig. 33.2 as $^{12}_{6}$C. The upper number is the nucleon number and the lower number is the proton number.

In general, we represent a nuclide as $^{A}_{Z}$X.

33.3 Isotopes

All atoms of the same element have the **same number of protons**.

Some atoms of the same element may have a different number of neutrons. These are called **isotopes** of the element. The two natural isotopes of carbon are $^{12}_{6}$C and $^{14}_{6}$C. In the second case we can see that the isotope contains eight neutrons instead of the more usual six. (This isotope is radioactive – see Unit 34.)

All the elements can be set out in a table called the **periodic table**, which you can find in a chemistry textbook.

Different elements have different numbers of protons. Any element in the table has one more proton than the one to the left of it. There are patterns in the chemical properties of atoms that depend on their structure.

33.4 Shell model of electrons in the atom

The electrons moving in orbits around the nucleus are arranged in groups or **shells**. The orbits have different shapes and radii. We find that elements in the same columns of the periodic table have similar chemical properties. This is usually the result of the number of electrons in the outer shell.

Lithium, sodium and potassium (all very reactive metals with similar properties) each have one electron in the outer shell.

Fluorine, chlorine and bromine (all very reactive gases) each have seven electrons in their outer shells.

Further discussion of the development of the modern view of the atom is found in Unit 35.

34 Radioactivity

[syllabus sections F3.2–4.2]

Around the year 1900 some substances were discovered that gave out three different, and then unknown, types of 'radiation'. They were given the names alpha (α) particles, beta (β) particles and gamma (γ) rays. Substances that give out these radiations are known as **radioactive** substances.

We now know that the three radiations are emitted from the **nucleus** of certain atoms.

34.1 Nature of radioactive emissions

Alpha particles are **helium nuclei** and are composed of two neutrons and two protons. They are positively-charged and their symbol is $_2^4$He. Velocity is $\approx 10\%$ c.

Beta particles are **high-speed electrons** and are negatively-charged and their symbol is $_{-1}^{0}$e. Velocity is $\approx 50\%$ c.

Gamma rays are high-energy, high-frequency **electromagnetic radiation** with no charge and their symbol is γ. Velocity is c, where c = the speed of light.

34.2 Properties of α-, β- and γ-rays

As they are positively-charged, α-particles are attracted towards negative charge in an **electric field**. Beta particles experience a force in the opposite direction. However, β-particles are deviated more than α-particles as the mass of the β-particles is much less (Fig. 34.1).

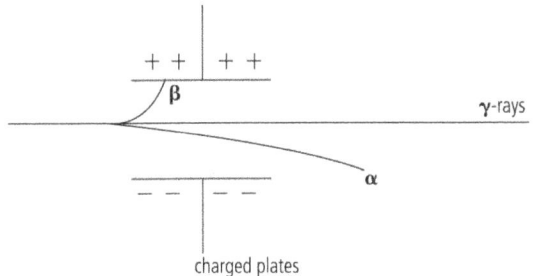

Fig. 34.1 *Properties of α-, β- and γ-rays in an electric field*

Alpha particles and beta particles are also deflected in opposite directions by **magnetic fields**. We predict the directions using the left-hand rule (Unit 29).

For the β-particles (electrons) the current is in the opposite direction to their motion.

For the positively-charged α-particles the current is in the same direction as their motion. With the magnetic field **into** the paper, the deflections are as shown in Fig. 34.2.

As γ-rays are uncharged they are not deflected by either electric or by magnetic fields.

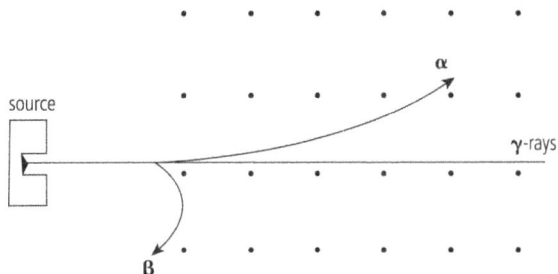

Fig. 34.2 *Properties of α-, β- and γ-rays in a magnetic field*

34.3 Detection of radioactivity

The Geiger-Müller tube (G-M tube) is used to detect the three types of radioactivity. It is a tube, filled mainly with argon gas, with a wire along the centre at high voltage (400 V). At one end is a thin mica window.

When α-, β- and γ-rays enter the tube they cause ionisation of the gas. This creates a burst of current that is registered by a counter. The mica is thin to allow the α-particles to penetrate (see below).

34.4 Penetration of α-, β- and γ-rays

α-particles

We place a G-M tube various distances (1 cm to 10 cm) away from an α-particle source. A large number of α-particles may be detected after passing through 1 cm of air. However, the number falls almost to zero after 5 or 6 cm of air. A single sheet of paper will also stop the α-particles completely.

β-particles

With a β-particle source we find that a large number of β-particles travel 30 or 40 cm in air before being stopped. We use aluminium sheets several millimetres thick to stop the β-particles.

γ-rays

Gamma rays are not absorbed by air and only to a small extent by aluminium. Gamma rays need several centimetres of lead, or several tens of centimetres of concrete, to ensure that they are absorbed.

34.5 Ionisation and penetration

Alpha particles do not travel far in air as they cause much ionisation. This is because they have a double positive charge and move relatively slowly past other atoms. Each ion created slows down the α-particle by a small amount.

Beta particles are moving at high speed, near to the speed of light, and cause less ionisation per centimetre than α-particles. They are thus able to travel further.

Gamma rays only cause ionisation if they directly hit an atom and eject an electron. The ejected electron then also causes ionisation – secondary ionisation.

34.6 Ionisation and the cloud chamber

In the diffusion cloud chamber the ionisation caused by the α-, β- and γ-rays creates a visible track. Alcohol vapour condenses on the ions formed.

The α-particles give bright, straight tracks. The fast β-particles give long, curving tracks. Gamma rays produce a confusion of tracks as the ejected electrons cause ionisation in short, curved tracks.

34.7 Nuclear changes in radioactivity

When α- and β-particles are emitted, the atom changes to another element. In α-particle emission the nucleus loses two protons and two neutrons. We write the emission of an α-particle from the uranium isotope $^{238}_{92}$U as follows:

$$^{238}_{92}\text{U} \rightarrow {}^{234}_{90}\text{Th} + {}^{4}_{2}\text{He}$$

uranium	thorium	α-particle
92 protons	90 protons	2 protons
146 neutrons	144 neutrons	2 neutrons

In α-decay the product moves two places down the periodic table.

Carbon 14, $^{14}_{6}$C, emits a β-particle ($^{0}_{-1}$e). In this case the number of protons **rises** by one and the number of neutrons **decreases** by one. It is as if a neutron decays into a proton and an electron. The electron is emitted as the β-particle.

$$^{14}_{6}\text{C} \rightarrow {}^{14}_{7}\text{N} + {}^{0}_{-1}e$$

carbon   nitrogen   β particle

In β-decay the product moves one place up the periodic table.

34.8 General radioactive equations

In general, α- and β-decays are represented as follows:

α-decay

$$^{A}_{Z}X \rightarrow {}^{4}_{2}He + {}^{A-4}_{Z-2}Y$$

parent nucleus   α-particle   daughter nucleus

β-decay

$$^{A}_{Z}K \rightarrow {}^{0}_{-1}e + {}^{A}_{Z+1}L$$

parent nucleus   β-particle   daughter nucleus

All radioactive decays are a result of **instability in the nucleus**.

34.9 Radioactive decay and the half-life

Radioactive decay is a random process. It occurs by chance. We cannot predict which atom will decay or when any particular atom will decay.

When we place a G-M tube near to an α-particle source the number of α-particles detected in a 10-second period may fluctuate as in Table 34.1.

Table 34.1 *α-particle readings*

Particles in ten seconds	22	17	19	23	20	20	21
Time/min	0	1	2	3	4	5	6

With a large number of atoms over a longer period of time we find that half of the atoms originally present decay in a certain time. This time is known as the **half-life**.

If the half-life is 6 hours and we originally have 12 g of the substance, then we would find that 6 g remains after 6 hours and 3 g after 12 hours. You should note that ½ remains after 1 half-life, ¼ remains after 2 half-lives and ⅛ remains after 3 half-lives. We can plot this as a graph (Fig. 33.3).

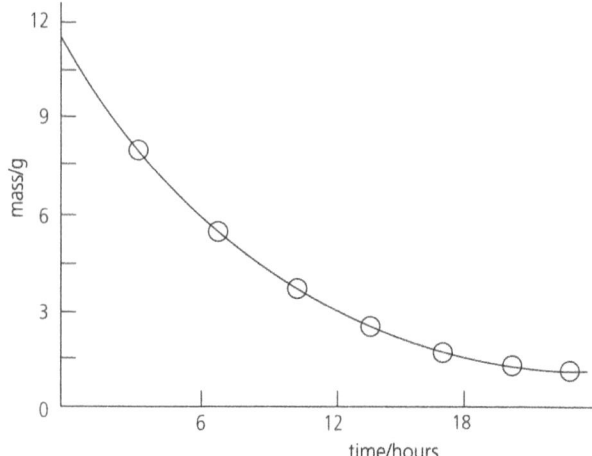

Fig. 34.3 *Half-life graph*

We actually measure the **activity** of the sample, not the amount present. The activity falls at the same rate that the amount remaining goes down.

We used 6 hours as an example of a half-live. In fact, half-lives vary in different radioactive substances from fractions of a second to millions of years.

The rate of radioactive decay is not affected by heating or cooling. It also makes no difference if an atom is an element or in a compound. Radioactivity is solely the result of instability of the nucleus. Physical and chemical processes have no effect on the rate of decay.

34.10 Model for random decay

We take a large number of dice, 100 or more, and throw all of them simultaneously. We remove all that show number 1(a dice showing 1 is said to have decayed). We record the number of dice remaining.

We repeat the process, say ten or more times and obtain a set of pairs of values of the number of dice remaining and the number of throws. We plot a graph of number remaining against number of throws (Fig. 34.4).

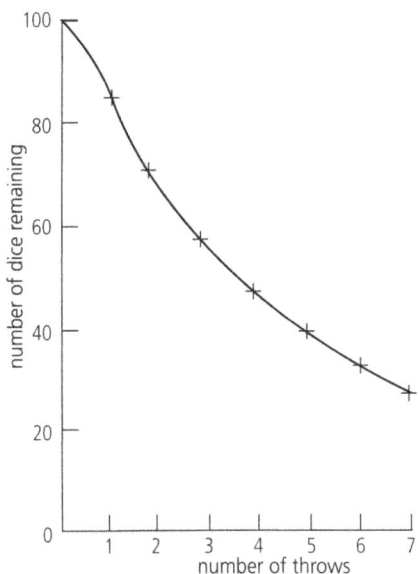

Fig. 34.4 *Random decay model*

In the graph the 'half-life' of the dice is the number of throws. We cannot predict which dice will decay but as each one has a random, one-in-six chance of decaying, the results are similar to those in radioactive decay.

34.11 Safety

Radioactivity can cause damage to cells with the long-term possibility of cancer and leukaemia. Genetic damage can occur and possibly lead to birth defects.

In the school laboratory we take the following precautions:
1. We always hold radioactive sources with forceps.
2. We do not point sources towards the body.
3. We store sources inside lead containers which are placed in a second container. The containers are then stored in a secure place.

34.12 Medical uses of radioactivity

1. Gamma rays are used to sterilise hospital equipment. They are particularly useful for sealed packets of equipment, e.g. needles, which then remain sealed until used.
2. Precisely directed γ-rays can be used to kill cancer cells in a patient's body.
3. Radioactive tracers in the blood are used. The radioactive substance is injected and a G-M tube can be used to follow the movement of the radioactive atoms. Diseased tissue takes up more radioactive atoms than healthy tissue and this can be seen from the G-M tube readings.

34.13 Industrial uses of radioactivity

1. Bacteria in food are killed by γ-rays. This does not reduce the nutritional value of the food, but the taste usually changes.
2. In conjunction with a photographic film, γ-rays can give evidence of defects in joints and castings. This is similar to X-rays but much more convenient as X-ray machines are quite large.
3. Beta particles and gamma rays are used to check the thickness of sheets of material during their manufacture. The amount of radiation passing through the film is monitored. If the reading falls, the thickness of the material has become too large.
4. The radioactive isotope $^{14}_{6}C$ is used in the dating of fossils.

34.14 Nuclear energy

Radioactive decays are examples of nuclear reactions. Many other nuclear reactions take place and in many of them a great deal of energy is given out. This energy is a result of the **destruction of mass** during the reaction. The total mass is less after the reaction.

The Einstein equation relates the energy released, E, with the mass destroyed, m, and the speed of light, c.

$$E = mc^2$$

34.15 Fission

Fission is the splitting of a large nucleus into two smaller nuclei. In the process mass is destroyed and energy released. It is the basis of the atomic bomb. For example:

$$^{235}_{92}U + ^{1}_{0}n \rightarrow ^{153}_{57}La + ^{80}_{35}Br + 3^{1}_{0}n + Q \text{ (energy)}$$

34.16 Fusion

Fusion is the process in which small nuclei join to form larger nuclei. Again mass is destroyed during the process and much energy is released. The Sun's energy is a result of the continuous fusion of hydrogen nuclei into larger nuclei. For example:

$$^{2}_{1}H + ^{2}_{1}H \rightarrow ^{3}_{2}He + ^{1}_{0}n + Q \text{ (energy)}$$

34.17 Advantages and disadvantages of nuclear energy: nuclear reactors

Nuclear power stations use nuclear energy as their energy source. The fission of large nuclei produces heat that is used to boil water and drive the turbines.

Although nuclear fuel is non-renewable, the quantities that we have available will last for many years. The cost of running a nuclear power station is less than the cost of those that use oil or coal.

However, nuclear power stations are expensive to build. The waste products are often radioactive and there are problems with the disposal of the waste products. High safety standards are necessary for the safety of the workers and the environment. Radiation leaks and the accidental discharge of radioactive waste can occur.

You may have heard of the accident at the Chernobyl power station in Russia when radioactive material was released into the atmosphere. Other accidents have occurred at other plants and some people argue that the risk of further accidents is too great.

Questions on Units 31 to 34

1. A nuclide of radon, Rn, has mass number 222 and atomic number 86.
   a Use this information to complete the symbol of this particular nuclide.
   b Use this information to describe the composition of one **atom** of the nuclide.
   c This radon nuclide decays by emission of an α-particle forming a nuclide of polonium, symbol Po. Write an equation to represent this decay.
   d In a given decay process, the total mass of the particles after the decay is less than the original mass by 11×10^{-18} kg. Calculate the corresponding quantity of energy released. (The speed of light in vacuo is 3×10^8 m s^{-1}.)

   (CAMB)

2. A given radioactive nuclide has a half-life of 0.5 hours. What fraction of the atoms in a sample of the nuclide will remain after 2.0 hours?

   (CAMB)

3. A radioactive source is making 2000 disintegrations per minute. Its half-life is 3 days. On a graph sheet, construct a graph showing the change in the disintegration rate over a reasonable period. From the graph, read off the disintegration rate after one week from the beginning.

   (CXC)

4. a i Distinguish between 'nuclear fission' and 'nuclear fusion'.
       ii Give **three** instances when large amounts of nuclear energy are produced.
   b Consider 1 g of matter converted to energy by nuclear fission and 1 g of water of 0°C converted to ice. Find the ratio of the two energies released. Comment on your result.
   c Suppose that your country has been at war with a neighbouring Caribbean country for several months. Discuss the feasibility of either side using nuclear bombs to settle the conflict. (Assume that such bombs can be obtained if required.) (SLH of water = 213×10^6 J kg^{-1}, speed of light = 3×10^8 m s^{-1})

   (CXC)

5 a A gold-leaf electroscope is represented by the diagram below.

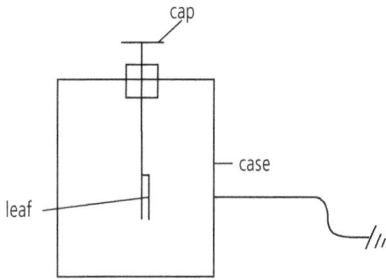

   i State how you would use the induction method to put a positive charge on the leaf, given a negatively-charged rod.
   ii Draw a diagram of the electroscope charged as in (i). On it show the sign of charges on the cap, leaf and case.
   iii A radioactive source, which emits strongly ionising radiation, is placed near to, but not touching, the cap. State what you would expect to observe, justifying your answer.
 b The diagram below shows an arrangement to identify the nature of the emission from a radioactive source. Assume a horizontal arrangement in the plane of the paper.

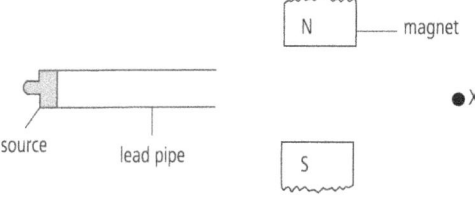

   A Geiger-Müller tube was moved around the point X, about 15 cm from the source. Carefully describe the position and orientation of the G-M tube when it responded if the source was (i) a β-emitter (ii) a γ-emitter.
 c Why would the investigation described in (b) be unlikely to give results with an α-emitter? Describe the changes you would make to allow the G-M tube to detect the radiation from such a source.

(CXC)

35 Some aspects of the historical development of physics

[syllabus sections B4.1; C2.1; D5.1; F1.1, 3.1]

It is important to study the history of physics to better understand scientific method. We look here at the lives and contributions of certain scientists.

35.1 Aristotle and his law of dynamics

Aristotle, a Greek, lived from 384–322 BC. He did not perform experiments but observed everyday events and tried to give explanations for them.

Aristotle felt that a force had to act on an object for it to keep moving. He also argued that a **greater** force was required for a **faster-moving** object, i.e. he suggested that

$$\text{velocity} \quad \alpha \quad \text{force}$$
$$v \quad \alpha \quad F$$

He compared a rock and a leaf falling and stated that heavy objects fall faster than light objects. Again, the velocity was supposed to be proportional to the force, in this case the weight.

Galileo and Newton realised the inadequacies of these arguments and from their ideas we get

$$\text{acceleration} \quad \alpha \quad \text{force}$$
$$a \quad \alpha \quad F$$

See Unit 6.

35.2 Galileo Galilei

Galileo Galilei was born in Pisa, Italy in 1564. In 1589, while working in the post of Chair of Mathematics at the University of Pisa, he carried out experiments on falling objects. He tried to **accurately describe** their motion.

He found that his results contradicted the views of Aristotle (outlined above) and that the rate of fall of a body was **independent** of the weight of the body. There was much opposition to his ideas and he had to resign his post in 1591.

As a Professor at Padua from 1592, he constructed telescopes, microscopes and air thermometers. He used the telescope to discover spots on the Sun and also discovered the four moons of the planet Jupiter. This latter discovery supported the theory of Copernicus. This was that the Sun, and not the Earth, was the centre of the solar system. This was opposed by the Church and he was ordered not to support Copernican theories. Eventually he had publicly to recant his views.

In 1982 the Roman Catholic Church absolved Galileo from any wrongdoing.

Galileo's methodology

Galileo was the first person to adopt the modern view of science in which theory and experiment come together. He saw that he could perform experiments and, from the results, obtain generalisations that predict future behaviour.

Galileo set out to **describe** situations before looking for explanations. He was the first to suggest that we should look at how a system would behave **under ideal conditions**, e.g. with no friction. These ideas greatly changed the methods of scientific enquiry.

35.3 Sir Isaac Newton

Isaac Newton was born in 1642 at Woolsthorpe in England. He attended Grantham public school for a while and was taken away to be a farmer. He later re-entered school and in 1660 went to Cambridge University to read physics and mathematics. Sir Isaac Newton made major contributions to physics and mathematics. They include

1. the three laws of motion
2. the universal law of gravitation and explanation of planetary motion
3. a particle theory of light, which was able to explain some of light's properties
4. the construction of a reflecting telescope
5. the dispersion of 'white light' (sunlight) into a beam of colours (the spectrum)
6. the foundation of calculus in mathematics.

Newton's methodology

While using a telescope Newton saw that the image had a fringe of colours. He then used a prism and obtained a spectrum from sunlight.

Newton investigated several possible causes of this spectrum. He varied the thickness of the glass, the size of the light ray and the position of the prism. He **changed one variable at a time** – a new method of experimentation.

Using a second prism he recombined the coloured light into white light. This suggested that the prism merely split up colours already present in white light.

He found no further dispersion with just one colour,

which was conclusive evidence for his argument about the composition of white light.

His methodology greatly influenced later scientists. He put forward a hypothesis, experimented, changed variables in a regular way, and was very thorough.

35.4 Joule and the conservation of energy

James Joule (1818–89) performed mechanical experiments that converted gravitational potential energy into thermal energy in water. He allowed weights to fall, which then rotated paddles in a container of water.

He calculated the work done by the falling weights ($E_P = m g h$) and the energy gained by the water ($E_H = m c \Delta\theta$). When he allowed for energy losses he found that the thermal energy gained was equal to the work done.

He spent many years making careful measurements and provided much evidence for the principle of conservation of energy; energy cannot be created or destroyed but is merely converted from one form into another.

35.5 Count Rumford and the nature of heat

In the eighteenth century there were two theories about the nature of heat.

The **caloric theory** suggested that heat was a fluid that permeated all matter. It was said that a hot object possessed more caloric than a cold object and that caloric would flow from a hot object to a cold object. Caloric particles were supposed to repel each other so they would tend to leave the hot object.

More caloric was also supposed to produce expansion.

The fact that two bodies when heated equally do not reach the same temperature was explained by assuming that one body did not allow the free passage of the caloric.

The **kinetic** or **mechanical theory** of heat interpreted heat as the kinetic energy of the particles of matter. However, there was at first little supporting evidence for this theory and it was not generally accepted.

Count Rumford (1753–1814) was not a scientist but was responsible for the production of guns and cannon for the Bavarian army. He performed experiments that showed weaknesses in the caloric theory.

Using blunt cannon borers he showed that an inexhaustible amount of heat could be produced while attempting to bore a hole. The heat produced depended only on the amount of work done by the horses that provided the energy for the machines. This suggested that heat could not be a material substance, present in a fixed quantity.

35.6 Michael Faraday and his achievements

Michael Faraday was born in 1791, the son of a London blacksmith. His first job, at age 13, was as an errand boy for a bookbinder. When he was 14 he became the bookbinder's apprentice. A few years later he started to attend lectures at the Royal Institution where, in 1812, he heard lectures by a chemist, Sir Humphrey Davy. At age 22 Faraday became Davy's assistant at the Royal Institution and eventually became the Director of the Institution.

Faraday investigated a wide range of topics in electricity and magnetism. His main contributions were the formulation of the laws of electrolysis and the discovery of electromagnetic induction. (See Units 25 and 30.)

Difficulties encountered in Faraday's electrolysis experiments

Faraday is likely to have had several difficulties in his experiments through which he established the laws of electrolysis. He needed precise values for the amount of water decomposed and the quantity of gas liberated. These would have been difficult to obtain. His results would have been difficult to interpret owing to the variation in the quality of the solutions used. He also would have had difficulty in obtaining a stable supply of electric current.

Electromagnetic induction

Faraday's discovery of electromagnetic induction was the result of a 10-year search for the appropriate apparatus and technique.

He knew that an electric current produced a magnetic field around the wire carrying the current and felt the reverse should be possible: a magnetic field should be able to produce an electric current. He found that a current was only induced when the magnetic field linked to the wire was **changing**.

He verified this in a variety of experimental situations.

He also developed the concept of magnetic lines of force from these experiments and stated precisely the conditions under which electricity could be produced.

35.7 Development of the modern view of the atom

For many years some scientists had argued that all matter was composed of a finite number of indivisible small particles called atoms.

More recently it has been realised that the atoms themselves are composed of other, still smaller particles.

JJ Thomson (1856–1940)

JJ Thomson showed that different materials, when heated, give off the **same** particles – electrons (thermionic emission). JJ Thomson used a cathode-ray tube before the nature of the emitted particles was known. He found that they all had the same charge-to-mass ratio and thus were the same particle.

He also showed that these emitted particles were 1/2000th of the mass of the smallest atom (hydrogen) and thus were **components** of atoms.

Thomson suggested a neutral, 'solid-ball' atom in which equal quantities of positive and negative charge were distributed throughout the ball.

Ernest Rutherford (1871–1937)

Ernest Rutherford suggested the **nuclear atom** from α-particle-scattering experiments (Unit 33).

Most of the α-particles passed straight through the gold foil, a few were deflected and a very small number were reflected.

From these results he inferred that most of an atom is empty space with a very small nucleus containing nearly all the mass and all the positive charge. Negative electrons are moving in orbits around the nucleus. Overall the atom is neutral.

James Chadwick

In 1932 James Chadwick examined the evidence that a very penetrating form of 'radiation' emitted by some light elements (boron, beryllium and lithium) when they were bombarded by α-particles. It was shown that this radiation could not be γ-rays.

Chadwick suggested a neutral particle with a mass similar to that of the proton – the **neutron**. They are found in the nucleus with the protons.

Radiation and atoms

The simple nuclear model did not adequately account for the emission of electromagnetic radiation from atoms.

When an atom emitted radiation it would be expected that the electrons would lose energy and quite quickly fall into the nucleus. It was also not clear why any given element emits only a particular set of wavelengths.

In 1913 **Neils Bohr** suggested that the orbiting electrons could only travel in particular orbits in which the electrons have a certain amount of energy.

This leads to the **shell** model of electrons in the atom (discussed in Unit 33).

As an electron moves from one orbit to another (from one energy level to another) it either emits or absorbs energy. The energy is emitted or absorbed in small packets of radiation known as **photons**.

As a photon is emitted, an electron moves from a higher to a lower energy level. The energy of the photon is equal to the difference in the energy of the levels. This leads to the particular wavelengths found in the spectra of many atoms.

Bohr's theory correctly predicted the spectrum of the hydrogen atom, although further modifications were needed to explain the spectra of more complicated atoms.

Marie Curie

Marie Curie was an early worker in the field of radioactivity. She spent the years 1898 to 1902 isolating the radioactive compound present in the uranium ore called pitchblende. Much patient work was required to identify the salt and describe its properties. She worked with no financial help in poor conditions.

In 1902 she identified radium, mass number 225. She was also able to describe its physical properties such as its density and melting point. She was awarded the Nobel Prize for these achievements.

She later received a second Nobel Prize, in Chemistry, in 1911, for isolating polonium and radium. She died in 1934, of leukaemia, which is likely to have been caused by regular exposure to radioactivity.

35.8 Albert Einstein

Albert Einstein's work in the early years of the twentieth century changed our understanding of the universe.

He was born in 1879 in Germany. His family encouraged him to read widely but he did not excel at school. He left Germany for Switzerland at the age of 17 to avoid regimentation at school.

His reading was mostly physics and mathematics. However, he failed an examination for Zurich Polytechnic as the range of his knowledge was small. Eventually he passed the examinations, graduated and became a teacher at the boarding school. He failed to keep this job as he encouraged the students to think and explore physics rather than just memorise facts for examinations.

In 1902 Einstein started working in the Patent Office in Berne, Switzerland. While there he developed three papers that were published in 1905: his special relativity theory, the theory of the photo-electric effect and an analysis of Brownian motion.

In 1909, after a post at the University of Bern, he was appointed a Professor at the University of Zurich. In 1916 he published his theory of general relativity which supplants Newton's theory of gravitation. Einstein received the Nobel Prize for his analysis of the photoelectric effect.

As he was a Jew, Einstein had to emigrate to the USA when Hitler came to power in Germany. Einstein died in 1955.

Einstein's work and influence

Relativity

Einstein's theory of **special relativity** concerns the relationship between space and time, which are not in fact, independent quantities. In this theory the speed of light is the maximum possible speed and is constant for all observers.

The theory of **general relativity** looks at the 'curvature of space' and revises earlier ideas of geometry. It compares gravitation and acceleration and puts the idea of a '**field**' as the basic concept in the universe.

Photoelectric effect

Einstein's explanation of the photoelectric effect suggested that light can be both a wave **and** a particle. The willingness to accept this duality was an important step forward. This duality has now been extended to include 'particles'.

The photoelectric effect was also important in the development of the quantum theory.

Einstein's work questioned some very basic concepts and moved scientists away from the idea that a physics theory might be finished and complete.

Einstein's involvement in the atomic bomb

The large amounts of energy released in an atomic explosion are the result of the conversion of matter to energy. In 1905 Einstein put forward the equation, $E = mc^2$ (Unit 34) and suggested the possibility of this conversion.

Uranium fission was discovered in the 1930s. In this process a uranium nucleus splits into two roughly equal, smaller nuclei with the destruction of some of the mass. This appears as energy.

A **chain reaction** is needed so that one of the products from the fission of one nucleus – the neutrons – causes fission in others. This was first achieved in December 1942 by Enrico Fermi and others at the University of Chicago.

After consultations with Neils Bohr and other scientists in 1939, Einstein wrote a letter to the then President of the United States, Franklin Roosevelt. In this letter Einstein suggested the development of an atomic weapon and argued that it would benefit the USA and its allies.

The 'Manhattan Project' developed the weapon and atomic bombs were first made in 1945. The only explosions of atomic bombs in war occurred in August of that year at the cities of Hiroshima and Nagasaki in Japan.

After these events Einstein opposed the use of atomic weapons and he adopted a pacifist approach in his later years.

Sample examination questions
CXC 1987

Section II
Answer any THREE questions.

1. a. Give a brief account of Aristotle's theory of motion. **(2 marks)**
   b. State Newton's THREE laws of motion. For EACH law give ONE example of its application and explain how EACH example given illustrates the law. **(9 marks)**
   c. In driving a rod 6.0 cm into the ground, a hammer with 4.8 J of kinetic energy is brought to rest with uniform deceleration. The mass of the hammer is 2.0 kg and it remains in contact with the rod throughout the blow.
      i. Calculate the resultant force that brings the hammer to rest. **(3 marks)**
      ii. What is the deceleration of the hammer? **(3 marks)**
      iii. What is the velocity of the hammer when it strikes the rod? **(3 marks)**
   Total 20 marks

2. a. Describe an experiment that demonstrates that molecules in a gas are in continuous, random motion. With the aid of a diagram describe what you would see and explain how you would interpret this observation. **(6 marks)**
   b. Explain the following observations on the basis of the KINETIC MODEL OF A GAS.
      i. A basketball or netball feels hard when it is fully inflated.
      ii. When you let some air out of the ball the pressure decreases.
      iii. If you leave the ball lying in the Sun the pressure will increase. **(7 marks)**
   c. Oxygen in a cylinder has a pressure of 1200 kPa when stored in the basement of a hospital at a temperature of 27° C. What does the pressure become when the cylinder is carried up to the operating theatre where the temperature is maintained at 17° C? **(7 marks)**
   Total 20 marks

3. a. An object 4.0 cm high is placed perpendicular to the axis of a converging lens and 50 cm from its centre. The focal length of the lens is 20 cm. By means of a scale drawing (on graph paper) find the position of the image and its size. **(9 marks)**
   b. i. We normally say that light travels in straight lines. As evidence for this belief, we note that it casts clear shadows and does not appear to bend round corners. Does this mean that light does not travel as a wave? Explain your answer. **(3 marks)**
      ii. Describe how you could demonstrate in the laboratory that light does, in fact, have a wave motion. **(4 marks)**
      iii. Even after the wave motion of light had been demonstrated by Thomas Young, Newton's corpuscular (particle) theory was still accepted by many scientists. What crucial experiment did Foucault perform and how did it settle the argument over the rival theories? **(4 marks)**
   Total 20 marks

4. a. i. Give TWO reasons why the lights in a house must be connected in parallel rather than in series. **(2 marks)**
      ii. Some appliances in the home have a three-pin plug connected to them. The plug is connected to the appliance by a three-core cable. ONE of these cores carries the earth-wire. What are the other TWO cores? What colour code is used for the insulation of EACH of the THREE wires? **(5 marks)**
      iii. The electric stove is one example of an appliance that needs an earth wire. What is the purpose of this earth wire and how does it function? **(3 marks)**
   b. The circuit diagram below shows three 120 V lamps connected to the 120 V mains. The power ratings of the bulbs are shown.

   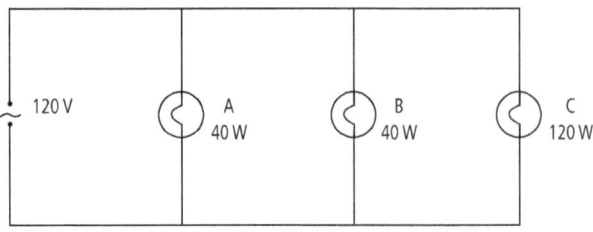

      i. How much current is supplied by the mains? **(3 marks)**
      ii. Find the resistance of the whole circuit. **(3 marks)**
      iii. Electricity costs 30 cents per kW h and the lamps are all used for 8 hours per day. What is the cost of the electricity used in a 30-day month? **(4 marks)**
   Total 20 marks

5 a A student needs a transformer to use a 330 W, 110 V soldering iron but the mains supply is 220 V. She uses a steel rod with two coils, as represented in the diagram below, to make a crude transformer. The transformer does not work very efficiently.

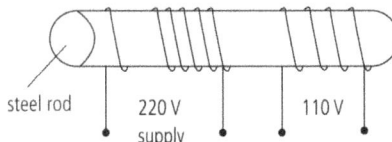

(Many more turns are wound than are shown on the diagram.)

   b Draw a labelled diagram showing a better design for the transformer. Give THREE reasons why your core will be more efficient than that of the student. **(11 marks)**
   c If the primary coil of your transformer has 300 turns, how many turns will you need on the secondary coil? Calculate the value of the current in the primary assuming 100% efficiency. **(4 marks)**
   d If another student borrows the transformer (in its redesigned form) to operate a 1500 W, 110 V kettle, what may happen to the transformer? What would you add to the circuit to ensure that no one uses it above its designed rating of 330 W? In your answer state where you would put this addition and how you would decide on its rating. **(5 marks)**

Total 20 marks

6 a Draw a diagram to represent the structure of a neutral helium atom. Clearly label the components. Taking the mass of the smallest component to be one 'unit', what are the approximate masses of the other components? **(8 marks)**

   b $^{X}_{92}U \longrightarrow {}^{234}_{90}Th + {}^{4}_{2}He$

   The equation above represents a nuclear decay.
      i What is the value of the mass number (represented by X) of the uranium?
      ii Write down the symbol for a nuclide, which is an isotope of $^{234}_{90}Th$.
      iii The thorium nuclide (Th) is not stable. It decays by β-emission to produce protactinium (symbol Pa). Represent this reaction in an equation like the one above. **(7 marks)**

   c The half-life for the β-decay of Thorium-234 is 24 days. The Physics Department of the U.W.I. in Jamaica bought a sample of this thorium from England. On the day of dispatch its activity was 4×10^5 Bq (i.e. 4×10^5 disintegrations per second).
      i What was the activity of the source when it arrived in Jamaica 72 days later?
      ii What safety precautions should the suppliers have taken to ensure that none of the dock-workers could be harmed? **(5 marks)**

Total 20 marks

January 1999 (2492)

1 **No more than 1/2 hour should be spent on this question.**

   DATA ANALYSIS

   When a driver of a car sees an obstruction in the road, the total stopping distance for the car is made up of two distances: the thinking distance and the braking distance.
   The **thinking distance** is the distance the car travels in the time it takes the driver to make the decision to stop.
   The **breaking distance** is the distance the car takes to stop while the brakes are applied.
   Data on these quantities at different speeds are shown in **Table 1**.

   TABLE 1

Car speed (v/m s^{-1})	Thinking distance (d/m)	Braking distance (x/m)	Total stopping distance (s/m)
16	12	12.8	24.8
20	16	20.0	36.0
24	20	28.8	48.8
28	24	39.2	63.2
32	28	51.2	79.2
36	32	64.8	96.8

   a A graph of thinking distance, d, against car speed, v, has been drawn for you (see *Graph for Question 1*). Determine the gradient, G, of this graph and give its unit. **(4 marks)**

   b Use the equation, $v = Gd + 4$, to find the value of d when v is 40 m s^{-1}. **(3 marks)**

   c Plot a graph of the total stopping distance, s, against the car speed, v. The graph line is a curve. **(9 marks)**

   d Use the graph of s against v to find the total stopping distance if an obstruction is seen when the speed of the car is 30 m s^{-1}. **(2 marks)**

   e If the mass of the car is 800 kg, calculate the kinetic energy of the car when it is travelling at 24 m s^{-1}. **(3 marks)**

   f The average force exerted by the brakes is 7 000 N. Determine how much work is done **by the brakes** to stop the car when the car is initially travelling at 24 m s^{-1}. **(3 marks)**

   g Explain why the answers to (e) and (f) are not the same. **(1 mark)**

   h If an extra load of 160 kg was put in the car, find the deceleration that the application of the brakes would cause. **(3 marks)**

   i Write down the main **energy change** that is occurring when a car is
      i moving along a level road at **constant** speed
      ii accelerating along a level road. **(2 marks)**

   Total 30 marks

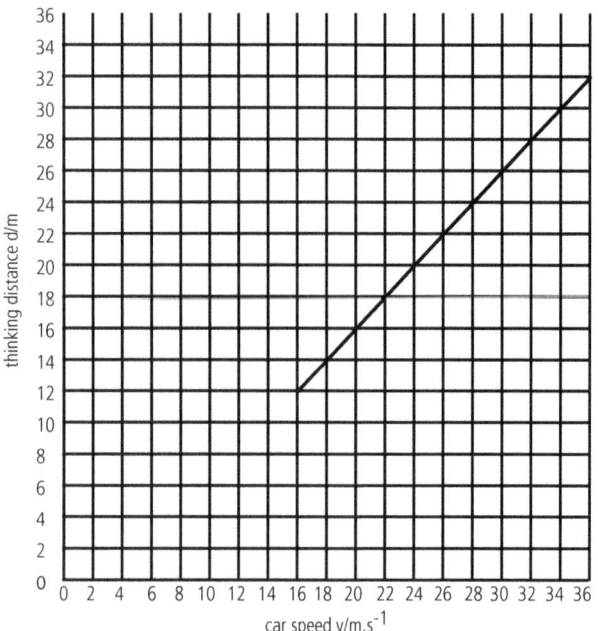

Graph for Question 1
(Use graph paper to plot your answer.)

2 a i Describe how you would determine the density of a small rock of an irregular shape. **(4 marks)**

      ii When astronauts landed on the Moon they collected pieces of rock. While on the Moon, one piece of rock was measured and found to have a volume of 6.4×10^{-5} m^3 and a mass of 0.36 kg. What was the density of the rock? **(2 marks)**

      iii On the Moon the acceleration due to gravity is 1.7 m s^{-2}. The rock was attached to a spring balance and lowered into water until it was completely submerged. The reading on the spring balance decreased due to the upthrust of the water. Calculate the upthrust of the water on the rock. (Density of water 1 000 kg m^{-3}) **(4 marks)**

   b On graph paper, draw a velocity-time graph for an object that is released from rest on the Moon, that falls for 3 s but that does **not** reach the ground. Label the axes and insert appropriate scales. **(2 marks)**

   c A small rock is thrown horizontally on the Moon with a speed of 3.4 m s^{-1}.
      i Write down the vertical component of its

velocity after one second. **(1 mark)**
ii Write down the horizontal component of its velocity after one second. **(1 mark)**
iii Sketch a vector diagram in the space below to show how you could determine the velocity of the rock after one second – you are not required to find the velocity.
(2 marks)
Total 16 marks

3 This question concerns the refraction of water waves and light.
a A block of glass is placed on the bottom of a ripple tank so that the water above the block is very shallow. Plane waves travel from the left across the deep water, through the shallow water and then continue into the deep water as shown in **Figure 1**.

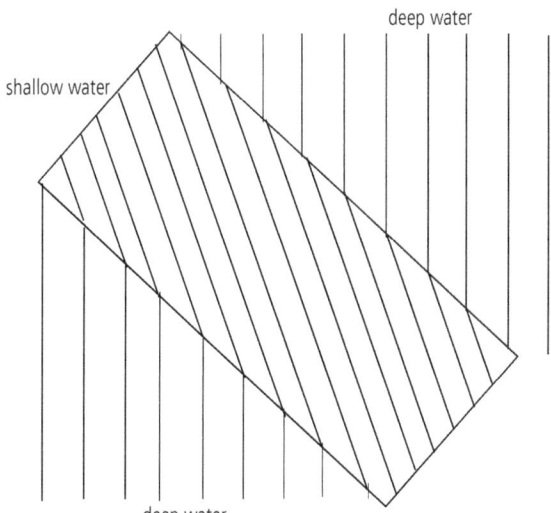
Figure 1

i As the waves approach the block they are travelling a speed of 6.4 m s^{-1}. Take measurements of the wavelengths, on the diagram, and use these measurements to determine the speed of the waves in the shallow water and in the deep water beyond the block.
Wavelength in shallow water
Wavelength in deep water **(1 mark)**
Speed in shallow water **(3 marks)**
Speed in deep water beyond block **(2 marks)**
ii Calculate the frequency of the water waves.
(3 marks)
iii Calculate the refractive index for water waves going from deep to shallow water.
(3 marks)
b The diagrams below show a coin in a porcelain cup – in **Figure 2** the cup is empty; in **Figure 3** water has been poured into the cup. Neither the coin nor the eye change position but in **Figure 2** the coin cannot be seen by the eye while in **Figure 3** the eye can see the coin.

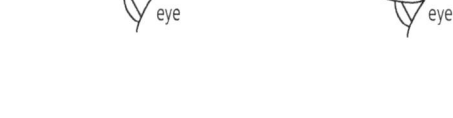

Figure 2   Figure 3

Draw ONE light ray from the coin (**Figure 2**) to explain why the coin cannot be seen by the eye. On **Figure 3** draw TWO rays that leave from the SAME point on the coin and enter the eye.
(3 marks)
Total 15 marks

4 Beta particles, in a vacuum, enter a region with a uniform magnetic field, which is perpendicular to the plane of their motion, as shown below in **Figure 4**.

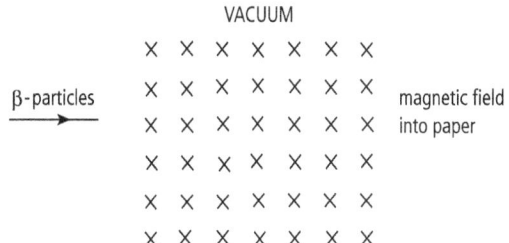

Figure 4

a What is a β-particle? **(1 mark)**
b On **Figure 4** draw the path of the β-particle in the magnetic field. What causes the β-particle to take this path? **(3 marks)**
c Write down TWO differences in the path that would be observed if the particle was an α-particle moving at the same speed. **(2 marks)**
d Describe how you would determine the range of α-particles in the air. **(4 marks)**
e What would be the range of α-particles in a vacuum? **(1 mark)**
f Alpha particles are emitted by radium – 226 ($^{226}_{88}$Ra) and a radon (Rn) nucleus is formed. Write the equation for this nuclear reaction.
(3 marks)
Total 14 marks

5 a State the name of the rule that allows us to predict the direction of the force on a current-carrying conductor perpendicular to a magnetic field. **(1 mark)**

b **Figure 5** is a diagram of a simple moving-coil loudspeaker.

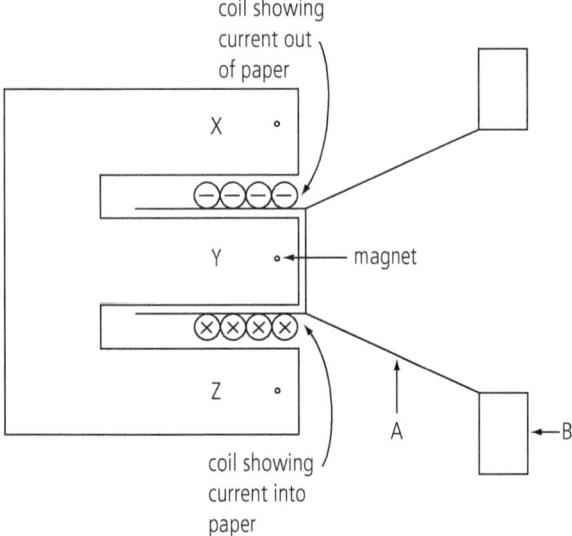

Figure 5

Identify the parts labelled **A** and **B** and indicate the polarity of the magnet at the points **X**, **Y**, **Z**.
A **(1 mark)**
B **(1 mark)**
X
Y
Z **(1 mark)**

c An alternating current is applied to the coil. Describe and explain the resultant motion of the coil. **(4 marks)**

d Sound is produced by the loudspeaker as a result of the motion referred to in part (c). What would be the effect of increased coil current on the
  i pitch of the sound produced? **(1 mark)**
  ii loudness of the sound produced? **(1 mark)**

e The coil is disconnected from the a.c. source and connected to a galvanometer (a sensitive, centre-zero instrument used to indicate the magnitude and direction of small currents). Part A in **Figure 5** is then made to vibrate at low frequency by displacing it by hand. State what you would observe on the galvanometer and explain your observation. **(5 marks)**

Total 15 marks

January 1999 (2493)

1 a Explain what is meant by a magnetic field. In your answer booklet, draw two bar magnets arranged as in **Figure 1**, and sketch the magnetic field pattern around and in between them.

Figure 1

An iron bar is placed near to a coil as shown in **Figure 2**.

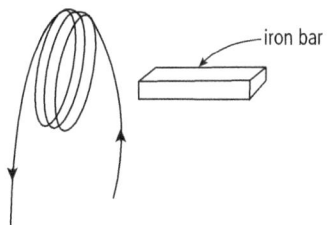

Figure 2

A steady current is passed through the coil. State and explain the effect on the iron bar. **(8 marks)**

b **Figure 3** below shows the parts of a meter that measure electric current.

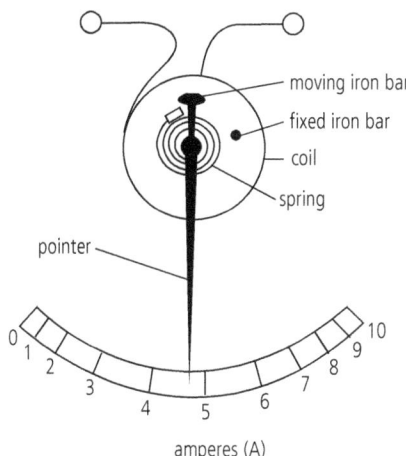

Figure 3

The current flows through a coil. Inside the coil there is a fixed iron bar and a second iron bar, which is attached to a pointer. A spring is also attached to the pointer. When current flows in the coil the pointer moves across the scale and then comes to a stop.

i Explain why the pointer moves when current flows and why the pointer stops moving at a particular scale reading. Explain why the pointer moves further before stopping when the current increases. Write down the reading on the meter on **Figure 3**.

ii Can alternating current be measured with this meter? Explain your answer. Why should you not pass a current greater than 10 A through this meter? **(12 marks)**
Total 20 marks

2 a Distinguish between **energy** and **power** and write an equation relating these two quantities. Explain what is meant by **work** and **gravitational potential energy**. What are the main energy transformations that occur when
i a person walks up a flight of stairs
ii an electric motor raises an object? **(8 marks)**

b i A girl of mass 45 kg walks slowly up a flight of stairs to the next floor in an hotel. Each step is 0.24 m high and there are 25 steps. How much work does she do against gravity? If it takes her 21 s to reach the top, what is her average power output? **(5 marks)**
ii On another occasion the girl runs up the stairs in 12 s. How much work does she now do against gravity and what is her average power output? **(3 marks)**
iii The hotel has an elevator of mass 240 kg. If, instead of using the stairs, the girl decides to take the elevator, what would be the total work done against gravity by the elevator motor? What is the efficiency of using the elevator when it is being used only to lift the girl? **(4 marks)**
(Acceleration due to gravity = 10 m s^{-2})
Total 20 marks

3 a In the past, different theories of light have been put forward by scientists. State any ONE property of light that could be used to support a particle theory of light and explain how the property supports the theory. Describe Young's double-slit experiment and show how this experiment supports a wave theory of light. **(8 marks)**

b An observer in a building looks down at a swimming pool at night. He notices that a lamp at the bottom of the pool produces a circle of light at the surface of the water.

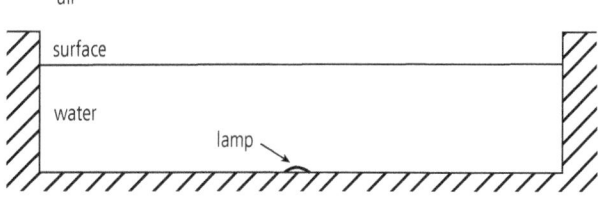

Figure 4

i Copy **Figure 4** and add the paths of THREE rays leaving the lamp, which strike the surface and continue. Choose your rays so that

ray 1 has an angle of incidence of zero
ray 2 has an angle of incidence of about 25°
ray 3 has an angle of incidence of about 60°.

(The critical angle for the water-air boundary is 49°.)

ii State which of these rays would be visible above the surface of the water.
iii Explain why a circle of light is seen and find the refractive index of water. **(12 marks)**
Total 20 marks

4 a A three-pin plug has live, neutral and earth wires attached. What is the purpose of the earth wire? To what is the other end of this earth wire attached and what is its International Colour Code? What is the purpose of a fuse and why is it particularly dangerous to have an earth wire fitted to an appliance without a fuse? What is the name and International Colour Code for the wire into which the fuse is fitted? **(8 marks)**

b An electric cooker draws a power of 9.5 kW when all burners are being used. If the cooker is operated on a 220 V supply, calculate the current that it draws when all the burners are being used. The cable that is used to connect the cooker to the mains supply has a resistance of 0.036 Ω m^{-1}. If the cable is 15 m long, calculate its total resistance and the power lost in this cable when the cooker is drawing maximum power. **(8 marks)**

c Electrical energy has to travel considerable distances from power stations to our homes. If the power station was 15 km from your home and the same type of cable was used, what would be the total resistance of the transmission cable? The house needs to be supplied with 220 V in order to operate the cooker. What would the supply voltage at the power station need to be?
(4 marks)
Total 20 marks

5 a State THREE differences between boiling and evaporation. Use the kinetic theory to explain how evaporation can take place at all temperatures but occurs more rapidly at higher temperatures. Why is there a drop in temperature in liquid when rapid evaporation occurs? **(8 marks)**

b Following an accident, a patient of mass 70 kg requires the transfer of 2 kg of blood. The blood is at 5° C when transferred to the patient and is warmed up to the patient's final temperature of 35° C. Calculate the energy transferred from the patient's body to the blood. Find also the change in the patient's body temperature.

This temperature change may cause 'shock' and to prevent this the patient is wrapped in a 500 W electrically-heated blanket. How long would it take for the patient's body temperature to be restored to its initial value?

It is found in practice that it takes more than the time calculated above for the patient's body temperature to be restored to its initial value. Account for this difference.
(Average specific heat capacity of blood = 4 500 J kg^{-1} K^{-1}; Average specific heat capacity for body tissue = 2 500 J kg^{-1} K^{-1}) **(12 marks)**
Total 20 marks

January 2002 (2492)

1 **You should not spend more than 30 minutes on this question.**

A 10 kg steel ball falls H metres from rest onto a light platform, which has a spring fastened underneath it. The maximum displacement, x, of the platform from its equilibrium position is measured and recorded. The procedure is repeated for different values of H and the results tabulated below.

Height H / metres	6.0	5.0	4.0	3.0	2.0	1.0
Displacement x^2/cm^3	324	250	196	157	112	49
Impact velocity $v^2/m^2\,s^{-2}$						

a By equating the kinetic energy at the moment of impact with the change in potential energy of the ball, we find that the velocity, v, at impact, is related to the initial height by
$v = \sqrt{20H}$ ∴ $v^2 = 20H$

Use this relationship to complete the table. **(2 marks)**

b On graph paper, plot the graph of the square of the displacement, x^2, against the square of the impact velocity, v^2. **(9 marks)**

c Find the slope, S, of the graph. **(5 marks)**

d Given that the spring constant k = 10/S N m⁻¹, find k. **(2 marks)**

e If you place (NOT DROP) the ball onto the platform, to what extent will the ball compress the spring? **(4 marks)**

f The graph you plotted in part (b) is obtained by assuming that the kinetic energy of the ball at the moment of impact, is converted completely into the potential energy stored in the spring. Identify the error involved in this assumption. **(1 mark)**

g From what height should the ball fall in order to displace the platform by 10 cm? **(4 marks)**

h Calculate the potential energy lost by the ball before coming to rest after the impact in part (g). **(3 marks)**

Total 30 marks

2 a i State TWO differences between sound waves and electromagnetic waves. **(2 marks)**

ii Relate the terms 'pitch' and 'loudness' to the physical properties of a sound wave. **(2 marks)**

iii Describe an experiment to show that sound does not travel in a vacuum. **(7 marks)**

b
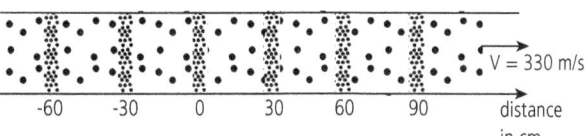

Figure 1

Figure 1 shows how a sound wave travelling through a long air-filled tube sets up a periodic pattern of rarefraction and compression.

i Determine for this sound wave the
a) wavelength **(1 mark)**
b) frequency. **(3 marks)**

ii Is this frequency in the audible range? Justify your answer. **(1 mark)**
(Speed of sound in air = 330 m/s)

Total 16 marks

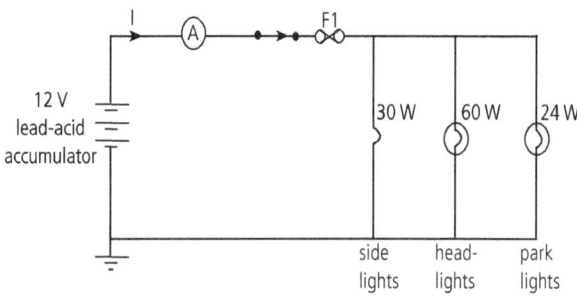

3 a Figure 2

i **Figure 2** shows a very simplified wiring diagram of part of an automobile electrical system. Calculate the effective resistance of the headlights. **(3 marks)**

ii Compute the magnitude of the current, I, when all three sets of lights are on. **(5 marks)**

iii Explain the function of the fuse, F1, in **Figure 2**. **(1 mark)**

iv If fuses are available in only 5 A, 10 A and 15 A denominations, select a fuse rating for F1. Explain your selection. **(2 marks)**

b i State TWO advantages of connecting all electrical devices in parallel with the battery. **(2 marks)**

ii Give TWO reasons why a dry cell may NOT be used in place of the lead-accumulator battery in used cars. **(2 marks)**

Total 15 marks

4 a Explain the meaning of EACH of the following:
      i   radioactivity   **(2 marks)**
      ii the half-life of a radioactive nuclide.
                                                    (2 marks)
   b i   What is nuclear fission?   **(2 marks)**
      ii Why is energy released in the nuclear
          fission process?   **(1 mark)**
   c The graph in **Figure 3** shows the activity of
      Iodine-131 ($^{131}_{53}$I) observed over a 36-day
      period.
      i   What is the initial activity?   **(1 mark)**
      ii Determine the half-life of Iodine-131
                                                    (3 marks)
      iii Calculate the activity on day 48. **(3 marks)**

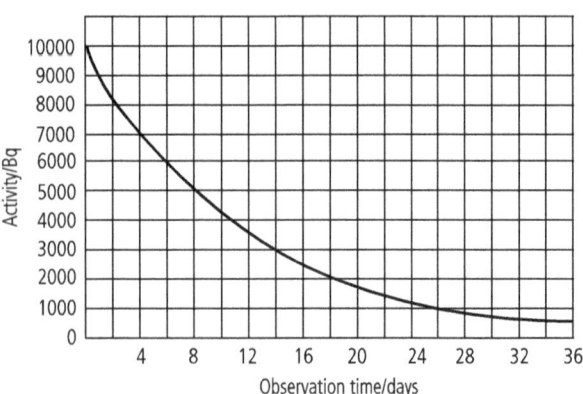

Figure 3

Total 14 marks

5 a Arrange the following in order of
      DECREASING wavelength.
      X-rays, radio waves, visible light rays.
                                                    (3 marks)
      ii Name TWO properties that these waves
          have in common.   **(2 marks)**
   b i   State the laws of reflection.   **(2 marks)**
      ii

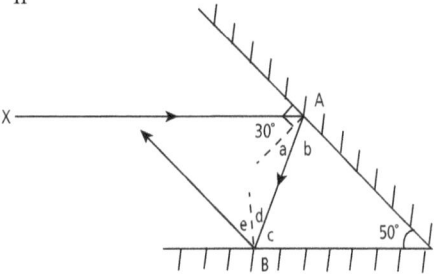

Figure 4

Figure 4 shows two plane mirrors: A and
B. The mirrors touch each other along one
edge and are oriented so that their surfaces
make an angle of 50° with each other. A
beam of light is directed towards A at an
angle of incidence at 30°. Calculate the
unknown angles, a, b, c and d in **Figure 4**.
Hence deduce the angle of reflection (e)
from B.   **(5 marks)**

c Zircon, a material used for manufacturing
   imitation diamonds, has a refractive index of
   1.9. Calculate the speed of light in Zircon.
   (Speed of light in vacuum 3×10^8 m s^{-1})
                                          (3 marks)
                                    Total 15 marks

January 2002 (2493)

1. a   i State Newton's second law of motion.
      ii Use Newton's second law of motion to
         a) distinguish between mass and weight
         b) define the unit of force.
      iii Identify the type of unbalanced force that acts on
         a) an electron moving around a nucleus
         b) a car going around a bend on a flat road.
   b The elevator in a high-rise building accelerates uniformly from rest to a speed of 4 m s⁻¹ in the first 2 s of its upward motion. It then continues at constant speed for 4 s and thereafter decelerates uniformly to a complete stop in 3 s.
      i Sketch a labelled velocity-time graph of this motion. (Do not use graph paper.)
      ii Calculate the acceleration in the first 2 s.
      iii Determine the distance travelled by the elevator while it is decelerating.
      iv Determine the total distance travelled by the elevator. **(12 marks)**
      Total 20 marks

2. a Explain the meaning of the following terms as they relate to a wave:
      i amplitude
      ii period. **(3 marks)**
   b i Draw a displacement-time graph to represent the movement of a floating buoy, which has an amplitude of 0.5 m as a water wave passes with a period of 3 s.
      ii Can the graph you drew in part (b)(i) be used to tell whether the wave is transverse or longitudinal? **(5 marks)**
   c The diagram in **Figure 1** shows the wavefronts in a ripple tank as water moves from deep water to water made shallower by a sheet of glass placed in the water.

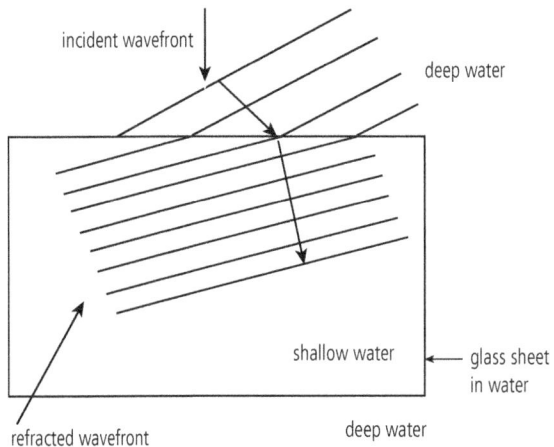

Figure 1

   i If the period of the incident wave is 0.1 s, the wavelength of the incident wave is 0.5 cm, and the wavelength of the refracted wave is 0.3 cm, calculate the
      a speed of the incident and refracted waves
      b refractive index at the deep-to-shallow water boundary.
   ii If the angle of incidence of the incident wave is 25°, determine the angle of refraction of the refracted wave.
   (12 marks)
   Total 20 marks

3. a Describe an experiment to show that a metal expands when heated. State the apparatus you would use, briefly describe your procedure, and say how you would arrive at your conclusions. **(8 marks)**
   b **Figure 2** shows a diagram representing the heating system of a domestic electric iron. The temperature of the iron is regulated by a bimetallic strip. At point C the bimetallic strip makes contact with the live wire of the supply.

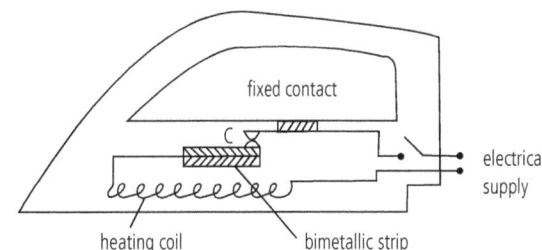

Figure 2

   i Use your knowledge of the thermal characteristics of bimetallic strips to explain how this system regulates the temperature of the iron.
   ii Sketch (no numbers required, just labelled axes and a shape) a graph showing how the temperature of the iron would vary with time. Indicate on your graph the times when the heating coil is ON or OFF.
   iii In a defective iron, the contacts stick together so that current flow is continuous, but the temperature of the iron does not increase indefinitely. Explain. **(12 marks)**
   Total 20 marks

4 a i Name the THREE methods by which thermal energy may be transferred. For EACH method describe ONE feature that is included in the design of the solar water-heater collector in order to minimise thermal energy losses.
      ii Describe TWO other design features that improve efficiency of solar water-heater collectors. **(8 marks)**
   b Six hundred and fifty watts of solar power is incident on every square metre of a solar water-heater collector with a length of 2 m and a width of 1.5 m. The solar water-heater is designed to heat 120 kg of water, which is placed in a storage tank.
      i Calculate the area of the solar water-heater collector and the power incident on it. **(4 marks)**
      ii Given that the power incident is sustained for 6 hrs, calculate the energy input to the solar water-heater collector. **(4 marks)**
      iii The solar water-heater collector supplies 18 MJ of energy to the water initially at 30°C. Calculate the temperature at which the water is stored. **(4 marks)**
      (Specific heat capacity of water = 4 200 J Kg^{-1} K^{-1})
      Total 20 marks

5 a i Sketch the magnetic field of a solenoid.
      ii **Figure 3** shows an electromagnetic relay. Describe the operation of this device. In your description you should refer to the components of the relay using the labels on the diagram.

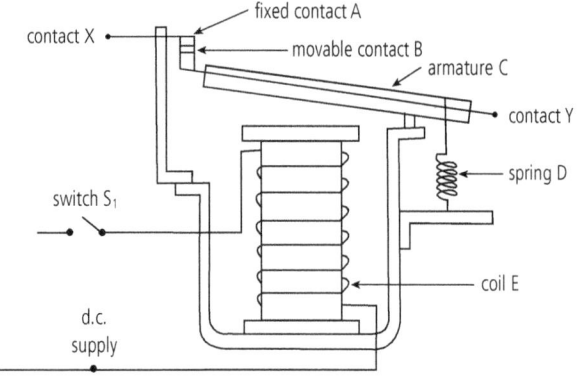

Figure 3

(8 marks)

b **Figure 4** shows an apparatus that may be used to demonstrate the phenomenon of magnetic levitation. A copper ring placed around a solenoid can be suspended in space without apparent support by adjusting the a.c. supply to the coil.

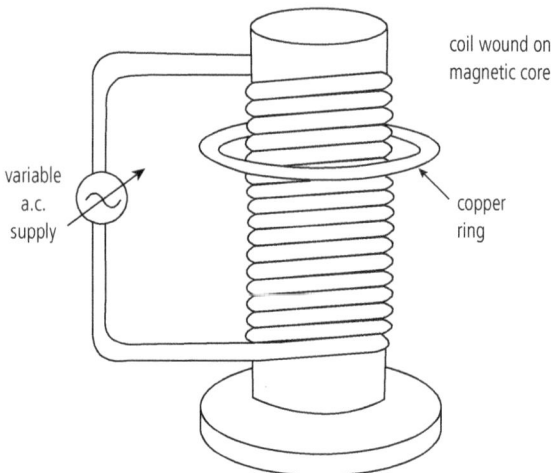

Figure 4

   i Explain why a varying supply causes a current to flow to the ring.
   ii At a given instant the a.c. supply voltage is increasing and the base of the coil is a north pole. **Figure 5** shows a sketch of the ring and the magnetic field around it at that instant.

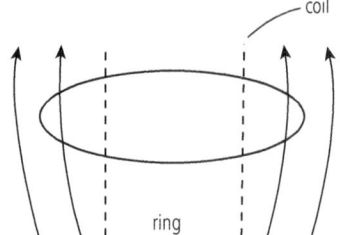

Figure 5

Redraw this diagram in your answer book. Show the direction of the induced current on your diagram. Explain how you arrived at your answer.
   iii On your diagram indicate the vertical forces acting on the ring when it is suspended and in equilibrium. State the nature and origin of these forces. **(12 marks)**
   Total 20 marks

Numerical solutions

Page 6 (Unit 2)
1. (a) 3×10^8 (b) 1.2 (c) 2×10^{-2} (d) $2 \times 10 = 20$
2. (c) 0.679 g cm^{-3}
3. (a) $\frac{2}{3}$ (b) 9 (c) –6 (d) No

Page 17 (Units 3 to 6)
1. (a) 12.5 m s^{-1} (b) 31.25 m
2. (b) 3 m s^{-2} (c) 48 m (d) 4 m^{-1}
3. (a) 6 s (b) 84 m (c) 4 m s^{-1}
4. 20 m
5. (a) 38.3 N (b) 24.5 cm (c) 14 cm (d) 24 cm
6. 50 N
7. 100 N; 53.1° to horizontal

Page 20 (Unit 7)
1. 24 J
2. 560 J
3. 800 J
4. (a) 3000 J (b) 11 m s^{-1}
5. 9×10^5 J
6. 750 W

Page 27 (Units 8 to 10)
1. (a) 480 N m (b) 300 N
2. 320 N
3. volume = 0.12 m^3, mass = 180 kg, weight = 1800 N, pressure = 9000 Pa

Page 36 (Units 12 and 13)
1. 350 K, 950 mm Hg
3. (b) 6 atmospheres

Page 42 (Units 14 and 15)
2. $300 \text{ J kg}^{-1} \text{ K}^{-1}$
4. $450 \text{ J kg}^{-1} \text{ K}^{-1}$
5. $1700 \text{ J kg}^{-1} \text{ K}^{-1}$
6. 11.25 K
7. 90 s

Page 55 (Units 18 and 19)
2. (b) (i) 250 mm (ii) 62.5 mm^2
3. 486 mm; 85.7 mm^2

Page 64 (Units 20 to 23)
1. (b) 4.8×10^{-7} m
2. (a) 1.4 m (b) (iv) 2×10^5 Hz

Page 74 (Units 24 to 26)
1. 0.5 J
2. (a) 1 A (b) 4 A (c) 4.5 Ω
3. (i) 3050 W (ii) 12.2 A (iii) 12.2 kW h (4.39×10^7 J)

Page 98 (Units 31 to 34)
1. (d) 0.99 J

Acknowledgements

Examination questions from papers set in previous years are reproduced by permission of the following:
The Caribbean Examination Council (CXC)
The University of Cambridge Local Examinations Syndicate (CAMB)
The Welsh Joint Education Committee (WJEC)

The University of Cambridge Local Examinations Syndicate bears no responsibility for the example answers to questions taken from its past question papers that are contained in this publication.

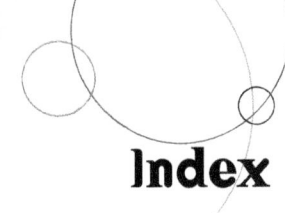

Index

absolute temperature scale 32
absolute zero 32
absorption of radiation and heat 38, 39
acceleration 7
    due to gravity 10, 11, 16
    equations of motion 9
    measurement of 9–10
accommodation of eye 53
accumulator 71
accuracy 4
air pressure 25, 26
alpha decay 96
alpha (α) particles 93, 95
alternating current 86
    advantage 87–88
    generator 86
    transforming voltage of 87
ammeter 68–69, 84
ampere, A 68
amplitude
    of simple pendulum 3
    of waves 56
angle of incidence
    light 47, 49
    water 57
angle of refraction
    light 49
anode 71
apparent depth 50
area 2
    under velocity/time graph 8
Archimedes' principle 27
Aristotle 100
atomic bomb 98
atomic mass 93
atomic number 93
atoms 65, 93–94

balance
    beam 2
    rule for balancing 21
    spring 12
balloons 27
barometer 25
batteries 70
beam balance 2
bell, electric 80
beta (β) particles 95–97
bimetallic strip 28
binoculars 51
Bohr, Neils 102
boiling 43–44
    and evaporation 44
Boyle's law 31, 36
brakes, hydraulic 24–25
breezes, land and sea 39
Brownian motion 34–5
brushes, carbon motor 83

calipers 1
vernier 1
caloric theory of heat 101
camera
    pinhole 46
    ray diagram of 53
crushing can experiment 25
cathode 71
cells, electric 70
Celsius scale 29
centre of gravity 22–3
centripetal force 17
Chadwick, James 102
chain reaction 103
charge, electric 68
charging an accumulator 70
charging by induction 66
Charles' law 31–2, 36
chemical energy 19
ciliary muscle 53
circuit breaker 73
circular motion 17
clinical thermometer 30
cloud chamber 96
coil, magnetic field of 79–80
colour code for wires 73
combined gas equation 33
compass 76
condensing 43
conduction
    electrical 68–72
    gases 67
    heat 38, 40
    liquids 71
    solids 68
conservation of energy 19
conservation of momentum 16–17
convection 38–9
conventional current 68
converging lens 52
convex lens 52
cooling curves 44
copper sulphate solution 71
coulomb, C 68
couple 82
critical angle 50
crowbar 22
current, see electric current
Curie, Marie 102

defects of the eye 54
demagnetisation 76
density 2
    relative 3
derived quantities 1
deviation of light 49
diffraction
    light 60
    sound 61–62
    water 58
diffusion 35

diode, semiconductor 89
direct current 68–72
direct current generator 86
direct current motor 82
dispersion 54
displacement 8
displacement can (eureka) 2–3
distance 7
diverging lens 52–53
domains, magnetic 77
dry cell 70

earth potential 66
earth wire 73
eclipses 47
efficiency 23
Einstein, Albert 97, 103
elastic limit 13
electric bell 80
electric charge 65–67
electric circuits 68–70
electric current
    alternating 86–88
    direct 68–72
electric field 66
electric motor 83
electricity, cost of 74
electrodes 71
electrolysis 71
electrolyte 71
electromagnetic induction 85–88
electromagnetic spectrum 61
electromagnets 80
electromotive force, emf 68, 70
electron shells 65, 93–94
electronics 89–90
electrons 65, 93
electroplating 71
electroscope 65, 66
emission of radiation 39
energy 19–20
equations of motion 9
evaporation 36
    and boiling 44
expansion
    force in expansion 28
    gases 29–30
    liquids 29
    solids 28
eye 53–54
    defects of 54

Faraday, Michael 101
Faraday's laws 85
fission, nuclear 98
Fleming's left-hand rule 82
Fleming's right-hand rule 85
floating objects 27
flux linkage 85
focal length 52
focus, principle 52
force 12–14
    between molecules 35
    and motion 16, 17
    turning 21

frequency 57
    audible range of 63
friction 15
fringes, interference 60
fulcrum 21
fundamental quantities 1
fusion, change of state 43
fusion, nuclear 98

g (acceleration due to gravity) 10, 16
Galileo 100
galvanometer 83
gamma (γ) radiation 61, 95–96
gas laws 31–3
gases 31–3
    electrical conduction of 66
    expansion of 29
    kinetic model of 35–6
Geiger-Muller (G-M) tube 95
gold-leaf electroscope 65–66
graphs
    distance/time 8
    drawing and interpreting of a
    velocity/time 8
gravitational potential energy 19
greenhouse (glasshouse) effect 40

half-life 96
heat
    and phase change 43–44
    and temperature 41–42
heat capacity 41
hertz, Hz 57
Hooke's law 13
hydraulic brakes 25

ice, latent heat of 43
images
    due to refraction 50–51
    in a plane mirror 47–48
    through a lens 53
incident ray
    reflection of 47
    refraction of 49
induced current 85
    magnetism of 77
induction
    electromagnetic 85–88
    electrostatic 67
    magnetic 77
inertia 13
infrared radiation 39, 61
insulators
    electrical 65
    heat 38
integrated circuits 90
interference
    light 60
    sound 62
    water 59
internal resistance 70
ion 67, 71
ionisation 67, 71
    by radioactive emissions 95–96

Joule 101
joule, J 19

Kelvin scale 32
kilogram, kg 1
kilowatt hour, kWh 74
kinetic energy 19
kinetic theory of matter 34-6

land and sea breezes 39
latent heat
   of fusion 43
   of vaporisation 44
lateral inversion 48
lead-acid cell (accumulator) 70–71
left-hand rule 82
length 1
lenses 52–53
Lenz's law 82
levers 22–23
light 46–55
   nature of 60
light pipes 51
lightning conductor 67
lines of force (field lines)
   electric 66
   magnetic 77
liquids
   and electrical conduction 71
   heat transfer in 38–39
   and kinetic energy 35
logic gates 91–92
long sight 54
longitudinal wave 56, 62
loudness of sound 63
loudspeaker 83

machines 22
magnetic compass 76
magnetic domains 77
magnetic fields 77–80
   due to coils 79
   in straight wire 79
   like and unlike poles 78
   and parallel conductors 79
   due to solenoid 80
magnetic materials 76
magnetic relay 80
magnetic screening 78
magnets 76–78
magnification 53
magnifying glass 52
manometer 25
mass 2
   and weight 13
mass number 93
mechanical advantage 23
metre, m 1
micrometer 1
mirrors
   image in plane 47–48
   plane 47
molecules, kinetic theory of 34–6
moment of force 21
   principle of 21

momentum 15
   conservation of 16–17
moon
   eclipse of 47
   weight on, 13
motion and forces 15–17
   equations of, 9
   Newton's laws of 15–16
motor, d.c. electric 82
motor rule, 82
moving-coil microphone 86–87
multiplier (voltmeter) 84

n-type material 89
neutral point in magnetic field 84
neutron 93
   discovery of 102
neutron number, N 93
newton, N 15
Newton, Sir Isaac 100–101
Newton's laws of motion, 15–16
no-parallax, 4, 48
nuclear energy 19, 97–98
nuclear fission 98
nucleons 93
nucleus 65, 93

Oested's experiment 79
Ohm's law 68–69
oil on water experiment 34
optical instruments 52–53
oscillation
   pendulum 3
   wave 56

p-n junction diode 89
p-type material 89
parallax 4, 48
parallel resistors 69
parallel circuits 69
parallel conductors in a magnetic field 79
parallelogram law 14
pascal, Pa 24
p.d., see potential difference
pendulum, simple 3
penetration of radioactive emissions 93
penumbra 46
period of oscillation 3, 57
periodic table 93
periscope 51
phase 57, 59
photoelectric effect 103
pipette 2
pitch (sound) 63
plug, electrical 73
pole, magnetic 76
potential 76
potential difference 68
   and emf 70
potential energy 19
   electrostatic 68
   gravitational 19
power 19
   electrical 70

power lines 87–88
prefixes 5
pressure 24–6
    in liquids 24
    of gases 25–6
pressure law 32
primary cell 70
principal axis 52
principal focus 52
prisms 49, 51
progressive waves 56
projector 52–53
proton 65, 93
proton number 93
pulley system 23

quality control 3
quality of sound 62–63

radar 61
radiant heat 38-9, 61
radiation
    electromagnetic 61
radioactive 95–97
radio waves 61
radioactive decay 96–97
    equations 96
    model for 97
    uses of 97
ray diagrams, lens 52
rectifier 87
reflection, plane mirror 47
refraction of light 49–50
refraction of sound 62–63
refractive index
    of light 50
    of waves 58
refrigerator 39
relative density 3
relativity 103
relay, magnetic 81
resistance
    electrical 68–69
    internal 70
    of wires 69–70
resistors
    parallel 69
    series 69
resultant force 14
rheostat 68
right-hand grip rule 79
right-hand rule 85
ripple tank 57
Rumford, Count 101
Rutherford, Ernest 102

scalars 7, 14
scales of instruments 4
scattering of alpha particles 93
screening, magnetic 78
second, s 1
secondary cell 71
semiconductors 89
    diode 89

series, resistors in 69
shadows 46
shell model 94
short sight 54
shunt 84
SI units 1
significant figures 4
silicon chip 90
simple pendulum 3
Snell's law 49
solar energy 20
solenoid 76, 80
solids
    expansion of 28–9
    kinetic energy in 35–6
sound waves 62, 63
    in a vacuum 62
sources of energy 20
specific heat capacity 41
    determination of 41–42
specific latent heat 43
    determination of 43–44
spectrum
    electromagnetic 61
    light 54
speed 7
    of waves 57
spring balance 12
stability 22
standard form 5
standing wave 56
starter motor 81
states of matter 35
static electricity 65–67
stationary wave 56
stopwatch 3
sun, eclipse of 47
superposition 59
switches 73
symbols
    electrical 68
    nuclear 93

temperature 28–9
thermocouple 30
thermometers 29–30
Thomson, J J 97
ticker-timer 9, 15
time 3
torque 21
total internal reflection 50
transformer 87
transistors 90
transmission of electrical power 87–88
turning forces 21–3

ultraviolet radiation 61
umbra 46
units, SI 1
    changing 5
upthrust 27

vacuum flask 40
vaporisation, latent heat of 43–44

vectors 7
velocity/time graphs 8
vernier calipers 1
volt, V 66
voltmeter 68, 69, 71, 83
volume 2
    gases and 31

water waves 57–58
watt, W 20
wave equation 57
wave front 57
wave length 57
wave-particle duality 60
waves
    diffraction 58
    interference 59
    longitudinal 56, 62
    progressive 56
    reflection 57
    transverse 56, 61
weight 13
    mass and 13
wiring, household 73
    colour code of 73
work 19

X-rays 61

Young's slits experiment 60